DRUG USE

A Reference Handbook

Other Titles in ABC-CLIO's
**CONTEMPORARY
WORLD ISSUES**
Series

Books in the Contemporary World Issues series address vital issues in today's society such as terrorism, sexual harassment, homelessness, AIDS, gambling, animal rights, and air pollution. Written by professional writers, scholars, and nonacademic experts, these books are authoritative, clearly written, up-to-date, and objective. They provide a good starting point for research by high school and college students, scholars, and general readers as well as by legislators, businesspeople, activists, and others.

Each book, carefully organized and easy to use, contains an overview of the subject; a detailed chronology; biographical sketches; facts and data and/or documents and other primary-source material; a directory of organizations and agencies; annotated lists of print and nonprint resources; a glossary; and an index.

Readers of books in the Contemporary World Issues series will find the information they need in order to better understand the social, political, environmental, and economic issues facing the world today.

DRUG USE

A Reference Handbook

Richard Isralowitz

**CONTEMPORARY
WORLD ISSUES**

A B C  C L I O

Santa Barbara, California • Denver, Colorado • Oxford, England

Library of Congress Cataloging-in-Publication Data

Isralowitz, Richard.
  Drug use : a reference handbook / Richard Isralowitz.
       p. cm.—(ABC-CLIO's contemporary world issues)
  Includes bibliographical references and index.
  ISBN 1-57607-708-X (alk. paper) ISBN 1-57607-709-8 (e-book)
1. Drug abuse—Handbooks, manuals, etc. 2. Drug
abuse—Prevention—Handbooks, manuals, etc. I. Title. II. Series:
Contemporary world issues.

  HV5801.I67 2004
  362.29—dc22

                                                        2004003047

08 07 06 05 04 10 9 8 7 6 5 4 3 2 1

This book is also available on the World Wide Web as an eBook. Visit abc-clio.com for details.

ABC-CLIO, Inc.
130 Cremona Drive, P.O. Box 1911
Santa Barbara, California 93116-1911

This book is printed on acid-free paper ∞.
Manufactured in the United States of America

Contents

Preface and Acknowledgments

The use of tobacco, alcohol, marijuana, heroin, cocaine, and other substances is a deeply imbedded characteristic of most societies. It often shows itself in the form of illness, death, crime and violence, police action and imprisonment, property confiscation, massive allocations of governmental resources, as well as many ways of human suffering. It tends to attract more concern and attention than any other social issue throughout the world.

In the United States, the scope and impact of drug use are profound. It is estimated that 11 percent of the adult population suffers from substance abuse or dependence during the course of a year. Nearly 14 million adults each year abuse or are dependent on alcohol, and about 5 million abuse or are dependent on illicit drugs. On a yearly basis, the cost of substance abuse to the U.S. economy has been estimated to be more than $414 billion; the illegal drug market is reported to be $150 billion and rising; the federal antidrug budget for law enforcement exceeds $12 billion; and more than $3 billion goes to conduct overseas drug wars, with more than half of that amount going to Colombia to eliminate opium and coca cultivation. The annual cost to the nation for each addict is about $30,000. And it has been estimated that substance use and addiction add more than $40 billion annually to the costs of elementary and secondary education due to class disruption and violence, special education and tutoring, teacher turnover, truancy, children left behind, student assistance programs, property damage, injury, and counseling.

More than ever before, governmental and nongovernmental

policy and program decision makers, educators, service workers, and ordinary people are aware of the damage caused by the use of drugs. People are exposed to research, evaluation reports, policy proclamations and debates, as well as education. Many are aware that drug problems involve intervention with interrelated factors, including those of a health, judicial, educational, and welfare nature, and understand that there is no short-term fix. And although there are considerable investment of resources and efforts to prevent and treat drug use, the drug problems show no signs of abating. There are no simple solutions to this complex issue.

This volume examines the drug-use problem from multiple perspectives. It defines terminology; reviews history; examines the scope of drug production, trafficking, and use in the United States, Europe, and elsewhere; describes the main substances of abuse; reviews the role of key people involved with shaping the problem and how it has been and is being addressed; and provides information sources for further inquiry. It is intended to be a starting point for study rather than a comprehensive theory, exhaustive history, or detailed policy analysis. I hope this book helps readers to begin considering, discussing, and studying the issue so that their input will contribute to informed and balanced decision making, organization, coordination of common concerns and effort, follow-up, and investment of prevention and treatment intervention at local, state, and national levels.

Many people have supported me throughout the preparation of this volume. Appreciation is expressed to the personnel of ABC-CLIO, including Mildred "Mim" Vasan for her steadfast support throughout the development phases of the book, Alicia Merritt who was instrumental in promoting my relation to ABC-CLIO, Vicki Speck for her cooperation and open-mindedness to suggestions, Jessica Bothwell for her administrative support, and Gina Zondorak who helped move this effort forward to publication. Gratitude is extended to Annette Wenda for her work as copyeditor. Thanks to Sofia Borkin, M.D., for her cooperation during the preparation of this effort.

1

What Is Needed to Understand the Drug Problem and Those Factors Associated with Use?

Harmful drugs destroy lives and communities, undermine sustainable human development, and generate crime. They affect all sectors of society in all countries; in particular, drug abuse affects the freedom and development of young people, the world's most valuable asset. Harmful drugs are a grave threat to the health and well-being of all humanity, the independence of states, democracy, the stability of nations, the structure of all societies, and the dignity and hope of millions of people and their families (United Nations 1998). They are a primary cause of illness, death, crime and violence, police action and imprisonment, property confiscation, and massive allocations of public resources. Harmful drug use is a social issue that generates considerable public concern and attention.

What Is a Drug? Its Use, Abuse, and Dependence

Drugs

A drug may be defined as any substance other than food that by its chemical nature affects the structure and function of the living

1

organism. Its meaning, however, often varies with the context in which it is used—from country to country and changing over time in response to social and economic pressures. Psychoactive substances like alcohol and tobacco were generally not regarded as drugs forty years ago. Today, most experts in the drug field believe both substances are drugs. A drug may be legal or illegal, harmful or helpful, such as those substances used in medical therapy. In most countries, tobacco and alcohol are legal drugs. Marijuana, amphetamines, barbiturates, heroin, and cocaine are regarded as illegal drugs in the United States.

Use

Use refers to those individuals who have tried or continue to use nicotine, alcohol, or illegal drugs but who are not dependent or addicted to the substances. The use of a drug is driven by one of two types of reasons. One group of people tends to use drugs just to feel good. They are seeking a good time and use drugs because their friends are doing it and they do not want to be left out. The second reason includes people who are suffering and use drugs to try to feel better or even normal. This group often includes people who live with poverty and/or who have been abused. It includes people with a variety of mental disorders like clinical depression, manic-depressive illness, panic disorders, and schizophrenia.

Many people use drugs to achieve a state of euphoria, pleasure, or relaxation, and it may be argued that they do not abuse the substances. They tend to fall into different subgroups: (1) those who have tried a substance but have discontinued use, (2) those who use infrequently and primarily in response to social circumstances, and (3) those who use periodically but infrequently enough to avoid dependence or addictions (Leshner 2001).

Abuse

Medical and governmental authorities have defined *abuse* as the nonmedical use of a substance. This includes the use of prescription drugs in a manner inconsistent with accepted medical practices, the use of over-the-counter drugs contrary to labeling, or the use of any substance (for example, marijuana, glue, and heroin) for psychic effect, dependence, or suicide attempt. In the

Diagnostic and Statistical Manual of Mental Disorders (DSM), *abuse* is referred to as a maladaptive pattern of repeated use that brings on significant adverse consequences, including the failure to fulfill obligations, repeated use in physically hazardous situations, as well as recurrent social, interpersonal, and legal problems (American Psychiatric Association 2000).

Dependence

Dependence involves compulsive use, usually accompanied by craving, increased tolerance, a pattern of compulsive use, and considerable impairment of health and social functioning. There is a pattern of repeated self-administration that usually results in tolerance, withdrawal, and compulsive drug-taking behavior. These terms are defined as follows: (1) *tolerance* is the need for greatly increased amounts of the substance to achieve intoxication (or the desired effect) or a markedly diminished effect with continued use of the same amount of the substance; (2) *withdrawal* is a maladaptive behavioral change, with physiological and cognitive consequences; and (3) *dependence* or compulsive drug-taking behavior is when an individual takes the substance in larger amounts or over a longer period than was originally intended (for example, continuing to drink until severely intoxicated despite having set a limit of only one drink).

What Are the Types of Drugs?

The *DSM* of the American Psychiatric Association lists eleven classes of pharmacological agents or drugs: alcohol, amphetamines or similarly acting agents, caffeine, cannabis, cocaine, hallucinogens, inhalants, nicotine, opiates, phencyclidine (PCP) or similar agents, and sedatives, hypnotics, and anxiolytics (that is, drugs such as benzodiazepines that have an antianxiety effect and are used widely to relieve emotional tension). There is a twelfth residual category for everything else, including anabolic steroids (substances like testosterone that increase muscle mass and strength), nitrous oxide, and so on (Erowid's Psychoactive Vaults 2003; Substance Abuse Mental Health Services Administration 2000; Falkowski 2000; Ray and Ksir 1990; World Health Organization 1992).

Types of Drugs: A Review

Alcohol

Beverage alcohol is a liquid obtained by fermenting or distilling various fruits, vegetables, or grains. The major types of alcoholic beverages are distilled spirits, beer, and wine. Like heroin, cocaine, and d-lysergic acid diethylamide (LSD), alcohol is a psychoactive substance. It is a central nervous system depressant that lowers inhibitions, impairs judgment, and is addictive. Alcohol affects the brain, coordination, judgment, reflexes, vision, and memory. It may cause blackout. It can damage every organ in the body, and it can increase the risk for a variety of life-threatening diseases, including cancer. Drinking can lead to risky behaviors, including unprotected sex that may expose a person to HIV/AIDS and other sexually transmitted diseases or cause unwanted pregnancy.

Amphetamines

Amphetamines are a group of drugs that stimulate the central nervous system. The substances produce an increased state of arousal accompanied by a sense of confidence and euphoria. Users tend to appear in a state of hyperactivity, agitation, or exhaustion; when amphetamines are used over prolonged periods of time, irrational and paranoid behavior may be evidenced. Medically, these substances are used to treat depression, obesity, attention disorders, narcolepsy, and other conditions. Most nonmedically prescribed amphetamines, however, are produced in backyard laboratories and sold illegally. Presently, two substances tend to define this category of substances: methamphetamine and Ecstasy.

Methamphetamine

Methamphetamine ("meth") is a relatively easily produced synthetic stimulant that is known as meth, crank, crystal, crystal meth, and speed. It is a powerfully addictive substance that affects the brain and the rest of the central nervous system. Easily made with relatively low-cost materials, meth is an odorless, bitter-tasting white crystalline powder that dissolves in water or alcohol. The active ingredient is either ephedrine or pseudoephedrine—a common ingredient found in prescribed or over-the-counter medicines. Methamphetamine in powder form is smoked, snorted, or injected intravenously. Crystal meth, or "ice," is a concentrated form of methamphetamine that resembles tiny chunks of translucent glass. As crack is to cocaine, ice is to methamphetamine. The effects of methamphetamine last six to eight hours, depending on the way it is used.

Ecstasy

Ecstasy is a synthetic psychoactive substance with stimulant and mild hallucinogenic properties; it is often used in pill form. The substance is structurally similar to methamphetamine and the hallucinogen mescaline. The substance has been associated with verbal memory impairments and poor memory performance, and it may have an effect on the ability to reason verbally or sustain attention. Ecstasy is used in social settings such as nightclubs and dance clubs, private homes, college dormitories, and bars. Ecstasy combines two opposite effects: stimulation and relaxation. The effects are similar, though more intense, to the popular anti-depressant Prozac (fluoxetine). It is often used in combination with other drugs—mostly alcohol, but also with other club drugs like gamma hydroxybutyrate (GHB), ketamine, marijuana, methamphetamine, psilocybin mushrooms, and LSD.

Caffeine

Caffeine, one of the oldest stimulants known, affects the central nervous system. It is capable of reversing the effects of fatigue on both mental and physical tasks. It is present in coffee, tea, soft drinks, and over-the-counter drugs such as No-Doz, Anacin, and Excedrine. The symptoms of caffeine overdose (caffeinism) will vary according to individual differences and the amount consumed. Excessive doses of caffeine from 250 to 750 milligrams (2 to 7 cups of coffee) or more can produce restlessness, dizziness, nausea, headaches, tense muscles, sleep disturbances, irregular heartbeats, anxiety attacks, drowsiness, ringing ears, diarrhea, vomiting, light flashes, difficulty breathing, and convulsions.

Cannabis (Marijuana and Hashish)

Marijuana refers to the leaves and flowering tops of the hemp (cannabis) plant. It is also known as cannabis, pot, weed, and ganja, among other names. Although sixty cannabinoids (certain chemical compounds) are found in marijuana, the psychoactive one that most affects the brain is tetrahydrocannabinol (THC). The THC level in marijuana has increased over the past quarter century from less than 1 percent to as much as 17 percent. Hashish and hash oil also come from the cannabis plant. Hashish is a resinous material that is extracted and pressed into different shapes. Marijuana and hashish are smoked and eaten. Marijuana is the most commonly used illegal substance. Use of the substance is a criminal offense under U.S. federal law. Local and state enforcement of marijuana violations varies from location to location. From a medical perspective, marijuana has been found to be beneficial in treating the symptoms of AIDS, cancer, multiple sclerosis, glaucoma, and other serious conditions.

Cocaine

Cocaine is a naturally derived central nervous system stimulant extracted and refined from the coca plant grown primarily in the Andean region of South America. Cocaine, a white powder with a bitter, numbing taste, is most often snorted. Converted to a liquid form, it can be injected with a needle. Because of the high temperatures present when smoking, powder cocaine tends to burn rather than vaporize. For this reason, freebase cocaine, also known as crack, is created from powder cocaine for smoking. Crack vaporizes at smoking temperatures, providing more effect with less substance; it provides a faster onset and a more intense high than powder cocaine. People who use cocaine often do not eat or sleep regularly. Among the symptoms experienced are increased heart rate, muscle spasms, and convulsions.

Hallucinogens

Hallucinogenic drugs are substances that distort the perception of objective reality. Under the influence of hallucinogens, the senses of direction, distance, and time become distorted. These drugs can produce unpredictable, erratic, and violent behavior in users that sometimes leads to serious injuries and death. Among the well-known hallucinogens is phencyclidine, otherwise known as PCP, angel dust, or love boat. This substance is described as a separate category in *DSM*. LSD is a powerful synthesized psychoactive substance. LSD use is unlikely to cause addiction in most people, and there is no physical addiction or withdrawal; however, it can become psychologically habit forming. Other substances in this category are peyote, a small button-shaped cactus that is dried and eaten; peyotillo; tsuwiri; sunami; donana; dolichothele; and San Pedro, a cactus that has gained considerable attention for its hallucinogenic effects. The effects of these plants come from their main active alkaloid, mescaline.

Inhalants

Inhalants are chemical products that are intentionally inhaled to cause an immediate high. Because they affect the brain with much greater speed and force than other substances, they can cause irreversible physical and mental damage. Inhalants include solvents (for example, gasoline, glues, nail-polish remover, lighter fluid, paint thinners, dry-cleaning fluid, markers, and correction fluid); gases and propellants used in butane lighters; and aerosols such as spray paints, hair spray, fabric protectants, refrigerants, and volatile nitrates found in room deodorizers. Chronic inhalant users may exhibit signs such as anxiety, excitability, irritability, or restlessness.

Nicotine

Nicotine is a naturally occurring liquid alkaloid that is colorless and volatile. Nicotine is the drug in tobacco that causes addiction. In the form of smoking, the substance is the most common cause of lung cancer and preventable death in the United States. The substance is found in cigarettes, cigars, pipe tobacco, and smokeless tobacco products. The pharmacological and biological processes that determine tobacco addiction are similar to those that determine addiction to drugs such as heroin and cocaine. Among the risks associated with nicotine use, especially in the form of smoking, are decreased senses of smell and taste, frequent colds, bleeding gums and frequent mouth sores, wheezing, coughing, bad breath, yellow stained teeth and fingers, gastric ulcers, chronic bronchitis, increase in heart rate and blood pressure, emphysema, heart disease, stroke, and cancer of the mouth, larynx, pharynx, esophagus, lungs, pancreas, cervix, uterus, and bladder.

Opiates

Substances derived from the opium poppy are opiates. The most commonly abused illegal substance is heroin. Prescription drugs, usually used for pain relief, include codeine, morphine, oxycodone (that is, OxyContin and Percocet), and others. Included in this category may be synthetic substances such as methadone and levo-alpha-acetylmethadol (LAAM), labeled "opioids," with the property to interact with opiate receptors in the brain. The substances may be eaten, but they are generally smoked, sniffed, or injected, subcutaneously or intravenously. The subcutaneous injection, referred to as "skin-popping," produces a slower absorption with a lower degree of euphoria but longer-lasting effects, including characteristic marks on the skin. People under the influence of opiates appear calm, sometimes sleepy, and have a tendency to take everything in stride. Pure opiates cause relatively little body damage; however, substances sold on the streets as "opiates" usually contain a large amount of contaminants, including poison, that can produce serious damage or even death to the user. Unlike stimulants, opiates do not produce a psychotic state when used in their pure form and have the ability to reduce or eliminate psychotic symptoms in mental patients.

Phencyclidine

PCP is a synthetic substance that was developed in the 1950s as an intravenous anesthetic. The substance affects the user at different times as a stimulant, hallucinogen, analgesic, or sedative. It can be snorted, smoked, or eaten. For smoking, PCP is often applied to a leafy material such as marijuana, cigar tobacco, mint, parsley, or oregano. Among the names given for the substance are "angel dust," "wack," and "rocket fuel." PCP is addictive, leading to psychological dependence, craving, and compulsive PCP-seeking behavior. Numbness or rigidity of extremities, large motor dysfunction, jerking eye movements, auditory hallucinations, nausea, drooling, dizziness, and memory loss have been reported as well.

Sedatives, Hypnotics, and Anxiolytics

This class of drugs when abused is commonly known as "downers." They include prescription drugs used to reduce anxiety or facilitate sleep. The most commonly abused drugs in this class are benzodiazepines (Valium, Xanax, Ativan, Halcion, and others) and barbiturates (phenobarbital, Seconal, Nembutal, and Amytal). Other substances in this category have been referred to as "date-rape drugs." They include two substances: GHB and flunitrazepam (Rohypnol). GHB is a central nervous system depressant usually sold as an odorless, colorless liquid in springwater bottles or as a powder and mixed with beverages. In addition to being used in drug-assisted rapes, GHB is used as a muscle-stimulating growth hormone, sleep aid, and aphrodisiac. Flunitrazepam, a benzodiazepine that is smuggled into the United States primarily from Mexico because it is no longer sold in the United States, is used mostly with beer as an "alcohol extender" and disinhibitory agent. Also, it is used in drug-assisted rape.

Who Uses Drugs? What Are the Risk Factors?

A host of often interrelated sociological, biomedical, and psychological factors underlies the problem of drug use and dependence. The following review describes some of the major considerations.

Society and Social Order

People are often referred to as deviant when they do not share the values or adhere to the social norms regarding conduct and personal attributes prescribed by society. Although the process of identifying deviance involves the use of normative definitions that may vary over time, the essential nature of deviant behavior associated with the use of drugs and problem behavior is that it reflects a departure from the norms of a particular society (Goode 1989).

Social Forces: Physical Environment, Values, and Morals

The environment where a person lives can influence the use and abuse of drugs. An environment that is deteriorating and poverty-stricken serves as a breeding ground for such behavior.

Living in this type of setting are people usually beset with a huge assortment of personal and family problems. Lower-class values and morals and the disproportionate amount of crime and drug problems found among poor people have been widely covered by sociological research and literature. Such problem behavior, however, is also indigenous to the middle and upper classes. Facts and statistics reveal that drug use and abuse are problems that traverse all social classes.

Interpersonal Relations

Family

The family has a major role in shaping the personality and behavior of children. Factors such as parental divorce, arrest, a lack of closeness between parents and children, parent and sibling drug use, family disorganization, mental illness, low educational aspirations for the children, lack of parental involvement in the child's activities, weak parental control and discipline, death or absence of a parent, and emotional, physical, and/or sexual abuse are factors that have been found to be linked to drug use.

Peers

Peer relations are often linked to drug use and dependence. Such behavior may be learned through association and interaction with others who are already involved with drugs. A person's relationship with peers may serve as a means of providing the individual with an escape from other undesirable dealings such as family, school, or work. Interaction with peers may also be a means by which a person can receive emotional gratification, recognition, reinforcement, security, self-protection, and defense for problem behavior. Association with substance-using peers tends to be a very strong predictor of substance use.

Education

The school is a major agent of status definition in society and has a significant role in the socialization process of people; consequently, it tends to be an important factor associated with drug use. The relationship between a negative school experience and drug use is strong. For example, negative attitudes toward school, low academic aspirations and educational achievement, and disciplinary problems often precede the onset of drug use and/or dropping out of school. Furthermore, teenage pregnancies and frequent school absenteeism are associated with increasing levels of drug use.

Media

Since the 1920s when motion pictures became a major source of mass entertainment, the effects of the media have been subject to scientific inquiry and public concern. It has long been recognized that movies, television, and popular "hard rock" music portray an excessive amount of drug-use behavior. Research has found that youths who spend more time watching television and listening to drug-related music are more likely to use drugs.

Labeling-Criminalization Process

The labeling process is a method that determines the fate of a person. It often reinforces problem behavior rather than ameliorates it. In terms of drug use, a consistent pattern of events tends to take place, resulting in a feedback cycle involving more deviations, more penalties, and still more deviations. Hostilities and resentment are built up, culminating in official reactions that label and stigmatize the addict. This situation is often used by authorities to justify even greater penalties that close offenders noncriminal options and coerce them into a career of systematic norm violations, including drug use.

Biological and Psychological Characteristics

Certain individuals are predisposed to drug and alcohol use because of their genetic makeup. Also, it appears that genetic loading in combination with environmental and personality factors can make for a significantly higher level of drug abuse or alcoholism in certain individuals or groups of people. The National Institute of Drug Abuse reports that genetic factors play a major role in the progression from drug use to abuse and dependence.

From a psychological perspective, drug use and dependence may be viewed in two ways: (1) drugs have addictive reinforcement properties, independent of personality factors, and (2) personality pathology, defect, or inadequacy points to problems of an emotional or psychic nature of certain individuals, leading them to drug use. Drugs are used to escape from reality as a means of avoiding life's problems and retreating into a state of indifference. It has been found that people who use drugs tend to lack responsibility, independence, and the ability to defer gratification in order to achieve long-range goals. They exhibit difficulties controlling emotions such as rage, shame, jealousy, and anxiety; have low self-esteem; and have feelings of peer rejection and parental neglect. It has been found that drug users are less religious, less attached to parents and family, less achievement-oriented, less cautious, ambivalent to authority, compulsive, confused over sex roles, narcissistic, defiant, and resentful, and they have unrealistic expectations for achievement (Lettieri, Sayers, and Pearson 1980; Petraitis et al. 1998).

Which Drugs Define the Problem?

Brief History

The use of an addictive substance is a complex phenomenon that includes the history of the drug, the social strata of society who use it, the kinds of situations in which the substance is used, and the publicity and public opinion associated with its use. Five legal and illegal substances tend to define the drug problem over time: tobacco (nicotine), alcohol, cannabis (marijuana and hashish), heroin, and cocaine (Isralowitz 2002).

Tobacco (Nicotine)

Tobacco is a leafy plant, a stimulant, indigenous to North, Central, and South America. Introduced to Columbus by natives of the New World, the substance found its way to Europe, and its importance was closely tied to economic interests. The Spanish, for example, had a monopoly on tobacco sales for more than one hundred years until the British colonies, notably Virginia, were able to produce sufficient quantities from the seventeenth century onward. Tobacco use has taken the form of cigarette, cigar, and pipe smoking; snuff; and chewing.

Tobacco is a psychoactive drug, and its use is one of the major causes of debility and premature death. Midway into the nineteenth century and long before scientific evidence emerged about the extent of the health risks they posed, cigarettes were labeled "coffin nails." In 1963, cigarette use in the United States reached an all-time high, precipitating the 1964 surgeon general's

report that definitively linked cigarette smoking to health problems. In 1980, the surgeon general said that cigarette smoking is
the single most important preventable cause of death and disease.
Additional facts revealed that cigarettes and other forms of
tobacco are addictive, nicotine is the drug in tobacco that causes
addiction, and pharmacological and behavioral processes that determine addiction are similar to those that determine addiction to
drugs such as heroin and cocaine.

Tobacco production and sales have represented big business
for hundreds of years, not only for growers and manufacturers but
also for governments in the form of tax revenues. During the colonial period of the seventeenth century, tobacco was an important
cash crop, and it was a federally taxed commodity that was used
to help finance the Civil War. More recently, it has been estimated
that the tobacco industry directly generates more than $40 billion
of the gross national product and provides employment for more
than 700,000 people. Additionally, reports show that $12 billion to
$35 billion is spent each year in the United States alone to treat
smoking-related diseases—a significant revenue source for health-
related services and industries. It has been estimated that the
tobacco industry and its suppliers generate about $10.6 billion in
federal taxes and $8.3 billion in state and local taxes each year. Fur-
thermore, when the trade deficit is of concern, the billions of dollars' worth of cigarettes exported by the United States is not an
insignificant factor. In 1998, after years of legal suits claiming violations of antitrust laws, consumer fraud, conspiracy to withhold
information about the harmful health effects of tobacco use, and
even manipulation of nicotine levels to keep people addicted to
smoking, historic settlements totaling $246 billion were reached
between state attorneys general and the tobacco industry. Only a
few years after this victory, it is clear that many states faced with
economic downturn and decreased revenues have been forced to
use settlement compensation to maintain commitments and priorities other than those promised, such as drug-prevention and educational services (ibid.).

Alcohol

Over time, alcohol is the most prominent drug used to experience
special physical sensations. After tobacco, alcohol abuse and dependence are by far the most common form of drug addiction. Although it is not known exactly when alcohol and its effects on

human behavior were discovered, some experts believe that humans have been drinking alcoholic beverages since 6400 B.C. when beer and berry wine were discovered. Grape wines date from 300 to 400 B.C. The drinking custom is probably even older than that. Reference to alcoholism is in the Bible (1 Sam. 1). Leaders throughout history have encouraged moderation.

Early use of alcohol seems to have been worldwide; for example, the American Indians encountered by Columbus drank beer. In the "new continent," what American colonists considered normal drinking would be defined as deviant and intemperate from a contemporary viewpoint. In America, Benjamin Rush (1745–1813), a physician and signer of the Declaration of Independence, described in his work *An Inquiry into the Effects of Ardent Spirits upon the Human Body and Mind* (1785) that drunkenness was a disease resembling certain hereditary, family, and contagious diseases. In the United States in the nineteenth century, a temperance movement that "demonized" alcohol became an important social force and a rallying point for the expanding middle class; thus, the liquor problem became a focus of attention for a broader sector of U.S. society that would bring social, political, and religious activism together, culminating in Prohibition.

In the United States, an amendment to the Constitution in 1919 made it illegal to manufacture or sell any alcoholic beverage. This amendment remained in effect until 1933 and had a significant impact on the nation's social patterns, economy, and underground life during those years and after. It has been suggested that the end of Prohibition was the result of corporate interests that saw the restoration of liquor taxes as a means of lowering personal and business taxes. Once Prohibition was repealed, the windfall from taxes on alcohol was used to fund depression-relief projects. No record of alcohol sales was kept in the United States from 1920 to 1933; nevertheless, there is a general perception that alcohol consumption rose during this period and that Prohibition was a failure. Contrary to this belief, death by cirrhosis of the liver, which is very closely correlated with alcohol consumption, decreased during Prohibition and increased once alcohol use was legal again. The number of people arrested and jailed on charges of public drunkenness and the number of automobile fatalities, another factor strongly related to the consumption of alcohol, declined as well. Exaggeration, myths, and the media probably account more for the misunderstanding of Prohibition's effect on people's drinking behavior than any other factor. For the most part, it has been noted that most Americans did not drink during the Prohibition years, and those who did drank less and less often than before or after the period.

Cannabis (Marijuana and Hashish)

Cannabis (marijuana and hashish) has generated much controversy and investigation in terms of its impact on individual behavior and society. Cannabis may have been cultivated as long as ten thousand years ago. It was grown in China by 4000 B.C. and in Turkistan by 3000 B.C. It has long been used as a medicine in India, China, the Middle East, Southeast Asia, South Africa, and South America. By A.D. 1000, the social use of the plant spread to the Muslim world and North Africa, and in the region of the Middle East its use was associated with a religious cult that committed murder for political reasons. The cult was called Hashishiyya, from which the word *assassin* developed.

The chemical compounds responsible for the intoxicating and medicinal effects of cannabis are found mainly in a sticky golden resin taken from the female plants. The three varieties are known as bhang, ganja, and charas. The least potent and cheapest preparation, bhang, is produced from the dried and crushed leaves, seeds, and stems. Ganja, prepared from the flowering tops, is two or three times as strong as bhang. Charas, also known as hashish in the Middle East, is the pure resin. Any of these preparations can be smoked, eaten, or mixed in drinks. Cannabis has been used as an analgesic, a topical anesthetic for the mouth and tongue, and for problems and discomfort related to tetanus, neuralgia, dysmenorrhea (painful menstruation), convulsions, childbirth pain, asthma, postpartum psychosis, gonorrhea, chronic bronchitis, preventing migraine attacks, certain kinds of epilepsy, depression, asthma, rheumatism, gastric ulcer, and drug addiction, particularly of morphine and other opiate substances.

A considerable amount of medical attention was given to cannabis from 1840 to 1900, recommending it for a variety of illnesses and discomforts. By 1890, the medical use of cannabis was on the decline. Among the reasons were that the potency of the preparations was too variable, and the invention of the hypodermic syringe in the 1850s made opiates more effective in pain relief since hemp products are insoluble in water and cannot be easily administered by injection. Also, synthetic drugs such as aspirin, chloral hydrate, and barbiturates that are chemically more stable became attractive for medicinal purposes in spite of their disadvantages.

In the 1930s, marijuana received much negative attention. It was claimed that the substance would cause users to go crazy and become violent, men would rape and kill under the influence, and women would become promiscuous. Today, these supposed effects receive no attention, even in the most vigorous antimarijuana polemics. The illegal status of marijuana may be attributed to four primary reasons: (1) certain special-interest organizations and labor unions were against cheap migrant workers; therefore, attributing the use of cannabis to immigrants was a productive means of keeping them out of the United States; (2) pharmaceutical companies interested in the marketing of profitable medicines may have seen the multipurpose benefits of cheap cannabis as a threat to profitability; (3) the alcohol industry and government, with big profits as well as local, state, and federal tax revenues at stake, were not interested in having any competition from cannabis; and (4) cannabis appears to have served as a powerful theme for government officials and politicians to generate support for a variety of reasons, including election to public office and the funding of governmental initiatives ranging from education to law enforcement.

After years of debate and controversy, there is an abundance of information regarding the characteristics of marijuana. What is known about the substance tends to be presented in ways that are contradictory, supporting the special interests of those who advocate legal regulation of marijuana because of its alleged harmful effects or who advocate legalization because of its helpful and benign characteristics. In 2002, after a two-year study, the Canadian Senate Special Committee on Illegal Drugs reported that scientific evidence indicates that cannabis is substantially less harmful than alcohol and should be addressed as a social and health issue. Essentially, the report called for the legalization, with controls, of cannabis use in Canada—a policy supported by a growing number of nations throughout the world who tend to say that the time has come to no longer have the "made in America" problem be their problem. The response from officials of the U.S. Drug Enforcement Administration (DEA) and White House Office of National Drug Control Policy (ONDCP) has been uniform, expressing disappointment and disdain for any policy decision that is contrary to that expressed by U.S. government officials who call for more research and information gathering on the potential harmful effects of the substance.

Heroin

If one substance were to be labeled the "king" of illegal drugs, most people would say it is heroin. Since the turn of the century when it was created, heroin has virtually defined the drug problem. Heroin addicts are the most stigmatized of all drug users. Its association in the public mind with street crime, in spite of competition from crack, is stronger than for any other drug. Heroin is chemically derived from morphine, which in turn comes from the opium poppy grown primarily in Afghanistan; the Golden Crescent, which is between Afghanistan, Pakistan, and Iran; the Golden Triangle, located in parts of Thailand, Laos, and Burma (now Myanmar); the Middle East, most notably Lebanon; and Latin American countries, including Colombia and Mexico.

In 1806, the primary active ingredient in opium was identified—an ingredient ten times more potent than opium itself. The substance was named *morphium,* after Morpheus, the god of dreams. In 1874, a chemical bonding process for morphine was discovered that produced heroin—a substance about three times as potent as morphine. Initially marketed by Bayer Laboratories of Germany in 1898 as a nonaddictive substitute for codeine derived from opium, it took nearly a decade of research before heroin was found to be the most addictive of the opiates, able to affect brain functioning faster than anything yet known. With a ban on non-medical use of opiates caused by the Harrison Narcotics Act of 1914, addicts began seeking the substance by illegal means. This provided an incentive for illegal organizations to enter the market for making a quick profit. Until the mid-1960s, laboratory facilities to transform morphine base into heroin were available only in Europe and the United States. This meant that most of the product had to be transported to be refined, and the refining process put a great deal of money into Western hands. In the mid-1960s, the situation changed, especially when Hong Kong–based drug entrepreneurs succeeded in establishing a series of laboratories in fields along the Mekong River. They started refining the product locally. It is rumored that those organizations foresaw the massive U.S. intervention in the Vietnam War and readied themselves to profit from the American soldiers coming to the area. Others claim that the Vietcong foresaw U.S. intervention and assisted the Chinese in establishing the laboratories so that heroin could be easily available in order to support the war effort.

Since the end of the cold war between the United States and the former Soviet Union, drugs have been financing some religious and ethnic conflicts. According to Interpol, the warlords have become the drug lords. The opening of borders in the European Union afforded unprecedented access to a vast untapped market. Aggressive criminal gangs in Africa and South America have been quick to seize the initiative, too. Capitalizing on skills in dealing marijuana or cocaine, they have expanded their product lines to include heroin, with a significant amount coming from South America. In 1994, it accounted for 32 percent of the heroin seized in the United States; by 1995, it was up to a staggering 62 percent.

Cocaine

Categorized as a stimulant, cocaine use dates back more than 2,000 years to the Andes Mountains in South America. The ancient Incan civilization worshiped cocaine. Despite efforts by Spanish invaders in the sixteenth century to stamp out its use, the coca leaf found its way to Europe, where scientists and physicians studied its effects. The Indians from the region, now Colombia, Peru, and Bolivia, still chew the leaves that contain about 1 percent cocaine to ward off fatigue and hunger, enabling them to work long hours without stopping.

Isolated from coca leaves in about 1860 (the exact date is uncertain), cocaine became popular through a concoction consisting of quality coca leaves steeped in good red wine, known as "Mariani's Coca Wine." Also during that time, in 1885, the Parke-Davis Pharmaceutical Company (now part of the Pfizer pharmaceutical conglomerate) started to market cocaine as a promising tonic, noting that it was a wonder drug that could take the place of food. There were many competitors to Mariani's cocaine-laced wine. None were more famous, however, than an Atlanta pharmacist by the name of John Pemberton who developed the formula for Coca-Cola. Pemberton sold only 160 gallons of the syrup, and soon the drink was taken over by Asa Griggs Candler, a pharmacist who made history with Coca-Cola.

Available in a large number of products for drinking, snorting, or injection, cocaine became identified with despised or poorly regarded groups—blacks, lower-class whites, and criminals—at the turn of the twentieth century. The regulatory actions eventually taken by the United States against the manufacture, sale, distribution, and use of cocaine were at variance with the drug's wide acceptability. When the Harrison Narcotics Act (1914) was used as a means of controlling drug addiction, cocaine became less available and more expensive. During this period, musicians, songwriters, and singers soon accepted cocaine, and the substance became indelibly connected in the public mind with elements in every branch of show business, including the brand-new radio scene.

The use of cocaine declined in the 1930s with the introduction of inexpensive and easily available amphetamine substances. It did not increase again until the end of the 1960s when amphetamines became harder to obtain. Three factors have been pointed to as contributing to an increase of demand: (1) there was a law-enforcement initiative against American-made amphetamines, which had an immediate effect on demand for the more natural imported product—cocaine; (2) the jet aircraft revolutionized travel and drug trafficking between the southern states in the United States and the Caribbean and Latin America; and (3) there was a strong revolt in the 1960s against any suggestion that government had the right to prescribe what people should or should not consume. During the early 1980s, cocaine abuse in the United States maintained epidemic status.

Until the late 1970s, the usual form of cocaine available on the street was cocaine hydrochloride, a salt form of cocaine that is usually sniffed (snorted) nasally or injected intravenously when mixed with water. Since the hydrochloride salt is quickly destroyed at high temperatures, it cannot be smoked unless it is in a freebase alkaloid form. When cocaine hydrochloride and sodium bicarbonate (baking soda) are mixed and then heated, the solution becomes a solid. The resultant pieces of the solid, also called "rock," release vaporized cocaine when heated. Since 1990, a lump, or rock, of crack costs about ten dollars, which makes it available to the poor. Cocaine and crack have become synonymous with the so-called War on Drugs.

Prevention and Treatment Factors

Prevention

Although there is no single definition of prevention, it may be defined as those efforts that keep alcohol, tobacco, and other drug problems from occurring by reducing risk factors. Ensuring that at-risk populations do not use these substances prevents some problems. Also, when these substances are not used, other problems are prevented such as drinking and driving (Center for Substance Abuse Prevention 1993). The first line of defense is often referred to as primary prevention, and the goal is to foster an environment in which: (1) alcohol use is acceptable only for those of legal age and only when the risk of adverse consequences is minimal; (2) prescription and over-the-counter drugs are used only for the purposes for which they were intended; (3) other abusable substances such as inhalants, including gasoline and aerosols, are used only for their intended purposes; and (4) illegal drugs and tobacco are not used at all (Center for Substance Abuse Prevention 1994).

When a person is in the early stages of problem behaviors associated with the use of alcohol, tobacco, and other drugs (ATOD), secondary prevention or early intervention efforts such as counseling and treatment may be used to cease use of the harmful substances by the person. Tertiary prevention refers to efforts that try to end compulsive use of ATOD and/or ameliorate their negative effects through treatment and rehabilitation. This is most often referred to as treatment but includes elements of rehabilitation and relapse prevention (Office of Substance Abuse Prevention 1991).

Numerous strategies are used to prevent drug use. Generally, they are associated with information, education, alternative behaviors, and primary and early intervention activities. These interventions focus on reducing risk factors and building protective factors and may be directed at any segment of the population. Several prevention activities or strategies may be used effectively in combination. Substance abuse prevention strategies reported by the White House Office of National Drug Control Policy include:

- Alternatives—This approach calls for the participation of target populations in constructive and healthy activities such as drug-free dances, youth/adult-leadership activities, community drop-in centers, and community service activities that exclude drug use. Constructive and healthy activities are designed to offset the attraction to, or otherwise meet the needs usually addressed by, alcohol and other drugs.

- Community-Based Process—This strategy enhances the ability of the community to more effectively provide prevention and treatment services for alcohol, tobacco, and drug-abuse disorders. Activities in this strategy include organizing, planning, enhancing efficiency and effectiveness of service implementation, interagency collaboration, coalition building, and networking. Some examples include community and volunteer training, multiagency coordination and collaboration, accessing programs and funding needed services, and community team building.
- Early Intervention—This approach uses activities that are designed to modify the behavior of an early substance abuser. It includes a wide spectrum of activities ranging from user education to formal intervention and referral to treatment provided by a substance-abuse professional.
- Education—This strategy builds critical life and social skills through structured learning processes. Critical life and social skills include decision making, peer resistance, coping with stress, problem solving, interpersonal communication, and systematic and judgmental abilities. Examples of this strategy include classroom and/or small group sessions, parenting and family-management classes, peer-leader/helper programs, educational programs for youth groups, and groups for children of substance abusers.
- Environmental—Programs of this nature challenge and change community standards, codes, and attitudes that tend to tolerate, accept, or support the use of drugs in the general population. This strategy is divided into two subcategories to permit distinction between activities that center on legal and regulatory initiatives and those that relate to the service and action-oriented initiatives. Some examples include promoting the review of drug-use policies in school; technical assistance to communities to maximize local

enforcement procedures governing availability and distribution of alcohol, tobacco, and other drugs; modifying alcohol and tobacco advertising practices; and product-pricing strategies.

- Information—This approach provides knowledge and increases awareness of the nature and extent of drug use, abuse, and addiction, and their effects on individuals, families, and communities. Knowledge and awareness are promoted of available prevention and treatment programs and services. Some examples include clearinghouse/information resource centers, resource directories, media campaigns, brochures, radio/TV public-service announcements, speaking engagements, health fairs/health promotion, and telephone/computer information lines.

- Problem Identification and Referral—This strategy includes activities that identify those who have engaged in illegal or age-inappropriate use of tobacco or alcohol and persons who have begun to use illicit drugs. Effort is generated to assess whether the early alcohol and drug use of the individual can be reversed through education. It does not include any activity designed to determine if a person is in need of treatment. Some examples include employee-assistance programs, student-assistance programs, and educational programs related to driving while under the influence or driving while intoxicated. Increased chances of substance use, stress, violence, trauma, and posttraumatic stress are among the reasons people are at greater risk of substance abuse, including relapse to alcohol and drug abuse, addiction, and cigarette smoking. Emotional strain caused by the September 11, 2001, terrorist attacks on the United States and threats of bioterrorism have led large numbers of Americans to seek treatment for substance-abuse problems. For example, "one year after the Oklahoma City bombing three times as many residents of that city reported increased drinking compared with residents of comparatively sized Indianapolis, Indiana. Understandably, rescue workers in Oklahoma City also experienced significant rates of substance abuse, depression, and suicide months and years after the bombing." (Columbia University Center of Addiction and Substance Abuse 2001)

According to the Center for Substance Abuse Prevention, such events are important reasons for promoting effective prevention efforts in every community. The Center for Substance Abuse Prevention publication *Science-Based Prevention Programs and Principles: Effective Substance Abuse and Mental Health Programs for Every Community* (2002) summarizes more than two decades of research on prevention programs. It delineates the broad range of influences that can lead to substance abuse or other potentially dangerous behaviors and presents practical community-based ways to curb the risk factors for these behaviors. Effective interventions are identified at the individual, family, peer group, school, community, and society level; a state-of-the-science review of substance-abuse prevention theory and practice is provided; and a compendium is included of tested and effective model substance abuse–prevention and mental health–promotion programs. The following programs, selected for universal appeal, are a few examples of "model" prevention initiatives.

Keep a Clear Mind (KACM) is a take-home drug-education program for upper-elementary-school students (eight to twelve years old) and their parents. The take-home material consists of four weekly sets of activities to be completed by parents and their children together. The program also uses parental newsletters and incentives. KACM lessons are based on a social-skills training model designed to help children develop specific skills to refuse and avoid the use of "gateway" drugs. This early intervention program has been shown to positively influence known risk factors for later substance use. Specifically, the program aims to increase students' ability to resist peer pressure to use tobacco, alcohol, and marijuana; increase student recognition of the harmful effects of tobacco, alcohol, and marijuana; help students identify and choose positive alternatives to substance use; decrease students' actual use of tobacco, alcohol, and marijuana; help parents become effective drug educators; increase parent-child communication about substance use; and strengthen relationships with adults and peers.

Evaluation of KACM activities compared parents who participated in the program to those who were not involved. Results of those involved with KACM show that 20 percent of parents indicated that their children had an increased ability to resist peer pressure to use alcohol, tobacco, and marijuana; 29 percent indicated a decreased expectation that their children would try substances; and 14 percent expressed a more realistic view of drug use among young people and a greater realization of its effects. Outcomes reported by children who participated show a 9 percent decrease in the KACM students' perceptions of extensive substance use among peers compared to an 18 percent increase in the control group's perceptions; a 15 percent decrease in KACM participants' expectations that they would use tobacco, compared to more than a 100 percent increase in the control group; and a 59 percent increase in the number of children who indicated that their parents did not approve of the use of marijuana. Further information about the Keep a Clear Mind program may be obtained by contacting Michael Young, Ph.D.; Health Education Projects Office (HP 326A); University of Arkansas; Fayetteville, AR 72701 (e-mail: meyoung@comp.uark.edu; Web site: http://www.uark.edu/depts/hepoinfo/clear.html).

Project ALERT is a drug-prevention curriculum for middle-school students eleven to fourteen years old that reduces both the onset of substance abuse and regular use. The two-year fourteen-lesson program focuses on the substances that adolescents are most likely to use: alcohol, tobacco, marijuana, and inhalants. Project ALERT uses participatory activities and videos to help motivate adolescents against drug use, teach adolescents the skills and strategies needed to resist pro-drug pressures, and establish non–drug-using norms.

Guided classroom discussions and small group activities stimulate peer interaction and challenge student beliefs and perceptions, while intensive role-playing activities help students learn and master resistance skills. Homework assignments that also involve parents extend the learning process by facilitating parent-child discussions of drugs and how to resist using drugs. These lessons are reinforced through videos that model appropriate behavior.

Evaluation of Project ALERT shows that it was effective in schools with both large and small minority populations from a variety of socioeconomic backgrounds, with youths experimenting with drugs and at risk for becoming regular users, as well as those who had not tried drugs before the program began. It substantially decreased pro-drug attitudes and beliefs, including intentions to use drugs, beliefs that drug use is not harmful, and perceptions that many peers use drugs. It also increased beliefs that one can successfully resist both internal and external pressures to use drugs. The program markedly reduced the use of marijuana and cigarettes and the initiation of marijuana use. Fifteen months after the baseline information was collected, compared to a control group of youths who did not receive Project ALERT, results of the program's effect show that marijuana initiation rates were 30 percent lower for ALERT students, current marijuana use was 60 percent lower in adult-led programs, current and occasional cigarette use was 20 percent to 25 percent lower, regular and heavy cigarette use was one-third to 55 percent lower, and antidrug beliefs were significantly enhanced, with many effects persisting into the tenth grade. Further information about this prevention effort may be obtained by contacting Project ALERT; 725 South Figueroa Street, Suite 970; Los Angeles, CA 90017-5416 (e-mail: info@projectalert.best.org; Web site: http://www.projectalert.best.org).

Community Trials Intervention to Reduce High-Risk Drinking (RHRD) is a multicomponent community-based program developed to alter alcohol-use patterns of people of all ages (for example, drinking and driving, underage drinking, acute or binge drinking, and related problems). The program uses a set of environmental interventions including community awareness, responsible beverage service (RBS), preventing underage alcohol access, enforcement, and community mobilization.

For RHRD to be successful, the implementing organization must first determine which program components will best produce the desired results for its community. The RHRD program uses five prevention components:

- Alcohol Access—Assists communities in using zoning and municipal regulations to restrict alcohol access through alcohol outlets (bars, liquor stores, and so on), density control, and RBS. Through training and testing, RBS assists alcohol beverage servers and retailers in the development of policies and procedures to reduce intoxication and driving after drinking.
- Responsible Beverage Service—Through training and testing, RBS assists alcohol beverage servers and retailers in the development of policies and procedures to reduce intoxification and driving after drinking.
- Risk of Driving and Drinking—Increases actual and perceived risk of arrest for driving after drinking

through increased law enforcement and sobriety
checkpoints.
- Underage Alcohol Access—Reduces youth access to
  alcohol by training alcohol retailers to avoid selling to
  minors and those who provide alcohol to minors, and
  through increased enforcement of underage alcohol-
  sales laws.
- Community Mobilization—Provides communities with
  the tools to form the coalitions needed to implement
  and support the interventions that will address the
  previous four prevention components.

Outcome results show that the RHRD program generated a 51 percent decline in self-reported driving when "over the legal limit" in
those communities that had the program compared to those who
did not participate, a 6 percent decline in self-reported amounts
consumed per drinking occasion, a 49 percent decline in self-
reported "having had too much to drink," a 10 percent reduction in
nighttime injury crashes, a 6 percent reduction in crashes in which
the driver had been drinking, a 43 percent reduction in assault injuries observed in emergency rooms, and a 2 percent reduction in
hospitalized assault injuries. Further information about RHRD
may be obtained by contacting Andrew J. Treno, Ph.D.; Prevention
Research Center; 2150 Shattuck Avenue, Suite 900; Berkeley, CA
94704 (e-mail: andrew@prev.org; Web site: http://www.PREV.org).

Treatment

According to the National Institute on Drug Abuse (1999), there
are many addictive drugs, and treatments for specific drugs can
differ. Treatment also varies depending on the characteristics of
the patient. Problems associated with an individual's drug addiction can vary significantly. People who are addicted to drugs
come from all walks of life. Many suffer from mental health, oc-
cupational, health, or social problems that make their addictive
disorders much more difficult to treat. Even if there are few associated problems, the severity of addiction itself ranges widely
among people. A variety of scientifically based approaches to
drug-addiction treatment exist. Drug-addiction treatment can include behavioral therapy (such as counseling, cognitive therapy,
or psychotherapy), medications, or their combination. Behavioral
therapies offer people strategies for coping with their drug crav-

ings, teach them ways to avoid drugs and prevent relapse, and help them deal with relapse if it occurs. When a person's drug-related behavior places him or her at higher risk for AIDS or other infectious diseases, behavioral therapies can help to reduce the risk of disease transmission. Case management and referral to other medical, psychological, and social services are crucial components of treatment for many patients.

The best programs provide a combination of therapies and other services to meet the needs of the individual patient, which are shaped by such issues as age, race, culture, sexual orientation, gender, pregnancy, parenting, housing, and employment, as well as physical and sexual abuse.

Treatment medications, such as methadone, LAAM, and naltrexone, are available for individuals addicted to opiates. Nicotine preparations (patches, gum, and nasal spray) and bupropion are available for individuals addicted to nicotine.

Medications, such as antidepressants, mood stabilizers, or neuroleptics, may be critical for treatment success when patients have co-occurring mental disorders, such as depression, anxiety disorder, bipolar disorder, or psychosis. Treatment can occur in a variety of settings, in many different forms, and for different lengths of time. Because drug addiction is typically a chronic disorder characterized by occasional relapses, a short-term one-time treatment often is not sufficient. For many, treatment is a long-term process that involves multiple interventions and attempts at abstinence.

The National Institute of Health's MEDLINEplus *Medical Encyclopedia* (2003) offers this additional definition of drug-abuse treatment: "Treatment for a person with drug abuse or dependence begins with the recognition of the problem. Though previously 'denial' was considered a symptom of addiction, recent research has shown that this symptom can be dramatically reduced if addicts are treated with empathy and respect, rather than told what to do or 'confronted.'"

Treatment of drug dependency involves detoxification, support, and abstinence. Emergency treatment may be indicated for acute intoxication or drug overdose. Often, support of the respiratory system is needed as there may be a loss of consciousness. This usually entails being on a mechanical respirator temporarily. The specific treatment depends on the drug.

Detoxification is the gradual withdrawal of an abused substance in a controlled environment. Sometimes a drug with a

similar action is substituted during the withdrawal process to reduce the unpleasant symptoms and risks associated with withdrawal. The process can be managed either on an inpatient or on
an outpatient basis. Rehabilitation is the process that occurs after
detoxification and is often needed to prevent relapse. Individual,
group, or family therapy is usually part of this process, which
may continue for a month or longer. Information and support
may also be sought from local twelve-step groups such as Alcoholics Anonymous (AA) and Narcotics Anonymous (NA), which
can be located through the phone directory or on-line. There are
also alternative programs for those who do not like or do not do
well in twelve-step programs. These include SMART Recovery,
Women for Sobriety, and LifeRing Recovery, which can also be
found on-line.

If a depression or other mood disorder exists, it should be
treated appropriately. In the past, addiction-treatment providers
discouraged use of antidepressant medications, which actually
made relapse to addiction more likely. Very often, drug abuse develops from efforts to self-treat mental illness.

Aftercare often involves lifelong abstinence from drug abuse.
Self-help groups such as Narcotics Anonymous can offer support.
For heroin addicts, long-term methadone maintenance is the treatment with the best track record of reducing relapse, improving
functioning, and restoring health (MEDLINEplus 2003). Nearly
three decades of scientific research have yielded thirteen fundamental principles that characterize effective drug-abuse treatment:

1. No single treatment is appropriate for all individuals.
    Matching treatment settings, interventions, and services
    to each individual's particular problems and needs is
    critical to his or her ultimate success in returning to
    productive functioning in the family, workplace, and
    society.
2. Treatment needs to be readily available. Because
    individuals who are addicted to drugs may be
    uncertain about entering treatment, taking advantage
    of opportunities when they are ready for treatment is
    crucial. Potential treatment applicants can be lost if
    treatment is not immediately available or is not readily
    accessible.
3. Effective treatment attends to multiple needs of the
    individual, not just his or her drug use. To be effective,

treatment must address the individual's drug use and any associated medical, psychological, social, vocational, and legal problems.

4. An individual's treatment and service plan must be assessed continually and modified as necessary to ensure that the plan meets the person's changing needs. A patient may require varying combinations of services and treatment components during the course of treatment and recovery. In addition to counseling or psychotherapy, a patient at times may require medication, other medical services, family therapy, parenting instruction, vocational rehabilitation, and social and legal services. It is critical that the treatment approach be appropriate to the individual's age, gender, ethnicity, and culture.

5. Remaining in treatment for an adequate period of time is critical for treatment effectiveness. The appropriate duration for an individual depends on his or her problems and needs. Research indicates that for most patients, the threshold of significant improvement is reached at about three months in treatment. After this threshold is reached, additional treatment can produce further progress toward recovery. Because people often leave treatment prematurely, programs should include strategies to engage and keep patients in treatment.

6. Counseling (individual and/or group) and other behavioral therapies are critical components of effective treatment for addiction. In therapy, patients address issues of motivation, build skills to resist drug use, replace drug-using activities with constructive and rewarding non–drug-using activities, and improve problem-solving abilities. Behavioral therapy also facilitates interpersonal relationships and the individual's ability to function in the family and community.

7. Medications are an important element of treatment for many patients, especially when combined with counseling and other behavioral therapies. Methadone and levo-alpha-acetylmethadol (LAAM) are very effective in helping individuals addicted to heroin or other opiates stabilize their lives and reduce their illicit-drug use. Naltrexone is also an effective medication for

some opiate addicts and some patients with co-occurring alcohol dependence. For persons addicted to nicotine, a nicotine replacement product (such as patches or gum) or an oral medication (such as bupropion) can be an effective component of treatment. For patients with mental disorders, both behavioral treatments and medications can be critically important.

8. Addicted or drug-abusing individuals with coexisting mental disorders should have both disorders treated in an integrated way. Because addictive disorders and mental disorders often occur in the same individual, patients presenting for either condition should be assessed and treated for the co-occurrence of the other type of disorder.

9. Medical detoxification is only the first stage of addiction treatment and by itself does little to change long-term drug use. Medical detoxification safely manages the acute physical symptoms of withdrawal associated with stopping drug use. While detoxification alone is rarely sufficient to help addicts achieve long-term abstinence, for some individuals it is a strongly indicated precursor to effective drug-addiction treatment (National Institute on Drug Abuse 1999).

10. Treatment does not need to be voluntary to be effective. Strong motivation can facilitate the treatment process. Sanctions or enticements in the family, employment setting, or criminal justice system can increase significantly both treatment entry and retention rates and the success of drug-treatment interventions.

11. Possible drug use during treatment must be monitored continuously. Relapses to drug use can occur during treatment. The objective monitoring of a patient's drug and alcohol use during treatment, such as through urinalysis or other tests, can help the patient withstand urges to use drugs. Such monitoring can also provide early evidence of drug use so that the individual's treatment plan can be adjusted. Feedback to patients who test positive for illicit-drug use is an important element of monitoring.

12. Treatment programs should provide assessment for HIV/AIDS, hepatitis B and C, tuberculosis (TB), and other infectious diseases, and counseling to help

patients modify or change behaviors that place themselves or others at risk of infection. Counseling can help patients avoid high-risk behavior. Counseling can also help people who are already infected manage their illness.

13. Recovery from drug addiction can be a long-term process and frequently requires multiple episodes of treatment. As with other chronic illnesses, relapses to drug use can occur during or after successful treatment episodes. Addicted individuals may require prolonged treatment and multiple episodes of treatment to achieve long-term abstinence and fully restored functioning. Participation in self-help support programs during and following treatment is often helpful in maintaining abstinence.

References

American Psychiatric Association. 2000. *Diagnostic and Statistical Manual of Mental Disorders.* 4th ed. Washington, DC: American Psychiatric Association.

Center for Substance Abuse Prevention (CSAP), Substance Abuse and Mental Health Services Administration. 1993. *A Discussion Paper on Preventing Alcohol, Tobacco, and Other Drug Problems.* Rockville, MD: United States Department of Health and Human Services.

———. 1994. *Prevention Primer: An Encyclopedia of Alcohol, Tobacco, and Other Prevention Terms.* Rockville, MD: United States Department of Health and Human Services.

———. 2002. *Science-Based Prevention Programs and Principles: Effective Substance Abuse and Mental Health Programs for Every Community.* Rockville, MD: United States Department of Health and Human Services.

Columbia University Center of Addiction and Substance Abuse. 2001. Results of post-September 11 survey of substance use in the United States. Available at http://www.casacolumbia.org/absolutenm/templates/PressReleases.asp?articleid=114&zoneid=48 (accessed January 9, 2004).

Erowid's Psychoactive Vaults. 2003. Available at http://www.erowid.org/psychoactives/psychoactives.shtml (accessed January 9, 2004).

Falkowski, C. 2000. *Dangerous Drugs.* Center City, MN: Hazelden.

Goode, E. 1989. *Drugs in American Society.* New York: McGraw-Hill.

Isralowitz, R. 2002. *Drug Use, Policy and Management.* Westport, CT: Auburn House.

Leshner, A. 2001. "Why Do Sally and Johnny Use Drugs?" Available at http://www.drugabuse.gov/Published_Articles/Sally.html (accessed January 12, 2004).

Lettieri, D., M. Sayers, and H. Pearson, eds. 1980. *Theories on Drug Abuse: Selected Contemporary Perspectives.* Rockville, MD: National Institute on Drug Abuse.

MEDLINEplus. 2003. *Medical Encyclopedia: Drug Abuse and Dependence.* Available at http://www.nlm.nih.gov/medlineplus/ency/article/001522.htm (accessed February 1, 2003).

National Institute on Drug Abuse (NIDA). 1999. *Principles of Drug Addiction Treatment: A Research-Based Guide.* Rockville, MD: National Institute on Drug Abuse.

Office of Substance Abuse Prevention (OSAP), Alcohol, Drug Abuse, and Mental Health Services Administration. 1991. *Prevention Plus III: Assessing Alcohol and Other Drug Prevention Programs at the School and Community Level.* Rockville, MD: United States Department of Health and Human Services.

Petraitis, J., B. Flay, T. Miller, E. Torpy, and B. Greiner. 1998. "Illicit Substance Use among Adolescents: A Matrix of Prospective Predictors." *Substance Use and Misuse* 33, no. 13: 2561–2604.

Ray, E., and C. Ksir. 1990. *Drugs, Society and Human Behavior.* St. Louis: Times Mirror/Mosby.

Substance Abuse Mental Health Services Administration (SAMHSA). 2000. *Tips for Teens Series.* Washington, DC: SAMHSA.

United Nations General Assembly Political Declaration. 1998. "Declaration on the Guiding Principles of Drug Demand Reduction." June 8–10.

White House Office of National Drug Control Policy. Available at http://www.whitehousedrugpolicy.gov/prevent/strategies.html (accessed February 1, 2003).

World Health Organization. 1992. *The ICD-10 Classification of Mental and Behavioural Disorders: Clinical Descriptions and Diagnostic Guidelines.* Geneva: World Health Organization.

2

Problems, Controversies, and Solutions: U.S. Drug Policy in Perspective

In this chapter, the drug problem is examined in terms of its impact and cost to society and people. The effectiveness of programs and policies to address the problem are discussed as well. The president's National Drug Control Strategy (2003) is presented, followed by a review of the pros and cons about legislation and an examination of the marijuana controversy. Thoughts are offered about the need for reform, including possible solutions.

Problems

U.S. society has a major drug problem on its hands; the condition is undesirable and it appears that policies must be changed and new programs instituted (Goode 1989). This statement was made more than a decade ago and little has changed based on observations and reports regarding patterns of drug use and addicted behavior, criminal activity, emergency hospital visits, and violence. The opinions expressed by antidrug leaders, a wide range of respected judicial and government officials, social scientists, and commentators on social order tend to agree that national drug policy and the War on Drugs is a "dismal failure," "monumental error," and "utter futility" (Russell 1992; Sweet 1996).

Opinions show:

- More than 50 percent of those surveyed in a 1999 Gallup poll said that their concern about illicit-drug use had grown in the past five years, and adolescent drug use and crime are among the top concerns.
- Most Americans view the nation's drug war as a failure. According to a 2001 survey by the Pew Research Center, no less than 90 percent say drug abuse is a serious problem in the nation, with a quarter calling it a national crisis. Nearly three-quarters of Americans say the drug war is being lost, and just as many say that insatiable demand will perpetuate the nation's drug habit.
- According to *Drug Wars,* a four-hour *Frontline* report aired on television by the Public Broadcasting Service (PBS) in 2000, little has been accomplished over the past three decades to stem the use and availability of illegal drugs.
- Other reports and commentary show that the U.S. antidrug campaign is waning. Americans are tired of wasting billions of dollars on a drug war that is not working, especially when clear, pragmatic alternatives exist. Wealthy businessmen have joined together to find ways of ending the drug war since their belief is that the federal government has proved incapable of reform, living in fear of the right-wing moralists.
- Editorials from leading newspapers such as the *New York Times, Washington Post,* and *International Herald Tribune* express criticism of drug policy, including the fact that it appears to be a war on civil liberties in which black men are being imprisoned for drug offenses at thirteen times the rate of white men.
- After five years as the U.S. "drug czar" Gen. Barry McCaffrey refers to the drug problem as a "cancer," not a war, calling for new drug courts, methadone, and access to insurance for drug abuse and mental health, which he believes will lower the level of spousal abuse and violence as well as save immense resources.

Numbers: What Do They Show?

The most revealing evidence about the state of the U.S. drug policy lie among the numbers of people involved and affected. Facts and numbers show:

- The national rate for past-year dependence on or abuse of alcohol or illicit drugs among persons aged twelve or older tends to be about 6.3 percent, slightly higher than the rate for just alcohol dependence or abuse (5.4 percent), which is three times larger than the rate for illicit-drug dependence or abuse only (1.9 percent).
- An estimated 14.5 million Americans aged twelve or older have been classified with dependence or abuse of either alcohol or illicit drugs. Most of these persons (10.2 million) are dependent on or abuse alcohol only. Another 1.9 million are dependent on or abuse both alcohol and illicit drugs, while 2.4 million are dependent on or abuse illicit drugs only.
- Throughout the United States (in 2000), almost half of the Americans aged twelve or older reported having a drink in the past month (46.6 percent), and about one-fifth (20.6 percent) of them participated in "binge" drinking in the past thirty days. Moreover, among youths, 16.4 percent reported using alcohol in the past month, and 10.4 percent of them reported past-month "binge" alcohol use.
- In 1997, more than 2.5 million arrests were made for alcohol offenses and more than 1.5 million for other drug offenses.
- About half of the state prison inmates and 40 percent of the federal prisoners incarcerated for committing violent crimes reported that they were under the influence of alcohol and/or drugs at the time of their offense. Alcohol is more likely to be involved in crimes against people, including homicides, rapes, and sexual assaults.
- From 1985 to 1995, the proportion of drug offenders in state prisons increased from 9 percent to 23 percent, and the proportion of federal inmates sentenced for drug offenses grew from 34 percent to 60 percent.

- More than one in three women in state prisons was serving a sentence for drug offenses in 1997, up from one in eight in 1986. The increases in incarcerated drug offenders are related, in part, to mandatory minimum-sentencing laws for drug offenses and are often cited as major reasons for prison overcrowding.

Additional information shows:

- The number of hard-core users of cocaine remained steady during the past decade, at around 3.5 million.
- The number of hard-core heroin users rose from 600,000 in the early 1990s to 980,000 in 2001.
- In 1960, the U.S. inmate population (counting those locked up in long-term prisons but not counting illegal immigrants and minors) stood at 333,000. During the next two decades, it rose at a comparatively modest pace, to 474,000. Then, from 1980 to 2000, the number of incarcerated quadrupled to 2 million. Regarding incarceration, 9.7 percent of black males in their twenties are imprisoned, compared with 2.9 percent of Hispanic men and 1.1 percent of white men in the same age group.
- According to the U.S. Department of Justice's Bureau of Statistics, 38,288 drug offenders were referred to federal prosecutors in 1999, an increase from 11,854 in 1984. Furthermore, 84 percent of the 38,288 suspects were subsequently charged in a U.S. court, and 90 percent of the drug offenders were convicted, the majority for drug trafficking.
- One-third of the federal drug offenders in 1999 had never been previously arrested, and two out of three had no prior felony convictions. Of that minority of drug offenders with previous convictions, 32 percent had only prior drug convictions. Fewer than 10 percent of all drug offenders convicted in 1999 had previous felony convictions.
- About 90 percent of the people convicted on federal drug charges in 1999 were nonviolent offenders, and two-thirds of those convicted were first-time felony offenders. Nine out of ten first-timers (92 percent) went to prison anyway.

- Almost 2 million Americans are either in prison (after conviction) or jail (waiting for trial). Of every 100,000 Americans, 481 are in prison. By comparison, the incarceration rate for Britain is 125 per 100,000, for Canada 129, and for Japan 40. Only Russia, at 685, has a higher rate of lockup.
- In the United States, 1.5 million children have at least one parent in prison. The 1999 figures mean that 500,000 more children have a parent in prison compared to 1991. There is a 98 percent increase over the past eight years in the number of minors with a mother in prison.
- Among the children with a parent in prison, 58 percent were younger than ten, with the average age of eight. Fathers are most likely to be the imprisoned parent—representing 93 percent of all imprisoned parents—with the children generally living with their mothers. In addition, half of the parents in prison are African American, one-quarter are white, and one-fifth are Hispanic.
- National estimates of the need for drug-abuse treatment suggest that only two in five illicit-drug abusers who need treatment for severe problems actually receive care. In 1996, about 5.3 million people with serious drug-abuse problems needed treatment, while only about 2 million received it.
- A fundamental building block for an antidrug strategy is treatment, yet in the past decade funds for treating drug addiction dropped from 25 percent of the federal drug budget—well before the cocaine epidemic created millions of new addicts—to only 14 percent. In the same period, arrests for drug crimes doubled, while violent crime jumped by more than one-third.
- Most offenders arrested for homicide or aggravated assaults were using cocaine or heroin, as were three-quarters of those arrested for burglary or robbery.
- More than three-quarters of all state prison inmates are drug users—at least 500,000 offenders—but only 10 to 20 percent receive any help. Although addicts maintained on methadone will give up heroin and commit fewer crimes, such treatment is available to less than 20 percent of the nation's heroin addicts. (Isralowitz 2002, 173–174)

Money: What Does All This Cost?

- The economic cost of substance abuse to the U.S. economy each year is staggering. In 2001, the White House Office of National Drug Control Policy estimated the annual economic impact of substance abuse to be $373 billion. This figure includes the costs of health care, social services, and criminal justice systems, as well as losses due to crime, impact of premature death and disability, and spending on prevention, treatment, and law enforcement. In terms of this amount, alcohol abuse is the most costly (44 percent), followed by smoking (37 percent) and illicit-drug abuse (19 percent).
- In 1992, the total cost to society for alcohol and illegal drug use was $965 for every person in the United States; the per-person cost for drug abuse alone was $383 (Swan 1998).
- The drug market in the United States was estimated to be at $150 billion a year in 1996.
- In 1996, the jails and prisons cost $20 billion a year; in 2001, the expense was in the area of $40 billion a year to construct and operate federal, state, and local prisons. The cost to taxpayers for the federal prison system alone that cares for 150,000 prisoners was estimated to be $4.66 billion in 2001. This means that the annual cost per prisoner is $31,000. In 1986, when federal mandatory minimum sentences were enacted, the budget of the Bureau of Prisons was $0.7 billion, according to the president of the Criminal Justice Policy Foundation.
- The annual federal antidrug budget grew from roughly $53 million in 1970 to $10 billion in fiscal year 1997. In 2002, the budget was approximately $11.5 billion.
- Since 1970, the United States has invested roughly $77 billion in domestic and foreign drug enforcement—$74 billion since 1981.
- In 1996, it was reported that the United States spent more than $3 billion a year on its overseas drug wars alone; in 2001, nearly $1.3 billion went to Colombia.
- Most of the federal government's annual drug-fighting

budget is spent on interdiction and enforcement. The
national drug control spending budget for 2002 was in
excess of $18 billion. By function, approximate amounts
show $9.5 billion for domestic law enforcement, $3.8
billion for treatment (with research), $2.4 billion for
prevention (with research), $2.1 billion for interdiction,
and $1 billion for international activities. A California
study has shown that on average, every dollar invested
in treatment saves $7 in crime and health care costs.

- In a Rand Corporation study of drug-treatment
spending by U.S. governmental agencies, a $1 billion
overstatement was found. Although the White House
Office of National Drug Control Policy estimated that
U.S. agencies spent $2.8 billion on drug treatment,
authors of the Rand study said in 2001 that the actual
amount was closer to $1.8 billion, or 36 percent less
than reported.

- It has been reported that substance abuse and addiction
added at least $41 billion—10 percent—to the costs of
elementary and secondary education in 2001 due to
class disruption and violence, special education and
tutoring, teacher turnover, truancy, children left behind,
student-assistance programs, property damage, injury,
and counseling.

- The National Association of State Alcohol and Drug
Abuse Directors estimates that the annual cost to
incarcerate a drug offender is up to $50,000 per inmate
compared to the annual cost of outpatient drug-free
treatment at $2,300, methadone maintenance at $3,000
per patient, and residential drug-free treatment at
$14,000. (ibid., 174–176)[1]

Effectiveness of Prevention and Treatment Programs

In the war against drugs, a major battlefront involves prevention
and treatment. At best, drug use–prevention and –treatment programs tend to reflect a mixed bag of results. It appears that a
number of intervention strategies have demonstrated the ability
to reduce or prevent drug use and drug-related crime. They
include school- and community-based education and prevention,

various methods of treatment, drug testing and employee-assistance programs in the workplace, organized neighborhood action to drive out dealers, media campaigns, parenting skills, grassroots coalitions, and other efforts to change attitudes and promote norms that rule out drug use.

For the most part, drug-prevention and -treatment efforts have been fragmented, underfunded, less than comprehensive, and poorly planned and integrated for a variety of historical, political, and economic reasons. In spite of this, it has been found that better outcomes tend to exist when treatment is individualized, promotes client motivation, and extends the amount of time the client is involved in the program.

Drug addicts are not a homogeneous group, and, in theory, the needs of each client should be matched, preferably to a service system characterized by rational, flexible, responsive, well-defined, and short- and long-term integrated service plans developed on dependable funding sources with ongoing monitoring and evaluation. The fact remains, however, that such approaches are, for the most part, absent in the United States. Additionally, over the past three decades, commitment to drug-abuse treatment has waxed and waned under different administrations with different funding priorities and in response to changing patterns of drug use, drug availability, and perceived national threat. Despite sporadic efforts by national commissions, policy advisory panels, and federal agencies to develop policies and plans to improve treatment—many of which have detailed the same or similar recommendations for what is needed—the development of drug treatment has more often than not been reactive rather than proactive, piecemeal rather than planned, and fragmented rather than integrated. Current policy and practice tend to isolate the drug abuser from mainstream health care. Also, legislation and general policy, including funding priorities, have created often insurmountable barriers to treatment for many people with drug problems (ibid, 176–178).

Drug Abuse Resistance Education (DARE)

Drug-prevention efforts tend to reflect a muddled scene of policy and practice. Specifically, the U.S. government invests annually hundreds of millions of dollars in an antidrug program known as Drug Abuse Resistance Education. In one evaluation of the program, it was found that the level of drug use among kids who had gone through DARE was virtually identical to the level among kids who had not and that the program does not produce any long-term prevention effects on adolescent drug-use rates. In 1994, a National Institute of Justice–sponsored study concluded that while many teachers and participants loved the program, it had no effect on drug use. In response to this finding, the Justice Department refused to release the peer-reviewed study; however, the *American Journal of Public Health* accepted it for publication. In a 1996 study published in *Preventive Medicine,* it was found that any results from DARE were extremely short-lived and that there was no evidence that the prevention program reduces drug use. More recently, elected officials throughout the country have called DARE a fraud on the people of the United States that has wasted opportunities to develop school programs that can work. Also, a survey released by the National Center on Addiction and Substance Abuse (CASA) in 2001 said that the popular DARE program presented little evidence of any extended impact.

After years of debate and controversy about the DARE program, the U.S. Government Accounting Office in January 2003 reported that based on six long-term evaluations of the DARE elementary-school curriculum, no significant differences were found in illicit-drug use between students who received DARE and students who did not. All of the evaluations suggested that DARE had no long-term effect on preventing youth illicit-drug use. The report also noted that in spite of the evidence regarding DARE's failure, the program continues to operate in about 80 percent of all school districts across the United States and in numerous foreign countries.

It has been noted that there is uncertainty about the real costs of DARE because there is no centralized accounting of the funds, expenditures, and resources used to support the program. According to the *New York Times,* in 2001 the Department of Justice gave DARE about $41.7 million; police departments (taxpayers) gave DARE approximately $215 million in indirect benefits in the form of officer salaries for speaking appearances and other duties, and DARE received around $15 million in private money. Officials in the U.S. Department of Education, who administer more than $500 million of safe-schools federal grant money annually to state education and governors' offices, do not know and do not keep records of how much goes to support the DARE program. The Institute of Industrial Relations in 2001 reported the annual costs for the program, including local expenses, may range as much as $1 billion to $1.3 billion (Shepard 2001).

National Youth Anti-Drug Media Campaign
The National Youth Anti-Drug Media Campaign is a U.S. government–funded initiative to reduce and prevent drug use among young people. Through the use of television, radio, and other advertising, complemented by public-relations efforts including community outreach and institutional partnerships, the campaign addresses youths directly and indirectly as well as encourages their parents and other adults to take actions known to affect drug use. The campaign was initiated under the Treasury-Postal Appropriations Act of 1998 with Congress-approved funding (P.L. 105-61). Annually, the campaign receives about $180 million to deliver its messages. The Drug Reform Coordination Network (http://www.drcnet.org) reported that this taxpayer-funded advertising campaign had cost $929 million by 2002 and included more than 200 TV commercials using popular performers such as the Dixie Chicks and Mary J. Blige in an effort to turn kids away from drugs.

Under contract from the National Institute on Drug Abuse, Westat (a private consulting group) in cooperation with the Annenberg School for Communication at the University of Pennsylvania conducted an evaluation focused on evidence of the campaign's effects on youths and parents, including recall of campaign messages, effects on parents, and effects on youths. From the final evaluation, little evidence was found supporting a favorable effect of the campaign on youths, either directly or through their parents' exposure to the campaign. In fact, there was evidence consistent with an unfavorable direct effect of the campaign on youths' cognizance of marijuana.

National Research Council Report on Drug Enforcement Activities
In 1998, the White House Office of National Drug Control Policy sponsored a study by the National Research Committee to review the entire range of data and research that might contribute to informed policy making about illegal drugs. The National Research Council reported in 2001 that although the federal government invests about $12 billion each year in drug-enforcement programs, little evidence exists to determine the programs' effectiveness. It was noted that the nation's ability to evaluate whether its drug policies work is no better now than it was twenty years ago, and the assessment of drug-enforcement activities is severely hampered by an absence of adequate, reliable data on both drug

consumption and the cost of illegal drugs. According to the chairman of the committee, "It is unconscionable for this country to continue to carry out a public policy of this magnitude and cost without any way of knowing whether, and to what extent, it is having on the desired result" (The National Academies News 2001).

Drug Enforcement Administration (DEA)

The Drug Enforcement Administration is responsible for enforcing the controlled-substances laws and regulations of the United States. The DEA is the lead agency responsible for the development of overall federal drug-enforcement strategy, programs, planning, and evaluation.

Does the DEA work? According to the White House Office of Management and Budget (OMB), which released its evaluation of the agency in early 2003, the answer is no. The report says that the DEA spends $1.56 billion each year on drug law enforcement, but it has no idea whether it has an effect on its mission. According to the report, the DEA is unable to demonstrate progress in reducing the availability of illegal drugs in the United States, it lacks clear long-term strategies and goals, its managers are not held accountable for problems, and its financial controls do not comply with federal standards. In a *New York Times* article (February 5, 2003), it was noted that DEA critics say that drug purity has increased and drugs are easier to buy than ever before. Additionally, it was noted by President Bush in his report on drug strategy for 2003 that use among young people was at "unacceptably high levels" and that "in recent years we have lost ground in reducing illegal use."

Support for the DEA has more than doubled since 1995; now, the agency's financing is to remain virtually the same, while other law enforcement agencies are receiving increases of 10 percent or more. Furthermore, with the Federal Bureau of Investigation (FBI) moving four hundred agents off drug cases to terrorism, the DEA is being asked to pick up the slack. According to the president of the Criminal Justice Policy Foundation, the DEA emperor has no clothes and the White House report should really shake up our national revelry with drug enforcement and generate a major reevaluation of our antidrug efforts. Others say the OMB critique was long overdue and could start a debate about how the War on Drugs is working.

Current Policy in the United States: The President's National Drug Control Strategy

In Febrary 2003 director of the White House Office of National Drug Control Policy, John Walters, unveiled the president's new National Drug Control Strategy. The strategy reports progress toward meeting the president's goals of reducing drug use by 10 percent over two years, and 25 percent over five years, highlighted by reductions in drug use among young people for the first time in nearly a decade. The strategy also highlights a new treatment initiative funded with $600 million over three years to help addicted Americans find needed treatment and support services from the most effective programs, including faith-based and community-based organizations.

Key Points of the National Drug Control Strategy

The strategy proposes a fiscal year 2004 budget of $11.7 billion for drug control serving three core priorities: (1) stopping drug use before it starts, (2) healing America's drug users, and (3) disrupting the market.

Stopping Drug Use before It Starts
Continuing the initial reductions in drug use by young people will require action by all Americans through education and community involvement. In homes, schools, places of worship, the workplace, and civic and social organizations, Americans must set standards that reaffirm the values of responsibility and good citizenship while dismissing the image that drug use is consistent with individual freedom. America's children must learn from an early age that avoiding drug use is an expectation and lifelong responsibility.

- The strategy ties national leadership with community-level action to help re-create the formula that has helped the United States succeed against drugs in the past. The president's budget backs up this goal with a $10 million increase in funding for the expanded Drug-

Free Communities Support Program, along with providing $5 million for a new Parents Drug Corps.
- In fiscal year 2004, the strategy proposes that tools such as student drug testing be available in communities where parents and educators deem them appropriate, and funds them with $8 million.

Healing America's Drug Users

Despite substantial drug-prevention efforts, some 16 million Americans still use drugs on a monthly basis, and roughly 6 million meet the clinical criteria for needing drug treatment. Yet the overwhelming majority of users in need of drug treatment fail to recognize their need. The second core priority of the strategy emphasizes the crucial need for family, friends, and former addicts to intercede with and support those fighting to overcome substance abuse. Drug users also need the support of institutions and the people who run them—employers, law enforcement agencies, faith-based and community-based organizations, and health care providers, among others—to help them recognize their drug addiction and to seek treatment.

- Overall, for 2004, the administration proposes $3.6 billion for drug treatment, an increase of 8.2 percent over 2003.
- The 2004 request includes new funding of $200 million ($600 million over three years) for a new treatment initiative to provide drug treatment to individuals otherwise unable to obtain access to services. People in need of treatment, no matter where they are— emergency rooms, health clinics, the criminal justice system, or schools—will receive an evidence-based assessment of their treatment need and will be issued vouchers to obtain help at effective treatment organizations, including faith-based and community-based organizations.

Disrupting the Market

Priority 3 of the strategy, disrupting the market, seeks to capitalize on the engagement of producer and transit countries like Colombia and Mexico in order to address the drug trade as a business—one that faces numerous and often overlooked obstacles that may be used as pressure points. The drug trade is not an unstoppable force of nature but rather a profit-making enterprise where costs and rewards exist in an equilibrium that can be disrupted. Every action that makes the drug trade more costly and less profitable is a step toward "breaking" the market. As the strategy explains, drug traffickers are in business to make money. We intend to deny them that revenue.

- To help secure U.S. borders, the president's budget includes $2.1 billion for drug interdiction, an increase of 7.3 percent from 2003. Internationally, the Bush administration will continue to target the supply of illegal drugs in the source countries.
- The administration is requesting $731 million in dedicated funds in 2004 for the Andean Counterdrug Initiative to be applied in Bolivia, Brazil, Colombia, Ecuador, Panama, Peru, and Venezuela.
- To ensure unity of effort, the strategy advocates the use of a single list identifying high-level targets (the Consolidated Priority Organization Targeting list) among the various agencies involved in domestic drug law enforcement.

Progress toward Two- and Five-Year Goals

Only the first year of the two-year goal period has elapsed, yet already the goal of reducing current use by 10 percent among eighth, tenth, and twelfth graders, as measured by the Monitoring the Future survey, is well on the way to being met.[2] Adjustments to the measuring baseline for the goals have been prompted by discontinuities in the National Household Survey on Drug Abuse (NHSDA). As a result, the goal of reducing drug use among adults will still be measured by the NHSDA, but the baseline has been reset to the 2002 survey, which is not released until midyear 2003.[3] For detailed data tables related to the National Drug Control Strategy, visit http://www.whitehousedrugpolicy.gov. Information about the Monitoring the Future report is available at http://monitoringthefuture.org.

Legislating Reform: What Are the Perspectives?

Legislation is a route to drug-policy reform. Two perspectives are presented. The first is from Asa Hutchinson, who served as President Bush's director of the Drug Enforcement Administration and resigned his position in March 2003. Mike Jay, a journalist and author, presents another view of the issue.

"Drug Legalization Doesn't Work," by Asa Hutchinson

This column by Asa Hutchinson first appeared in the *Washington Post* on October 9, 2002.

> On a recent summer tour through south London, I saw the future of drug legalization. A young couple injected heroin inside the filthy ruins of an abandoned building. In this working-class neighborhood, residents weave in and out of crowded sidewalks, trying to avoid making eye contact with dealers who openly push heroin, marijuana and crack.
>
> Scotland Yard aggressively targets international drug traffickers, and I applaud its strong overall antidrug policy. But last year, a local police commander initiated a pilot program in which people caught possessing marijuana are warned rather than arrested. Often, they're just ignored. In news reports and my interviews, residents criticize the program for bringing more drug dealers, more petty criminals and more drug use.
>
> The one-year Lambeth pilot ended Aug. 1, but Britain has announced it will relax the country's marijuana laws. That move has given fuel to those in the United States who believe we should follow suit. Some have called for the outright legalization of marijuana. People could buy dope over the counter, as they do in the red-light district of Amsterdam.
>
> What these legalization advocates do not talk about are the disturbing problems that people in Lambeth lived with every day. They ignore the sad misery of young people addicted to drugs. They ignore the seri-

ous problems that countries such as the Netherlands are experiencing—problems that are leading them to reconsider their own liberal drug laws.

The culture of drug use and acceptance in the Netherlands has played a role in that country's becoming the world's top producer of Ecstasy. It's interesting that, in a 2001 study, the British Home Office found that violent crime and property crime increased in the late 1990s in every wealthy country except the United States. No doubt effective drug enforcement had a part in declining crime in the United States.

Maybe it's time Europeans looked to America's drug policy as their model. Our approach—tough drug laws coupled with effective education programs and compassionate treatment—is having success. It's a great myth that there's been no progress in our antidrug effort. To the contrary, there's been remarkable success. Overall drug use in the United States is down by more than one-third since the late 1970s. That's 9.5 million fewer people using illegal drugs. We have reduced cocaine use by an astounding 70 percent in the past 15 years.

This is not to say we have done enough. Drugs are still readily available, and a new National Household Survey on Drug Abuse shows that American kids are increasingly using drugs such as Ecstasy. As long as we have despair, poverty and frustration, as long as we have teenage rebellion, we're going to have problems with drugs. But we must keep in mind our success and also keep some perspective about U.S. drug use. Less than 5 percent of the population uses illegal drugs. That's 16 million regular users of all illegal drugs, compared with 66 million tobacco users and 109 million alcohol users.

Emerging drug threats such as Ecstasy and methamphetamine are going to require even more resolve and innovation. We need a renewed dedication by all Americans to help our kids stay away from the misery and addiction of drugs. In fighting drugs, we do have new ideas: from drug courts to community coalitions; from more investment in education to more effective treatment; from drug testing in the workplace to drug counselors in schools. These are ideas that work.

What doesn't work is legalization. It's a well-kept secret that we have tried it before in this country. In 1975, Alaska's Supreme Court held that under that state's constitution, an adult could possess marijuana for personal consumption at home.

The court's ruling became a green light for marijuana use. A 1988 University of Alaska survey showed that the state's teenagers used marijuana at a rate more than twice the national average for their age group. The report also showed a frequency of marijuana use that suggested it wasn't experimental but was a well-incorporated practice for teens. Fed up with this dangerous experiment, Alaska's residents voted in 1990 to recriminalize the possession of marijuana. But 15 years of legalization left its mark—increased drug use by a generation of our youth.

Legalizing drugs is simply a surrender. It's giving up on the hope of a drug-free future for our next generation. It's writing off those still in the grip of addiction and despair. Isn't every life worth fighting for?

"Legalisation: The First Hundred Years: What Happened When Drugs Were Legal and Why They Were Prohibited," by Mike Jay

The following paper was presented at a conference in London on July 17, 2002, organized by the Institute for Public Policy Research (IPPR).[4]

Today, as the notion of legalising drugs is making its way into the mainstream political agenda for the first time in living memory, one of the most common objections to it is that it represents a high-risk experiment whose outcome cannot be accurately modelled or predicted. Yet within the context of history, the opposite is true: it is the prohibition of drugs that is the bold experiment without precedent. A hundred years ago, any of us could have walked into our high street chemist and bought cannabis or cocaine, morphine or heroin over the counter. At this point, mind-altering drugs had been freely available throughout history and across almost every culture, and their prohibition, pressed forward largely by the goal of eliminating alcohol from modern societies, was a radical break with the traditional wisdom of public policy.

Nor was it the case that the prohibition of drugs was a response to their sudden emergence in Western societies. In 1800, virtually the only drugs familiar to the West were alcohol and opium; but by 1900, the constellation of substances that form the modern category of illicit drugs—opiates, cannabis, cocaine, stimulants and psychedelics—had all found their niches within a consumer culture driven by scientific discovery and the expansion of global trade. The nineteenth century, typically regarded as an era of repression, moral probity and social control, could also be billed as "Drug Legalisation—The First Hundred Years."

There is much that today's policy makers can learn from this era. Not only were most of the policies now being debated—statutory control and regulation, medical supervision and legal exclusion—all pioneered with varying degrees of success, but the legal availability of drugs offers a glimpse of how the general public originally negotiated their benefits and dangers, and how the various substances found their own levels within the society at large. History, of course, has its limits: it cannot tell us everything, and cannot be expected to repeat itself exactly. Cannabis, for example, was legal throughout the nineteenth century, and its levels of use remained for various reasons quite low: if it were legalised tomorrow, we would hardly expect its prevalence to fall to nineteenth-century levels. But history nevertheless illuminates many of the underlying dynamics in the modern drug debate, not least by offering the possibility of distinguishing between the consequences of drugs themselves and those that only followed once their use had been prohibited.

Perhaps the most significant difference was that today's prime distinction between "medicinal" and "recreational" drugs was, in a society without illicit drugs, at best embryonic. Opiate and cocaine preparations, like alcohol and tobacco, were both intoxicant and medicine, and the distinction between "use" and "abuse," "feeling good" and "feeling better" was vague and subject to medical and social fashion. Today's Class A substances were not typically understood as drugs of "abuse" but as tonics, pick-me-ups or mild sedatives, medicines "for the nerves" inhabiting a middle ground perhaps similar to that occupied today by health supplements, over-the-counter stimulants or energy drinks. This was not because they were only available in mild preparations like opium tinctures and coca teas: even in the late nineteenth century, when pure cocaine and injectable morphine were readily available, the great majority of the public chose to continue consuming these drugs in dilute and manageable preparations.

Even in this era of mild plant and patent preparations, though, there was a clear need for some types of statutory drug controls. Until the 1860s, the market was unregulated: anyone could sell any substance to anyone, and make whatever claims they wished for it. Although most doctors were not overly preoccupied with the dangers of opiate addiction—which was typically seen as a marginal side-effect of the most effective medicine in their pharmacopeia—accidental poisonings and overdoses were a risk that was clearly exacerbated by preparations that labelled their contents inaccurately or not at all. The emergent pharmacy profession began to lobby for control of the sale of such substances, and in 1868 the Poisons and Pharmacy Act was passed. This limited the sale of arsenic, cyanide and opium, previously sold everywhere from grocers' to pubs, to registered pharmacists; the pharmacists, in turn, were obliged to record details of their sales (date, quantity and purchaser).

In retrospect, this initial level of statutory regulation was perhaps the most effective public policy initiative of the era. Public confidence in the drug business rose, and misuse fell. Deaths by accidental overdose, suicide or poisoning remained steady from the 1870s to the 1900s at less than 200 a year in Britain—a figure that today's doctors would gladly trade for the thousands associated with modern prescription drugs. The combination of reliable health information and trace-able sales provoked a modest public reaction against opiate drugs, the first indication that a population presented with a credible assessment of the dangers of drug use will to some extent regulate their use on their own initiative.

But there were two initially unrelated dynamics in nineteenth-century culture that would, by the end of the century, have dovetailed to put the outright prohibition of drugs on the political agenda. The first was a growing set of racial anxieties at the prospect of a multicultural society; the second was the extension of medical science into the notion that drug addiction, and by extension all drug use, was a disease that needed to be addressed under medical supervision.

It was the racial anxieties that bit first. In 1874, the Opium Exclusion Act passed in San Francisco became the first drug prohibition in the modern West; but this was a prohibition to the Chinese population only. It was represented as being for the immigrants' own good as well as for the protection of the whites who might be contaminated by the foreign habit, but the most obvious driving force was the fear of miscegenation between Chinese and whites in the informal and disinhibited surroundings of Chinatown opium dens. Around the same time, the political mood in Britain was turning against the imperial adventures of the Opium Wars, and images of a China "enslaved" by addiction to British opium became prevalent through the reports of missionaries and campaigning journalists. Although these images have subsequently been shown to have been greatly exaggerated, they transformed the perception of opium from indigenous medicine to foreign poison, and anti-opium groups (including Quakers and Temperance activists) promulgated the fear that the growing Chinatowns in Britain might become breeding-grounds for the new "plague."

Metaphors of "plague" and "contagion" were, simultaneously, being given new and literal force by a medical profession for whom the addictive qualities of opium, morphine and cocaine were becoming more significant. The development in the 1870s of the hypodermic syringe, and consequent wider use of potent alkaloidal extracts like morphine, fuelled medical concerns about unprecedentedly powerful and dangerous drugs being available to the general public. Opium users like Thomas de Quincey had long since pointed out that constant use of the drug led to serious physical cravings, tolerance of high doses and withdrawal symptoms (in opposition to much of the medical opinion of the 1820s, which saw these effects simply as overindulgence or vice). But from the 1870s onwards the modern notion of addiction came to take shape, along with the still-familiar claim that this was a "disease" that required specialist treatment by professionals. This, particularly in the context of the contemporary "degeneration theory" that proposed that indulgence in drugs could pass on hereditary disorders to the users' offspring, gradually led to some doctors calling for all opiates to be prohibited to the general public without medical supervision.

There was an element of professional self-interest in all this: opium was the most common and effective remedy of its time, and the majority of the population understandably preferred self-medication with cheap patent pills and tinctures to paying doctors' fees. But there was also, in the new world of cocaine, morphine and needles, a pressing need for new medical advice and statutory controls: manufacturers' guarantees of strength and purity, professional guidance around the potentially hazardous issues of injection and dosage, and public information about the risks of addiction. Yet many medical voices went further, arguing for an outright ban with an urgency perhaps attributable to the fact that the largest group in the emerging addict population were medical professionals: from the 1870s to the 1920s, the profession's own surveys repeatedly suggested that around half of all addicts were doctors and their wives. As the medical profession grew in expertise and stature, calls for legal controls on opiates and cocaine became more authoritative. For the medical profession was not only becoming better organised to extend its remit into new arenas of public health—it was developing its new views against the background of a popular and influential Temperance movement.

Temperance had a diverse set of lobbying groups behind it—the church, the Women's Movement and, particularly in America, the moral high ground of politics—but at its core was an aspirational middle-class crusade to convert the alcohol-fuelled culture of the working classes to civic responsibilities, Christian virtues and "moral hygiene." Most campaigners, doctors and churchmen alike, were united in their belief that alcohol was by far the most significant root of social evil, and the dangers of drugs like opium and cocaine were only stressed in the particular contexts where ethnic minorities lived cheek-by-jowl with the white working classes. Nevertheless, the Temperance movement had the side-effect of carrying the drug debate in its wake. Medical diagnoses like "opium inebrity" were coined, and the urge to indulge in any form of intoxication was classified as "moral insanity," a condition whose ultimate recourse was confinement in an asylum. The public voices prepared to defend the traditional use of drugs were few, and the new medical taxonomy of drug use as a disease, and by extension a contagious "plague," dovetailed with broader fears about miscegenation and racial contamination to produce a climate where, led by the United States, the League of Nations began around 1900 to agree on international measures to prohibit the nonmedical use of opiates and cocaine.

The basic template for today's drug laws was hammered out at summits like the Hague Conference of 1911, and mostly passed into national law in the form of emergency wartime legislation like Britain's 1915 Defence of the Realm Act, later codified in the Dangerous Drugs Act of 1921. The initial effect most noticeable to the general public was that the range of preparations available over the chemist's counter— long-time staples like cannabis, opium or coca tinctures, as well as recently-developed brand medicines like Bayer Pharmaceuticals' new cough treatment, 'Heroin'—were replaced with synthetic alternatives like codeine or ephedrine, alongside useful new palliatives like aspirin. Despite their universal availability, the problematic use of the newly illicit drugs was little higher at this point than it had been a generation before, and the prohibition initially led only to a limited and regional illegal traffic in pure and concentrated substances like morphine, cocaine and heroin. The pressing drug issue of the day was the campaign for alcohol prohibition in America, which built up an irresistible head of steam until the 18th Amendment brought it into law, via the Volstead Act, in 1919.

Historically, there are clear examples of prohibitions that have worked. We only have to look around the world today to see that drugs that are prevalent in some countries have been prevented from gaining a foothold in other similar ones by legal exclusion. But the common denominator of successful prohibitions is that they have nipped a drug habit in the bud, interdicting supply before demand has been established. Once demand is present, the financial arbitrage presented to suppliers will always be a more powerful driver than government tools for interdiction and enforcement. Counterexamples are rare—the Japanese success in curtailing amphetamine use in the 1950s is perhaps the best—and American prohibition was not among them. Alcohol use was too widely established across the social spectrum to halt an illicit traffic that began on the day the law was passed and which proceeded, through financial muscle and the corruption of public officials, to develop a vast shadow economy, which in its centres like Chicago came virtually to amount to an alternative government.

The collapse of the American experiment with prohibition in 1932 left America both internally ravaged by organised crime and corruption and externally isolated from the rest of the world, which had balked at following its lead, and it was in this climate that much of today's drug legislation was assembled, driven through League of Nations Conferences and Geneva Conventions mostly by American initiatives. There were many interest groups in America who had much to gain by switching the focus from alcohol to drugs, and from rebranding traditional medicines as "new menaces." The U.S. Narcotics Bureau needed to shake off the stigma that attached to the Alcohol Bureau by showing that their new quarry was a genuine enemy, far more dangerous than alcohol, and that this time their goal was one that every citizen should support and respect. Medical opinion, too, was keen to backtrack from the less-than-credible excesses of their anti-alcohol warnings and to reverse the nineteenth-century consensus by insisting that substances such as cannabis were, in fact, more dangerous than alcohol. The press and other media, too, found their readers and listeners eager to believe that drugs might be the slippery slope to hell, which had been claimed of alcohol a generation before. Drugs were still prominently linked with ethnic minorities, and new anxieties led to the "anti-narcotic" laws being extended to control the sale of new substances such as cannabis, associated with the Mexican immigrant population, which had previously been assessed (by a British Royal Commission among others) as a minor public health issue. The new legislation left a picture almost unrecognisable from the one that had existed before prohibition. The thrust of the original drug prohibitions—to protect the majority white population from the habits of ethnic minorities—failed to stem demand as drugs flowed through the emerging multicultural societies in much the same way as other culturally specific tropes like fashion, music or food. Medically, new and serious problems emerged. The mild patent preparations, which had proved the most popular forms of the now-illicit drugs, had vanished: now opiates and cocaine were provided by illicit traffickers only in their most concentrated, lucrative and dangerous forms. The health costs of drugs increased in other ways, as risky procedures like injection moved away from the ambit of doctors and chemists and into more dangerous and unhygenic [sic] areas situated specifically beyond the reach of the law. Criminal organisations, many with their origins in alcohol prohibition, filled the vacuum left by patent and pharmaceutical companies, enforcing their illicit trade with violence. Drugs were not without their problems before prohibition, but the majority of the problems associated with them today only emerged fully under the legislation of the twentieth century.

These problems may have been produced by prohibition but, although many of them would not survive long without it, they cannot all be expected to vanish overnight with its repeal. The last century of public policy has transformed our traditional relationship with drugs into something new and uniquely problematic, for which history offers no tailor-made solution. It does, however, offer a reminder that the drug that presents the most obvious public health problems is alcohol, and that although alcohol policy remains highly problematic it has broadly proved to be best tackled not with prohibition but with socialisation under an umbrella of statutory regulation and education. History offers, too, an illustration of how a society legally permeated by today's illicit drugs used to function, and shows that high levels of overall drug prevalence can coexist with low levels of problematic use. . . .

Harm Reduction: An Alternative Approach

The Drug Policy Alliance is a major advocacy organization focused on promoting drug policies based on common sense, science, public health, and human rights. The Alliance and the Lindesmith Library (http://www.lindesmith.org) are supported by George Soros, a wealthy reformer who maintains a fundamental position about promoting human rights. Ethan Nadelmann, an outspoken critic of U.S. government drug policy, is director of the alliance. The following description about "harm reduction" is drawn from the alliance's Web site.

> Harm reduction is a public health philosophy that seeks to lessen the dangers that drug abuse and our drug policies cause to society. A harm reduction strategy is a comprehensive approach to drug abuse and drug policy. Harm reduction's complexity lends to its misperception as a drug legalization tool.
>
> • Harm reduction rests on several basic assumptions. A basic tenet of harm reduction is

that there has never been, is not now, and never will be a drug-free society. A harm reduction strategy seeks pragmatic solutions to the harms that drugs and drug policies cause. It has been said that harm reduction is not what's nice, it's what works.

- A harm reduction approach acknowledges that there is no ultimate solution to the problem of drugs in a free society, and that many different interventions may work. Those interventions should be based on science, public health, common sense, and human rights.
- A harm reduction strategy demands new outcome measurements. Whereas the success of current drug policies is primarily measured by the change in use rates, the success of a harm reduction strategy is measured by the change in rates of death, disease, crime, and suffering.
- Because incarceration does little to reduce the harms that ever-present drugs cause to our society, a harm reduction approach favors treatment of drug addiction by health care professionals over incarceration in the penal system.
- Because some drugs, such as marijuana, have proven medicinal uses, a harm reduction strategy not only seeks to reduce the harm that drugs cause, but also to maximize their potential benefits.
- A harm reduction strategy recognizes that some drugs, such as marijuana, are less harmful than others, such as cocaine and alcohol. Harm reduction mandates that the emphasis on intervention should be based on the relative harmfulness of the drug to society.
- A harm reduction approach advocates lessening the harms of drugs through education, prevention, and treatment. Harm reduction seeks to reduce the harms of drug policies dependent on an overemphasis on interdiction, such as arrest, incarceration, establishment of a felony record, lack of

treatment, lack of adequate information about
drugs, the expansion of military source control
intervention efforts in other countries, and
intrusion on personal freedoms.

- Harm reduction also seeks to reduce the harms
caused by an overemphasis on prohibition,
such as increased purity, black market
adulterants, black market sale to minors, and
black market crime.

- A harm reduction strategy seeks to protect
youth from the dangers of drugs by offering
factual, science-based drug education and
eliminating youth's black market exposure to
drugs.

- Finally, harm reduction seeks to restore basic
human dignity to dealing with the disease of
addiction.

The Cannabis/Marijuana Controversy: What Are the Perspectives?

Marijuana has generated more controversy and response to its
impact on individual behavior and society than any other illegal
substance in the United States. There is an abundance of information about marijuana. What is known tends to be presented in
ways that are contradictory, supporting the special interests of
those who advocate legal regulation of the substance because of
its harmful effects or who advocate legalization because of its
helpful and benign characteristics. Details presented in this section have been drawn from Washington, D.C.–based advocacy
groups for marijuana reform—the Marijuana Policy Project Foundation (http://www.mpp.org) and Common Sense for Drug Policy (http://www.drugwarfacts.org). Also, information published
by the U.S. Drug Enforcement Administration (http://www.
usdoj.gov/dea/ongoing/marijuana) has been used to provide a
comparison of what is communicated about marijuana. A brief review of "Cannabis: Our Position for a Canadian Public Policy—
Report of the Senate Special Committee on Illegal Drugs" (Nolin
and Kenny 2002) is added to this perspective of the marijuana
controversy.

For Policy Change: What the Reformists Say

The Marijuana Policy Project Foundation states the following:

General

Very few Americans had ever heard about marijuana when it was first federally prohibited in 1937. Today, nearly 70 million Americans admit to having tried it. . . . According to government-funded researchers, the perceived availability of marijuana among high school seniors has remained high and steady despite decades of a nationwide drug war. With little variation, every year about 85 percent consider marijuana "fairly easy" or "very easy" to obtain. . . .

Legal and Policy Perspectives

There have been more than 12 million marijuana arrests in the United States since 1970, including a record 704,812 arrests in 1999. About 88 percent of all marijuana arrests are for possession—not manufacture or distribution. . . . Cultivation of even one marijuana plant is a federal felony. . . . Lengthy mandatory minimum sentences apply to a myriad of offenses. For example, a person must serve a five-year mandatory sentence if federally convicted of cultivating one hundred marijuana plants. This is longer than the average sentences for auto theft and manslaughter. . . . Approximately 60,000 marijuana offenders are in prison or jail (June 1999). . . . Civil forfeiture laws allow police to seize the money and property of suspected marijuana offenders—charges need not even be filed. The claim is against property, not the defendant. The property owner must then prove that the property is "innocent"—and indigents have no right to appointed legal counsel. Enforcement abuses stemming from forfeiture laws abound. . . . [It is] estimated that the war on marijuana costs taxpayers more than $9 billion annually. . . . "Decriminalization" involves the removal of criminal penalties for possession of marijuana for personal use. Small fines may be issued (similar to traffic tickets) but there is no arrest, incarceration, or criminal record.

Marijuana use is presently decriminalized in 10

states—California, Colorado, Maine, Minnesota, Mississippi, Nebraska, New York, North Carolina, Ohio, and Oregon. In these states, cultivation and distribution remain criminal offenses.... Decriminalization saves a tremendous amount in enforcement costs. California saves $100 million per year....

Medical

Organizations that have endorsed medical access to marijuana include the AIDS Action Council, American Academy of Family Physicians, American Public Health Association, California Medical Association, California Society of Addiction Medicine, Lymphoma Foundation of America, National Association of People with AIDS, National Nurses Society on Addictions, the New England Journal of Medicine and others.... A few of the many editorial boards that have endorsed medical access to marijuana include: *Boston Globe, Chicago Tribune, Miami Herald, New York Times, USA Today....*

Facts compiled by Douglas A. McVay (2002) for Common Sense for Drug Policy are:

- In 2000, the FBI's Uniform Crime Reports for the United States show that 46.5 percent of the 1,579,566 total arrests for drug abuse violations were for marijuana—a total of 734,497. Of those, 646,042 people were arrested for possession alone. This is an increase over 1999, when a total of 704,812 Americans were arrested for marijuana offenses, of which 620,541 were for possession alone.
- According to the United Nation's Office for Drug Control and Crime Prevention estimate, 141 million people around the world use marijuana. This represents about 2.5 percent of the world population.
- A Johns Hopkins study published in the *American Journal of Epidemiology* (May 1999) examined marijuana's effects on cognition on 1,318 participants over a 15-year period. Researchers reported "no significant differences in cognitive

decline between heavy users, light users, and nonusers of cannabis." They also found "no male-female differences in cognitive decline in relation to cannabis use . . . These results . . . seem to provide strong evidence of the absence of a long-term residual effect of cannabis use on cognition," they concluded. Current marijuana use has been found to have a negative effect on global IQ score only in subjects who smoked five or more joints per week. A negative effect was not observed among subjects who had previously been heavy users but were no longer using the substance. Furthermore, it has been concluded that marijuana does not have a long-term negative impact on global intelligence. Whether the absence of a residual marijuana effect would also be evident in more specific cognitive domains such as memory and attention remains to be ascertained. These findings were published in the *Canadian Medical Association Journal* in April 2002.

- In March 1999, the U.S. Institute of Medicine's (IOM) Division of Neuroscience and Behavioral Research reported on various aspects of marijuana including the so-called Gateway Theory (the theory that using marijuana leads people to use harder drugs like cocaine and heroin). The IOM stated that there is no conclusive evidence that the drug effects of marijuana are causally linked to the subsequent abuse of other illicit drugs.

- The Institute of Medicine also explained that marijuana has been mistaken for a gateway drug in the past because patterns in progression of drug use from adolescence to adulthood are strikingly regular. Because it is the most widely used illicit drug, marijuana is predictably the first illicit drug most people encounter. Most users of other illicit drugs have used marijuana first. In fact, most drug users begin with alcohol and nicotine before marijuana—usually before they are of legal age.

- The Institute of Medicine found that for most people, the primary adverse effect of acute marijuana use is diminished psychomotor performance. It states that it is inadvisable to operate any vehicle or potentially dangerous equipment while under the influence of marijuana, THC, or any cannabinoid drug with comparable effects.

- In 1988, the DEA's administrative law judge, Francis Young, concluded that in strict medical terms marijuana is far safer than many foods we commonly consume. For example, eating ten raw potatoes can result in a toxic response. By comparison, it is physically impossible to eat enough marijuana to induce death. Marijuana in its natural form is one of the safest therapeutically active substances known to man. By any measure of rational analysis marijuana can be safely used within the supervised routine of medical care.

- Commissioned by President Nixon in 1972, the National Commission on Marijuana and Drug Abuse stated that "Marihuana's relative potential for harm to the vast majority of individual users and its actual impact on society does not justify a social policy designed to seek out and firmly punish those who use it. This judgment is based on prevalent use patterns, on behavior exhibited by the vast majority of users and on our interpretations of existing medical and scientific data. This position also is consistent with the estimate by law enforcement personnel that the elimination of use is unattainable." When examining the relationship between marijuana use and violent crime, the 1972 National Commission on Marijuana and Drug Abuse concluded, "Rather than inducing violent or aggressive behavior through its purported effects of lowering inhibitions, weakening impulse control and heightening aggressive tendencies, marihuana was usually found to inhibit the expression of aggressive impulses by pacifying the user, interfering with muscular coordination, reducing psychomotor activities and generally producing states of drowsiness, lethargy, timidity and passivity."

- When examining the medical affects of marijuana use, the National Commission on Marijuana and Drug Abuse concluded, "A careful search of the literature and testimony of the nation's health officials has not revealed a single human fatality in the United States proven to have resulted solely from ingestion of marihuana. Experiments with the drug in monkeys demonstrated that the dose required for overdose death was enormous and for all practical purposes unachievable by humans smoking marihuana. This is in marked contrast to other substances in common use, most notably alcohol and barbiturate sleeping pills." The WHO reached the same conclusion in 1995.

- The World Health Organization (WHO) released a study in March 1998 that states: "there are good reasons for saying that [the risks from cannabis] would be unlikely to seriously [compare to] the public health risks of alcohol and tobacco even if as many people used cannabis as now drink alcohol or smoke tobacco." The authors of the 1998 WHO report comparing marijuana, alcohol, nicotine and opiates quote the U.S. Institute of Medicine's 1982 report stating that there is no evidence that smoking marijuana "exerts a permanently deleterious effect on the normal cardiovascular system."

- Some claim that cannabis use leads to "adult amotivation." The World Health Organization 1998 report addresses the issue and states, "it is doubtful that cannabis use produces a well defined amotivational syndrome." The report also notes that the value of studies that support the "adult amotivation" theory are "limited by their small sample sizes" and lack of representative social/cultural groups.

- Since 1969, government-appointed commissions

in the United States, Canada, England, Australia, and the Netherlands concluded, after reviewing the scientific evidence, that marijuana's dangers had previously been greatly exaggerated, and urged lawmakers to drastically reduce or eliminate penalties for marijuana possession.

- The Canadian Senate Special Committee on Illegal Drugs recommended in its 2002 final report on cannabis policy that "the Government of Canada amend the Controlled Drugs and Substances Act to create a criminal exemption scheme. This legislation should stipulate the conditions for obtaining licenses as well as for producing and selling cannabis; criminal penalties for illegal trafficking and export; and the preservation of criminal penalties for all activities falling outside the scope of the exception scheme.

- UK Home Secretary David Blunkett announced in July 2002, "We must concentrate our efforts on the drugs that cause the most harm, while sending a credible message to young people. I will therefore ask Parliament to reclassify cannabis from Class B to Class C. I have considered the recommendations of the Home Affairs Committee, and the advice given me by the ACMD medical experts that the current classification of cannabis is disproportionate in relation to the harm that it causes."

- The Police Foundation of the United Kingdom stated in April 2000:

  Our conclusion is that the present law on cannabis produces more harm than it prevents. It is very expensive of the time and resources of the criminal justice system and especially of the police. It inevitably bears more heavily on young people in the streets of inner cities, who are also more likely to be from minority ethnic communities, and as such is inimical to police-community relations. It criminalizes large numbers of otherwise law-abiding, mainly young, people to the detriment of their futures. It has become a proxy for the control of public order; and it inhibits accurate education about the relative risks of different drugs including the risks of cannabis itself.

• According to the federal Potency Monitoring Project in 2002, supported by the U.S. National Institute on Drug Administration (NIDA), the average potency of marijuana has increased very little since the 1980s. The Project reports that in 1985, the average THC content of commercial-grade marijuana was 2.84 percent, and the average for high-grade sinsemilla in 1985 was 7.17 percent. In 1995, the potency of commercial-grade marijuana averaged 3.73 percent, while the potency of sinsemilla in 1995 averaged 7.51 percent. In 2001, commercial-grade marijuana averaged 4.72 percent THC, and the potency of sinsemilla in 2001 averaged 9.03 percent.

Against Policy Change: What The U.S. Drug Enforcement Administration Says

In "Exposing the Myth of Medical Marijuana: Marijuana the Facts," the DEA states the following:

Q: Does marijuana pose health risks to users?

• Marijuana is an addictive drug with significant health consequences to its users and others. Many harmful short-term and long-term problems have been documented with its use.
• The short term effects of marijuana use include: memory loss, distorted perception, trouble with thinking and problem solving, loss of motor skills, decrease in muscle strength, increased heart rate, and anxiety.
• In recent years there has been a dramatic

increase in the number of emergency room mentions of marijuana use. From 1993 to 2000, the number of emergency room marijuana mentions more than tripled.

- There are also many long-term health consequences of marijuana use. According to the National Institutes of Health, studies show that someone who smokes five joints per week may be taking in as many cancer-causing chemicals as someone who smokes a full pack of cigarettes every day. Marijuana contains more than 400 chemicals, including most of the harmful substances found in tobacco smoke. Smoking one marijuana cigarette deposits about four times more tar into the lungs than a filtered tobacco cigarette.
- Harvard University researchers report that the risk of a heart attack is five times higher than usual in the hour after smoking marijuana.
- Smoking marijuana also weakens the immune system and raises the risk of lung infections. A Columbia University study found that a control group smoking a single marijuana cigarette every other day for a year had a white-blood-cell count that was 39 percent lower than normal, thus damaging the immune system and making the user far more susceptible to infection and sickness.
- Users can become dependent on marijuana to the point they must seek treatment to stop abusing it. In 1999, more than 200,000 Americans entered substance abuse treatment primarily for marijuana abuse and dependence.
- More teens are in treatment for marijuana use than for any other drug or for alcohol. Adolescent admissions to substance abuse facilities for marijuana grew from 43 percent of all adolescent admissions in 1994 to 60 percent in 1999. Marijuana is much stronger now than it was decades ago. According to data from the Potency Monitoring Project at the University of

Mississippi, the tetrahydrocannabinol (THC) content of commercial-grade marijuana rose from an average of 3.71 percent in 1985 to an average of 5.57 percent in 1998. The average THC content of U.S. produced sinsemilla increased from 3.2 percent in 1977 to 12.8 percent in 1997.

Q: Does marijuana have any medical value?

- Any determination of a drug's valid medical use must be based on the best available science undertaken by medical professionals. The Institute of Medicine conducted a comprehensive study in 1999 to assess the potential health benefits of marijuana and its constituent cannabinoids. The study concluded that smoking marijuana is not recommended for the treatment of any disease condition. In addition, there are more effective medications currently available. For those reasons, the Institute of Medicine concluded that there is little future in smoked marijuana as a medically approved medication.
- Advocates have promoted the use of marijuana to treat medical conditions such as glaucoma. However, this is a good example of more effective medicines already available. According to the Institute of Medicine, there are six classes of drugs and multiple surgical techniques that are available to treat glaucoma that effectively slow the progression of this disease by reducing high intraocular pressure. In other studies, smoked marijuana has been shown to cause a variety of health problems, including cancer, respiratory problems, increased heart rate, loss of motor skills, and increased heart rate. Furthermore, marijuana can affect the immune system by impairing the ability of T-cells to fight off infections, demonstrating that marijuana can do more harm than good in people with already compromised immune systems.

- In addition, in a study by the Mayo Clinic, THC was shown to be less effective than standard treatments in helping cancer patients regain lost appetites.
- The American Medical Association recommends that marijuana remain a Schedule I controlled substance.
- A synthetic THC drug, Marinol, has been available to the public since 1985. The Food and Drug Administration has determined that Marinol is safe, effective, and has therapeutic benefits for use as a treatment for nausea and vomiting associated with cancer chemotherapy, and as a treatment of weight loss in patients with AIDS. However, it does not produce the harmful health effects associated with smoking marijuana.
- It's also important to realize that the campaign to allow marijuana to be used as medicine is a tactical maneuver in an overall strategy to completely legalize all drugs. Pro-legalization groups have transformed the debate from decriminalizing drug use to one of compassion and care for people with serious diseases. The *New York Times* interviewed Ethan Nadelmann, Director of the Lindesmith Center, in January 2000. Responding to criticism from former drug czar Barry McCaffrey that the medical marijuana issue is a stalking-horse for drug legalization, Mr. Nadelmann did not contradict General McCaffrey. "Will it help lead toward marijuana legalization?" Mr. Nadelmann said: "I hope so."

Q: Does marijuana harm anyone besides the individual who smokes it?

- Consider the public safety of others when confronted with intoxicated drug users.
- Marijuana affects many skills required for safe driving: alertness, the ability to concentrate, coordination, and reaction time. These effects

can last up to twenty-four hours after smoking marijuana. Marijuana use can make it difficult to judge distances and react to signals and signs on the road.

- In a 1990 report, the National Transportation Safety Board studied 182 fatal truck accidents. It found that just as many of the accidents were caused by drivers using marijuana as were caused by alcohol—12.5 percent in each case.
- Consider also that drug use, including marijuana, contributes to crime. A large percentage of those arrested for crimes test positive for marijuana. Nationwide, 40 percent of adult males tested positive for marijuana at the time of their arrest.

Q: Is marijuana a gateway drug?

- Yes. Among marijuana's most harmful consequences is its role in leading to the use of other illegal drugs like heroin and cocaine. Long-term studies of students who use drugs show that very few young people use other illegal drugs without first trying marijuana. Although not all people who use marijuana go on to use other drugs, using marijuana sometimes lowers inhibitions about drug use and exposes users to a culture that encourages use of other drugs.
- The risk of using cocaine has been estimated to be more than 104 times greater for those who have tried marijuana than for those who have never tried it.

In Summary:

- Marijuana is a dangerous, addictive drug that poses significant health threats to users.
- Marijuana has no medical value that can't be met more effectively by legal drugs.
- Marijuana users are far more likely to use other drugs like cocaine and heroin than nonmarijuana users.

- Drug legalizers use "medical marijuana" as a red herring in an effort to advocate broader legalization of drug use.

A Solution to the Marijuana Problem? What Canada Says

Following a two-year study of public policy related to marijuana, the Canadian Senate Special Committee on Illegal Drugs found that the drug should be legalized. Released on September 4, 2002, the Senate report, entitled, *Cannabis: Our Position for a Public Policy,* is a result of research, analysis, and extensive public hearings in Ottawa and communities throughout Canada with experts and citizens (Canadian Senate Special Committee on Illegal Drugs 2000).

Significant excerpts from the Commission report include:

- Clearly, current approaches are ineffective and inefficient. Ultimately, their effect amounts to throwing taxpayers' money down the drain in a crusade that is not warranted by the danger posed by the substance. It has been maintained that drugs, including cannabis, are not dangerous because they are illegal but rather are illegal because they are dangerous. This is perhaps true of other types of drugs, but not of cannabis. We should state this clearly once and for all, for public good: it is time to stop this crusade. (ibid., 34)
- As far as cannabis is concerned, only behaviour causing demonstrable harm to others should be prohibited: illegal trafficking, selling to minors and impaired driving. (ibid., 35)
- We were told that drugs were made criminal because they are dangerous. Analysis of debates in Parliament and in media accounts clearly shows how far this is from truth.
- When cannabis was introduced in the legislation on narcotics in 1923, there was no debate, no justification, in fact many members did not even know what cannabis was. (ibid., 21)

- Early drug legislation was largely based on a moral panic, racist sentiment and a notorious absence of debate. (ibid., 22)
- In our view, it is clear that if the aim of public policy is to diminish consumption and supply of drugs, specifically cannabis, all signs indicate complete failure. (ibid., 31)
- In effect, the main social costs of cannabis are a result of public policy choices, primarily its continued criminalization, while the consequences of its use represent a small fraction of the social costs attributable to the use of illegal drugs. (ibid., 27)
- In fact, more than for any other illegal drug, [marijuana']s criminalization is the principal source of social and economic costs. (ibid., 31)
- Billions of dollars have been sunk into enforcement without any greater effect. There are more consumers, more regular users and more regular adolescent users. Cannabis is more available than ever, it is cultivated on a large scale, even exported, swelling coffers and making organized crime more powerful. And there have been tens of thousands of arrests and convictions for the possession of cannabis and thousands of people have been incarcerated. However, use trends remain totally unaffected and the gap the Commission noted between the law and public compliance continues to widen. (ibid., 33)
- It is time to recognize what is patently obvious: our policies have been ineffective, because they are poor policies. (ibid., 33)
- Cannabis itself is not a cause of other drug use. In this sense, we reject the gateway theory. . . . Cannabis itself is not a cause of delinquency and crime; and Cannabis is not a cause of violence. (ibid., 15)
- Physical dependency on cannabis is virtually nonexistent. Psychological dependency is moderate and is certainly lower than for nicotine or alcohol. (ibid., 26)
- We have seen that approximately 50 percent of high school students have used cannabis within the past year. Nevertheless, a high percentage of them stop using, and the vast majority of those who experiment

do not go on to become regular users. Even among regular users, only a small proportion develop problems related to excessive use, which may include some level of psychological dependency. (ibid., 38)

- There are clear, though nondefinitive indications of the therapeutic benefits of marijuana in the following conditions: analgesic for chronic pain, antispasm for multiple sclerosis, anticonvulsive for epilepsy, antiemetic for chemotherapy and appetite stimulant for cachexia. . . . Measures should be taken to support and encourage the development of alternative practices, such as the establishment of compassion clubs [medical marijuana buyers' clubs]. . . . The practices of these organizations are in line with the therapeutic indications arising from clinical studies and meet the strict rules on quality and safety (ibid., 18–19). . . . The international drug control conventions are, at least with respect to cannabis, an utterly irrational restraint that has nothing to do with scientific or public health considerations. (ibid., 29)

- In our opinion, the data we have collected on cannabis and its derivatives provide sufficient grounds for our general conclusion that the regulation of the production, distribution and consumption of cannabis, inasmuch as it is part of an integrated and adaptable public policy, is best able to respond to the principles of autonomy, governance that fosters human responsibility and limitation of penal law to situations where there is demonstrable harm to others. A regulatory system for cannabis should permit, specifically:

  - more effective targeting of illegal traffic and a reduction in the role played by organized crime;
  - prevention programs better adapted to the real world and better able to prevent and detect at-risk behaviour;
  - enhanced monitoring of products, quality and properties;
  - better user information and education; and
  - respect for individual and collective freedoms, and legislation more in tune with the behaviour of Canadians. (ibid., 31–32)

The Canadian Senate Special Committee on Illegal Drugs report consists of eleven recommendations. Among the three that appear to be most far reaching are:

> Recommendation 5: The Committee recommends that the Government of Canada adopt an integrated policy on the risks and harmful effects of psychoactive substances covering the whole range of substances (medication, alcohol, tobacco and illegal drugs). With respect to cannabis, this policy should focus on educating users, detecting and preventing at-risk use and treating excessive use.

> Recommendation 6: The Committee recommends that the Government of Canada amend the *Controlled Drugs and Substances Act* to create a criminal exemption scheme. This legislation should stipulate the conditions for obtaining licenses as well a for producing and selling cannabis; criminal penalties for illegal trafficking and export; and the preservation of criminal penalties for all activities falling outside the scope of the exemption scheme.

> Recommendation 7: The Committee recommends that the Government of Canada declare an amnesty for any person convicted of possession of cannabis under current or past legislation.

The War: The Debate Goes On

The *National Review* has stated that the time had come to revise the laws on drug trafficking. "[The *National Review*] deplores the [use of drugs] and we urge the stiffest sentences against anyone convicted of selling a drug to a minor. But that said, it is our judgment that the war on drugs has failed, that it is diverting intelligent energy away from how to deal with the problem of addiction, that it is wasting our resources, and that it is encouraging civil, judicial, and penal procedures associated with police states." Based on a symposium of national experts sponsored by the magazine, the primary conclusions were: "(1) that the famous drug war is not working, (2) that crime and suffering have greatly increased as a result of prohibition, (3) that we have seen, and are countenancing, a creeping attrition of authentic civil liberties, and (4) that the direction in which to head is legalization" (Buckley 1996).

Efforts to reverse drug prohibition face formidable obstacles such as antidrug-warlords' control over the attitudes and behavior of those involved with all aspects of drug control, prevention, and treatment through the distribution of funding resources and the "bogeyman syndrome"—the need of people to use scapegoats to "embody their fears and take blame for whatever ails them. . . . Just as anti-Communist propagandists once feared Moscow far beyond its actual influence and appeal, so today antidrug proselytizers indict marijuana, cocaine, heroin and assorted hallucinogens far beyond their actual psychoactive effects and psychological appeal. . . . The evidence of history and of science is drowned out by today's bogeymen. No rhetoric is too harsh, no penalty too severe" (Nadelmann 1993).

In the United States, change is occurring, especially at the state level as evidenced by initiatives to reduce penalties for marijuana use and legal challenges against the tobacco industry for compensation of health costs and reform. A broad-based coalition of respectable special-interest groups and grassroots organizations may prove to be the vanguard for moving drug policy and practices to a more rational and pragmatic level for addressing the problem. Certainly, if this expectation does not come to fruition, there is always the issue of economic realities and constraints—Americans are not inclined to pay for the rising costs of enforcing laws, especially when substantial tax revenues can be generated through different methods of control and regulation (ibid.). In an effort to address the state of New York's $11.5 billion deficit, for example, Governor George Pataki and the state legislature have agreed that the Rockefeller-era drug laws are too harsh, especially in terms of mandating sentences for some first-time nonviolent drug offenses. Based on a study of the Legal Action Center, it has been reported that

> Three thousand eight hundred and eighty-four individuals incarcerated in 2001 would have been eligible for judicial diversion under the [State] Assembly's drug reform law (A-7078). For each offender diverted from prison to community-based treatment the state would save approximately $50,000 in total net criminal system–related spending and $10,000 in health care and welfare costs, and crime and increased tax contribution. Furthermore, New York State would save an additional $24,384,000 under the Assembly bill by reducing the sentences of individuals serving certain

drug offenses, potentially saving the state $164,244,000 a year. These calculations do not include savings that would result from decreased burden on the foster care system and increased local economic benefits resulting in higher employment and increased wages. . . . [T]his report shows that reforming New York's Rockefeller-era drug laws to make greater use of mandated community treatment would save taxpayers enormous sums of money. ("New Report" 2003)

The door is open for change in terms of how the problem of drug use is to be addressed; the only question is when and how that change will occur. Getting there will not be easy, and the effort should be taken incrementally. Such gradualism, which should begin with cannabis, would allow for a necessary shift in values so that more socially and economically pragmatic policies can be formulated and enacted. For some, such legislation may be a leap in the dark. Indeed, there will be unpredictable consequences as well as predictable ones. But that does not argue for doing nothing or talking tougher with words that are empty in terms of action and outcomes (Isralowitz 2002).

Notes

1. Cost figures vary according to sources of information.

2. In December 2003 the results of the Monitoring the Future survey showed current use (past thirty days) declined 11 percent over the previous year, from 31.8 percent to 28.3 percent.

3. The National Household Survey on Drug Abuse has been renamed the National Survey on Drug Use and Health [NSDUH]. The report was released in September 2003, and information from that report is used in chapter 3.

4. Jay, M. 2002. "Legalisation: The First Hundred Years: What Happened When Drugs Were Legal and Why They Were Prohibited." Reprinted with permission obtained from IPPR. Available at http://www.cedro-uva.org/lib/jay.legalisation.html (accessed January 22, 2004).

References

Buckley, W. 1996. "400 Readers Give Their Views." *National Review* 1 (July): 32.

Buckley, W., E. Nadelmann, K. Schmoke, J. McNamara, R. Sweet, T. Szasz, and S. Duke. 1996. "The War on Drugs Is Lost." *National Review* 12 (February): 35–48

Canadian Senate Special Committee on Illegal Drugs. 2000. "Cannabis— Our Position for a Canadian Public Policy." Available at http:// www.ukcia.org/research/CanadianPublicPolicy/default.html (accessed January 27, 2004).

Goode, E. 1989. *Drugs in American Society.* New York: McGraw-Hill.

Horgan, C. 2001. *Substance Abuse: The Nation's Number One Health Problem.* Princeton, NJ: Robert Wood Johnson Foundation.

Hornik, R. 2002. *Evaluation of the National Youth Anti-Drug Media Campaign: Fifth Semi-Annual Report of Findings, Executive Summary.* Rockville, MD: Westat.

Isralowitz, R. 2002. *Drug Use, Policy and Management.* Westport, CT: Auburn House.

McVay, D. 2002. "Updated Drug War Facts: Common Sense for Drug Policy." Available at http://www.drugwarfacts.org (accessed March 1, 2003).

Nadelmann, E. 1993. "Should We Legalize Drugs? History Answers." *American Heritage* 44 (February–March): 41–56.

The National Academies News. 2001. "Data Sorely Lacking on Effectiveness of Nation's Drug Enforcement Programs." Available at http://www.4.nas.edu/news.nf (accessed March 29, 2003).

"New Report on Savings to New York State under Law Reform Bill." 2003. Available at http://www.lindesmith.org (accessed March 20, 2003).

Nolin, P., and C. Kenny. 2002. "Cannabis: Our Position for a Canadian Public Policy—Report of the Senate Special Committee on Illegal Drugs." Special Committee on Illegal Drugs, Senate of Canada. Available at http://www.ukcia.org/research/CanadianPublicPolicy/default.html (accessed March 1, 2003).

Russell, A. 1992. "Making America Drug Free: A New Vision of What Works." *Carnegie Quarterly* 37, no. 3 (summer).

Shepard, E. 2001. *The Economic Costs of DARE.* Syracuse, NY: Institute of Industrial Relations.

Substance Abuse Mental Health Services Administration (SAMSHA). 2002. *National Household Survey on Drug Abuse.* Rockville, MD: United States Department of Health and Human Services.

Swan, N. 1998. "Drug Abuse Cost to Society Set at $97.7 Billion, Continuing Steady Increase Since 1975." NIDA Notes, NIH Publication No. 98-3478. Available at http://www.drugabuse.gov/NIDA_Notes/ NNVol 13N4/ Abusecosts.html (accessed January 27, 2004).

Sweet, R. 1996. "The War on Drugs is Lost." *National Review* (February 12): 35–48.

U.S. General Accounting Office. 2003. "Youth Illicit Drug Use Prevention." Publication number Washington, DC-03-172R. Available at http://www.drugpolicy.org.docUploads/DAREfinal.pdf. (accessed March 1, 2003).

U.S. Office of Applied Studies. 2002. "Summary of Findings from the 2000 National Household Survey on Drug Abuse." DHHS Publication no. SMA 01-3549. Rockville, MD: SAMSHA.

3

Illicit-Drug Use: What's Happening?

International and U.S. Developments

Illicit-substance use and its consequences (for example, crime and violence, military and police intervention, lost work, family destruction, property confiscation, and massive allocations of funding resources for treatment and health maintenance) constitute a major public concern. This is true for well-established modern Western democracies as well as developing nations and regions throughout the world.

From an international perspective, a limited history exists in terms of addressing the production and use of illegal substances. For example, the United Nations (UN) General Assembly has held only one special session devoted to this issue since its beginning in 1946. That special session was held in 1990 to address the drug-control issue. Eight years later, its current secretary general, Kofi Annan, said that the problem of illicit drugs remains with us and the trends are not slowing. Drug trafficking is a multibillion-dollar industry, a clandestine, criminal, cartel-driven enterprise, leaving no country untouched. Addiction is indiscriminate, crossing lines of class, gender, religion, and country.

At UN-sponsored meetings held during 1998 in Vienna and New York, the representatives from 130 governments agreed to a political declaration calling for a drastic reduction of both illicit supply and demand for drugs by the year 2008. Additionally, the main themes for the members' discussion and consideration included precursor chemicals used to manufacture illicit drugs; the manufacture, trafficking, and abuse of amphetamine-type stimulants that are the most abused synthetic drugs manufactured clandestinely; judicial cooperation such as strengthening the legal framework to improve application of drug-control laws regarding extradition and illicit traffic by sea; the laundering of money derived from illicit-drug trafficking and other serious crimes; the elimination of illicit crops and the promotion of alternative crop development; as well as other matters.

According to a report issued by the United Nations Office for Drug Control and Crime Prevention (UNODCCP), the 1980s and 1990s were a period that exhibited a surge of illegal drug activities (Kazancigil and Milani 2002). Activities such as the processing, export, production, and distribution of illicit drugs were taken over by major criminal organizations. These organizations are now present in all the major regions of the world. For the drug trade today, nationalities and borders do not exist.

This chapter provides information about the nature and extent of the illicit-drug problem that varies by drug type and region. Specifically, the production, trafficking, and consumption of cannabis, heroin, and cocaine are discussed in international and U.S. contexts. It concludes with overviews of the relation of illicit drugs to disease, with a focus on the former Soviet Union because of the rapid spread of problems there, terrorism, and youth attitudes and behavior in the United States.

Production, Trafficking, and Consumption

Cannabis (Marijuana and Hashish)

Cannabis is grown throughout the world; however, there is a lack of usable information to make an assessment about the extent of its cultivation at the global level, according to UNODCCP. Cannabis ranks first among all substances in terms of the amounts seized and number of seizure cases. In recent years, it has been given a low-priority status among law enforcement authorities in many countries, including the Netherlands, Great Britain, Germany, Switzerland, Italy, Portugal, and Canada. This factor along with increased levels of seizures lead to the assumption that there is an increased level of production and trafficking.

In terms of global seizures in metric tons of illicit substances, approximately 72 percent is cannabis and 17 percent cannabis resin (hashish).

Worldwide, cannabis is the most extensively trafficked drug. In 2000, more than half of the cannabis seized was in North America, mostly in Mexico. Nearly a quarter of the seizures were in southern Africa, particularly South Africa. Regarding hashish (that is, cannabis resin), there has been an increase of law enforcement efforts in Morocco, Near and Middle East countries, and southern Africa. Western Europe accounts for almost two-thirds of the global hashish seizures, of which nearly half comes in Spain alone.

In the United States, trafficking patterns show that cannabis is mainly imported from Mexico. Canadian-grown marijuana, including the seedless and potent "BC bud," is being reported in numerous locations. Domestic cultivation, especially indoor hydroponics, including those in private homes, exists in many areas. Other reports related to cultivation and trafficking in the United States indicate that some Latin American marijuana still enters Miami from Jamaica, the Bahamas, and other Caribbean transshipment points; trafficking patterns in certain locations have shifted from coastal marine and air smuggling to complex indoor growing with hydroponics and domestic interstate shipments; and Colombian marijuana-trafficking organizations are moving back into the marijuana market (National Institute on Drug Abuse 2001).

In Kentucky, it has been reported that the annual marijuana crop grown there generates about $4 billion revenue generated from markets of the Northeast willing to pay high street prices.

> It's kind of like the old moonshine days with neighbors making a living at it. . . . Everybody seems to know somebody who grows it, sells it, smokes. It's the dirty little secret of Kentucky. . . . More than 200,000 pot plants, each worth about $1,000 in retail produce, are seized each year alone in the sprawling beauty of the Daniel Boone National Forest. . . . The planters use hydroponics, growing lamps and scientific pruning techniques to produce a crop every 89 days in basements, silos, closets, and even underground bunkers, replete with booby traps and remote video monitoring. (Clines 2001)

In terms of consumption, cannabis is the most widely used drug in the world. It is estimated that 147 million people, or 3.5 percent of the global population, fifteen years and older, used cannabis from 1998 to 2000. The largest numbers of cannabis users are found in Asia where the people there account for more than 25 percent of the global consumption, followed by 25 percent in Africa, 25 percent in the Americas, and about 20 percent in Europe. The largest demand for the substance is in the United Kingdom, Spain, the Netherlands, and Sweden. When compared to opiates and cocaine, cannabis users are a lower proportion in treatment. Nevertheless, treatment demand for cannabis is far from negligible. On average, about 15 percent of all treatment demand at the global level is related to cannabis use. This rate is rising in many countries as consumption levels and the THC levels increase (United Nations Office for Drug Control and Crime Prevention 2002). In Europe, details about cannabis use include:

- At least 45 million Europeans (18 percent of those aged fifteen to sixty-four) have tried cannabis at least once. Around 15 million (about 6 percent of those aged fifteen to sixty-four) have used cannabis in the past twelve months.
- Use is higher among younger groups. About 25 percent of those aged fifteen to sixteen and 40 percent of those aged eighteen have tried cannabis. In some countries, use has doubled since 1990; in others, the rise is less marked; and in a few, it has stabilized.
- Curiosity is a primary motive for trying cannabis, and use is more experimental or intermittent than persistent.
- There is an increase in numbers, especially young people, attending treatment centers for cannabis use. Additional drugs are also involved.
- Cannabis remains the primary drug in drug offenses, mostly for possession rather than trafficking. (European Monitoring Centre for Drugs and Drug Addiction 2000)

In the United States, patterns of marijuana use over the past twenty years or so do not indicate that governmental efforts have been very successful in reducing or controlling the use of the substance. Since 1992, teenage marijuana use has grown considerably, and by one measure it has doubled. In 2002, it was used by

75 percent of the current population of 19.5 million illicit-drug users. Approximately 55 percent of current illicit-drug users (10.7 million) used only marijuana, 20 percent used marijuana and another illicit drug, and the remaining 25 percent used an illicit drug but not marijuana in the past month. During the past year, 12.2 percent of marijuana users used the drug on 300 or more days. This translates into 1.8 million persons using marijuana on a daily or almost daily basis over a twelve-month period. Among past-month users, about one-third (32.6 percent persons) used marijuana on twenty or more days. Of the 2.2 million current illicit-drug users aged twelve to seventeen, about 71 percent used marijuana—boys more than girls. The highest rate of illicit-drug use is among those eighteen to twenty-five years—20.2 percent, or 3.9 million users. About 86 percent of this age group use marijuana compared to 27 percent who use prescription-type drugs nonmedically, which is the next most common substance used; 9 percent use cocaine; and 9 percent use hallucinogens. Among adults aged twenty-six or older, 5.8 percent, or 1.1 million, reported current illicit-drug use: 69 percent used marijuana and 34 percent used prescription-type drugs.

In 1965 and 1966, only 1.8 percent of youths had ever used marijuana. Beginning in 1967, use increased until it reached the level of 19.6 percent in 1979. A period of decline followed until 1991, when the rate was 11.5 percent, after which the trend reversed, reaching a peak at 21.9 percent in 2001. The percentage of youths aged twelve to seventeen who had ever used marijuana declined slightly from 2001 to 2002 (21.9 to 20.6 percent). Regarding young adults aged eighteen to twenty-five who had ever used marijuana, the percentage was 5.1 percent in 1965, but increased steadily to 54.4 percent in 1982. Although the rate for young adults declined somewhat from 1982 to 1993, it did not drop below 43 percent and increased to 53 percent in 2001 and 53.8 percent in 2002 (Substance Abuse and Mental Health Services Administration 2003b).

From hospital emergency department (ED) information it has been found that the use of cannabis among adolescents is common, approaching that of cigarette use among young adults. The eighteen-to-twenty-five age group accounts for the highest rate of marijuana hospital ED mentions in most cities throughout the United States. Youths are increasingly dominating the marijuana treatment demographics. In most areas, primary marijuana users are generally younger than primary cocaine or heroin admissions. Males outnumber females nationally among marijuana ED mentions, accounting for 60 percent or more of the total. Treatment admissions are also more likely to be male than female. Racial/ethnic distributions of primary marijuana treatment admissions vary across the country (Willard and Schoenborn 1995; Schlosser 1997; NIDA 2001; NIDA 2002).

Marijuana users were asked in the National Survey on Drug Use and Health how, from whom, and where they obtained the marijuana they used most recently. In 2002, most users (56.7 percent) got the drug for free or shared someone else's marijuana. Almost 40 percent of marijuana users bought it. Most marijuana users obtained the drug from a friend; 79 percent who bought their marijuana and 81.8 percent who obtained the drug for free had obtained it from a friend. More than half (55.9 percent) of users who bought their marijuana purchased it inside a home, apartment, or dorm. This also was the most common location for obtaining marijuana for free (67.2 percent). The percentages of youth users who obtained marijuana inside a home, apartment, or dorm were 34.7 percent for buyers and 48 percent for those who obtained it free. Almost 9 percent of youths who bought their marijuana obtained it inside a school building, and 4.8 percent bought it outside on school property (Substance Abuse and Mental Health Services Administration 2003b).

Throughout the United States, the following routes of cannabis use have been reported. "Blunts" or "Vega"—gutted cigars refilled with marijuana—remain entrenched in the culture of adolescents and young adults in many areas. Blunt smoking is frequently accompanied by alcohol consumption. Marijuana tends to be used in combination with other substances, particularly alcohol and cocaine (usually crack) and sometimes PCP. The marijuana/PCP combination is called a "love boat," "wets," "lilies," "wacky sticks," "donk," or "dream team." Marijuana–crack cocaine combinations are referred to as "geek joints," "oolies," "diablitos," "primos," "woolies," and "turbo," depending on the city. Marijuana with PCP plus formaldehyde is called "fry," "amp," or "water-water" (National Institute on Drug Abuse 2001; Isralowitz 2002b).

Opium and Heroin

In the 1990s, Afghanistan became the world's leading opium producer, with about 80 percent (5,674 metric tons) of the substance by 1999. Other major producers are Myanmar, Laos, Colombia, Mexico, and Pakistan. Following the imposed ban by the Taliban in July 2000, Afghanistan opium poppy cultivation was down by 91 percent, and opium production dropped by 94 percent in 2001 compared to the 2000 levels. In global terms, opium poppy cultivation dropped by 35 percent, and the potential production of opium went down by 65 percent from 2000 to 2001. Such a large supply decrease would normally reduce trafficking and consumption unless large stocks were available. This was in fact the case, as confirmed by seizures and prices in the source region and further along the trafficking routes, according to UNODCCP.

With production curtailed in 2001, an opiate shortage was expected on the Western European market. Among the projected consequences were price increases, including a rise in crime by addicts to pay the higher prices; a reduction in purity of heroin sold in the streets, with health implications; a shift to legal opiate substitutes such as methadone or buprenorphine or to other illegal substances available on the market such as cocaine and amphetamine-type stimulants; and an increase in the demand for treatment. Many of these conditions could have happened if it had not been for the events of September 11 and the subsequent military campaign. Rather, consumer prices fell because of panic sales of opiate stocks, revealing that there was an ample supply for transport to Western Europe.

Afghanistan opium production is returning to the levels that existed in the mid-1990s. If it were not able to, illicit-opiate sources for Europe and western Asia would shift to other growing areas such as Myanmar, Laos, and Colombia to address consumer need. This has been happening for years as a result of factors such as drought, war, and law enforcement.

The history of heroin trafficking in the United States during the past twenty-five years is a prime example of how flexible heroin sources from one region to another can address market demand. UNODCCP reports that in 1972, the French connection that had been supplying Turkish heroin to the U.S. market was disbanded and Turkey enforced a ban on opium production. In response, Mexican heroin was brought in to fill the gap. The Mexican government soon initiated a process of eradication that led to the need for another source to be found—Southeast Asian heroin. With a decline of Mexican and Southeast Asian heroin because of a drought, combined with the development of the cocaine epidemic, there was a decreased level of heroin abuse in the United States.

For the next fifteen years, from 1979 to 1993, heroin-use levels remained stable at a relatively low level. During that time,
heroin from Southeast Asia, Pakistan, and then more from
Afghanistan dominated the U.S. market. In the early 1990s,
opium poppy cultivation started to develop in Colombia. This,
along with a number of heroin trafficking problems in Southeast
Asia, provided the opportunity for Colombian heroin to make its
entry into the United States, fueling a revived heroin demand.
The UNODCCP reports that during the past thirty years, the U.S.
market has been supplied, in succession, by all the main opium-
producing areas (United Nations Office for Drug Control and
Crime Prevention 2002).

Afghanistan is a focal point for the production and distribution of opium and heroin. The following description of drug trafficking in the Afghanistan region, including its border countries,
is based on a report prepared in 1999 by a senior military official
of the United Nations Anti-Drug Project "Osh Knot" in Osh, Kyrgyzstan (Isralowitz 2002a). More than four years later, violence
and instability in the country and region continue in spite of
large-scale intervention by the United States after September 11.

> Over time, the flow of drugs has gone through Iran to
> Turkey and then to Europe. In the mid-1980s, however,
> Iran proclaimed a jihad, or holy war, against drugs.
> The country's drug legislation was tightened, Islamic
> antidrug troops were formed, and a huge stone wall
> was built along the state borders. This situation along
> with the collapse of the Soviet Union, including a melt-
> down of its economy, ethnic clashes, as well as politi-
> cal and social upheaval, caused drug barons to move
> their trafficking efforts to the central Asian region. This
> region includes Tajikistan, which has a 1,200-kilometer
> common border with Afghanistan, 800 kilometers of
> which are in the Gorno-Badakhshan region. Here, a
> major "narco-beachhead" was created in 1991–1993
> where one kilo of raw opium could be easily ex-
> changed for a pair of soldier's boots, a pea jacket, or
> big iron pot. . . .
> Via the mountain road to Khorog (a small city center
> of the Gorno-Badakhshan region of Tajikistan) to Osh
> (a regional center in southern Kyrgyzstan), "made in
> Afghanistan" drugs made their way to the Kyrgyz Re-
> public, then to Uzbekistan, Kazakhstan, Russia, the

Baltic countries, and Europe. Drugs coming through the "Osh corridor" could be found in Germany, Greece, Poland, the Netherlands, and elsewhere throughout Europe.

By 1995, Osh was a major drug-trading center. According to experts at that time, the estimated weekly amount of raw opium being dealt with was up to 100 kilograms. One year later, trading had escalated to a level such that 726 kilograms were seized via the "overclouded route" of Osh-Khorog, meaning that vast amounts were being traded and moving westward. With the excess flow of drugs came an increase of weapons, counterfeit dollars, and corruption in the region. Although local government, armed forces, and domestic law enforcement agencies tried to keep the situation under control, they found themselves overwhelmed. For this reason, international agencies such as the UN were called on to help strengthen the antidrug enforcement capacities of Uzbekistan, Kyrgyzstan, and Tajikistan.

In order to close the "overclouded trafficking route," police and customs operative units were joined with governmental military troops, special task forces, and border troops. The narco-dealers, however, were organizationally superior and much more flexible in terms of responding to adverse conditions than those pursuing them.

Numerous small side roads along the distance of the Kyrgyz-Tajik border, more than 800 kilometers guarded by no one, became the new gateways for drugs. Heroin began to displace raw opium as the smuggled substance of choice, and the efforts of Uzbekistan and Turkmenistan in trying to guard hundreds of kilometers of joint borders with Afghanistan against the narco-smuggling were futile.

In 1997, opium production in Afghanistan was nearly 3,000 tons, sufficient to produce almost 300 tons of heroin. These figures have been reported by UN officials in a report issued by the International Narcotics Control Board titled "Taliban. . . . " Drugs were used to pay for weapons and food. And according to operatives in the region, heroin-producing laboratories were moved from Iran and Pakistan to borders areas with Tajikistan and Kyrgyzstan.

During the period of Taliban control of the region, its emissaries fanned out to the small Afghan Pamirs—an arduous mountain area inhabited by 3,000 ethnic Kyrgyz who have been wandering there with cattle for generations. In order to survive and protect their livestock interests, the inhabitants of the region were forced into the drug business—buying and selling opium. Meanwhile, those engaged in Afghan narco-traffic sought new directions for transporting drugs—for example, through China. The situation around the China-Afghanistan-Tajikistan borders has been reported to be similar to the wild barter scene that existed on the Tajik-Afghan border in Gorno-Badakhshan during 1991–1993. Over time, Chinese frontier guards arrested opium-smuggling citizens from Tajikistan and Kyrgyzstan. This situation generated considerable concern among Chinese authorities for two reasons. First, drugs were spreading into China. Second, there was the danger of Muslim radicals, "Mojaheddins," supplying weapons and instructors to people of the "explosive" Scin-Czyan-Uyghur region of China. According to specialists dealing with the drug problem, there was concern that international narco-mafia interests were moving in to gain control of the China Kara-Korum [Pass] and its seaports on the Pacific Ocean in order to transport drugs. This would have enabled them to move cheap Afghan drugs more easily to major markets in Japan, Europe, and the United States.

With a glut of readily available heroin on the market, marijuana and hashish addicts in the region switched to that substance as their drug of choice. The problem of heroin drug abuse, common to big cities, became a rural problem as well. Women became involved as drug couriers, drug-related criminal cases soared in Kyrgyzstan, and opium/heroin control in Tajikistan became a source of power for armed groups.

In 1997 to 1998, a large-scale military operation carried out by governmental forces uncovered a huge amount of opium traffic in the area. Russian border troops in Tajikistan intercepted 135 narco-smugglers, resulting in forty armed clashes and the death of thirty-five couriers. In retaliation, narco-barons targeted commanders of Russian frontier outposts and fortified zones for elimination. Because of the deteriorating situation, a decision was made to extend the UN antidrug presence in the region and to allocate $8 million for a special antidrug program establishing a security belt around Afghanistan.

Producing more than 3,000 metric tons of raw opium annually, Afghanistan moved its drugs through Uzbekistan via roads, rail, and waterways. Although some organized and well-equipped narco-smugglers were neutralized in Uzbekistan, Afghan heroin laboratories caused the greatest troubles for drug-control authorities of that country. In 1995 to 1998, Uzbek customs-service personnel cut off attempts to smuggle 72 tons of opium. Nevertheless, the number of drug abusers in the country increased rapidly, and like elsewhere, the problem spread from population centers to rural areas, affecting agricultural production.

Regardless of the extent of intervention, including the removal of the Taliban and the presence of U.S. and international forces, the region has remained a hotbed of instability, opium and heroin production, smuggling, and huge profit making for a few people. The internal armed conflict in Afghanistan is lasting. And it is wrong to believe that this conflict is "internal" only to Afghanistan. In his January 1998 report to the UN Security Council, the special UN resident-representative in Afghanistan at that time said that the presence and the activity of international humanitarian aid agencies could not be restored in the country in the near future because of insufficient security. The military presence of Pakistani armed groups in the country, international terrorists, as well as Osama bin Laden also aggravate the situation. He expressed his disappointment with results from the efforts of the "six + two" group—countries neighboring Afghanistan plus the United States and Russia.

Regarding consumption, opiates including heroin are the main problem drugs in the world. Those who use and abuse opiates make up about two-thirds to three-quarters of the people in need of treatment. In the United States, more people are admitted for treatment of opiates than for cocaine abuse.

The estimate of opiate users worldwide is about 13 million people—half of whom are in Asia, mainly in the areas of Afghanistan and Myanmar. The total number of opiate users in Europe is estimated to be about 4 million, accounting for 30 percent of the global number. The bulk of opiate use in Eastern Europe is found in countries of the former Soviet Union. The estimated rate of opiate use in Australia is comparable to that in Europe—about 0.62 percent of the population age fifteen and above.

In Europe, details about heroin use include:

- Known users are a largely aging population with serious health, social, and psychiatric problems.
- Heroin experience overall remains low (1 to 2 percent in young adults), and school surveys show pupils are highly cautious about using the substance.
- Some countries report anecdotal evidence of increased heroin smoking among young people, and some school surveys reveal greater experimentation.
- Heroin use is reported among young heavy "recreational" users of amphetamines, Ecstasy, and other drugs. Other high-risk groups include marginalized minorities, homeless young people, institutionalized youth and young offenders, prisoners (women in particular), and sex workers.
- New clients entering treatment for heroin use are less likely to inject and more likely to smoke the drug than clients returning to treatment.
- Numbers of heron seizures and the quantities involved are stable across the European Union, although variations exist among countries. (European Monitoring Centre for Drugs and Drug Addiction 2000)

In the United States, since the mid-1990s, the prevalence of lifetime heroin use increased for both youths and young adults. From 1995 to 2002, the rate among youths aged twelve to seventeen increased from 0.1 to 0.4 percent; among young adults aged eighteen to twenty-five, the rate rose from 0.8 to 1.6 percent. During the latter half of the 1990s, the annual number of heroin initiates rose to a level not reached since the late 1970s. In 1974, there were an estimated 246,000 heroin initiates. Between 1988 and 1994, the annual number of new users ranged from 28,000 to 80,000. Between 1995 and 2001, the number of new heroin users, annually, was consistently greater than 100,000.

Results from the 2002 National Survey on Drug Use and Health show that there are an estimated 166,000 current heroin users (generally defined in terms of use during the past thirty days) in the United States (0.1 percent of the population). This number reflects an increase from the 123,000 reported in the 2001 National Household Survey and the 130,000 in 2000. Other details about heroin use in the United States show that in 2000, about 2.4 million (1.1 percent) of the 218 million persons represented in the National Household Survey on Drug Abuse reported heroin use (that is, smoking, snorting or sniffing, or injecting) in their lifetime, and 308,000 persons (0.1 percent) used the substance in the past year. In the total population, males more than females and blacks more than whites and Hispanics were likely to report lifetime use of heroin. Lifetime use was higher among unemployed persons than those employed. Those aged twelve to twenty-five were more likely to report past-year heroin use than were those twenty-six or older. Heroin/morphine was the top-ranking drug among drug-related deaths reported to the Drug Abuse Warning Network in twenty-one metropolitan areas in 2000. Heroin/morphine was the third most commonly mentioned drug, constituting 16 percent of the hospital ED episodes.

Throughout the United States, the following routes of heroin use have been reported. Injecting remains the most common route of administration among heroin addicts in the majority of cities; however, intranasal use is popular in many locations. "Monkey water" and "shebanging" describe heroin nose drops. The drug is dissolved in water and then either sprayed up the nose using a squeeze bottle or squirted up the nose using a syringe. Due to high purity, snorting is the common starting route of administration for new and younger users, but progressions to injection are widely reported due to the increased effect from a given amount of heroin. There are reports of younger adults burning heroin in aluminum foil and inhaling the fumes—known as "chasing the dragon"—or snorting the powder form. These alternative methods of using heroin are seen in the sex-industry business and topless bars. Smoking heroin remains relatively rare, accounting for 1 to 3 percent of heroin hospital ED admissions in most eastern and central parts of the country.

Cocaine

Primary cultivation and production locations for coca leaf, the source for cocaine hydrochloride and crack, are Colombia, Peru, and Bolivia. In terms of production, Colombia produces about 74 percent, Peru 18 percent, and Bolivia 8 percent of cocaine, which totals 827 metric tons according to 2001 estimates. In these countries, an estimated 1 million people, including farmers and laborers, grow coca leaves and process and export cocaine products. At the growing and harvesting stages, those involved are simple farmers and rural laborers who are out to earn an income by growing a crop long consumed without great danger. For the most part, poor people involved with coca production know that they are breaking the law, but that is unfortunately common in societies with large informal sectors that have been forced by governmental rules to work illegally. The income from the cocaine industry grew in the late 1970s and early 1980s. Such a rise was associated with the deep economic troubles of Bolivia and Peru in terms of governmental deficits and rampant inflation. A vicious cycle was created for these two countries when the price for coca leaf soared while the legal economy was in a state of decline. In order to temporarily hide conditions, the Bolivian and Peruvian governments created massive overemployment in the government and in loss-making state-owned enterprises. With the major population centers no longer able to absorb migrants from the overcrowded and resource-poor highlands, people from those areas had little choice but to move to the coca-growing regions to grow coca (U.S. Department of State, Office of International Information Agency 1992).

Cocaine trafficking is concentrated in the Americas and Europe. More than 90 percent of all the cocaine seized in the world is in the Americas—about two-thirds of the seizures in that region equally shared between the United States and Colombia. It is estimated that 38 percent of the global supply of cocaine was intercepted in 2000. The need to bring cocaine (as well as other illicit drugs) to its principal market, the United States, has generated a considerable amount of ingenious illegal import activity. For example, one courier had a half of pound of cocaine surgically implanted under the skin of each of his thighs. The cocaine was divided into four one-square-inch packages of one-quarter pound each. Cocaine has been carried across the border in Arizona on the backs of mules or horses and on foot. Variable amounts of cocaine have been containerized and shipped out of Ecuador with such products as shrimp, cacao, and bananas. Tons of cocaine have been shipped from Venezuela to Miami inside concrete fencing posts, in false-bottomed metal boxes labeled as toilet seats and bathroom sinks, in counterfeit bottles of Pony Malta de Bavaria (a nonalcoholic malt drink from Colombia), in 55-gallon drums of guava pulp with the cocaine in plastic packets inside the fruit, in cardboard boxes packed with canned fruit stuffed with cocaine, in anchovy cans shipped from Argentina, and in stuffed teddy bears, Peruvian handicrafts, and cans marked "asparagus." Panamanian cocaine smugglers have developed a technology that combines cocaine with vinyl to produce a material that has been used in making luggage and sneakers. The cocaine is separated from the vinyl after reaching its destination. Cocaine has been smuggled in suitcases hidden behind interior panels of airplanes, hidden in a secret tank within the fuel tank of a cabin cruiser, and packed in 1-kilogram lots and placed inside a plastic pipe that was bolted to the bottom of a banana boat docked in the harbor of Bridgeport, Connecticut. It has been sewn into the interior roof of a family station wagon and transported during a family vacation, in a false compartment in the floor of a mobile home, and in the gas tank of a car equipped with a baffle that made the left side a separate compartment. With the disintegration of the former Soviet Union in the late 1980s came opportunities to expand Russian-speaking drug operations throughout the world. In one incidence, Colombia drug traffickers considered the purchase of a Russian-made submarine to transport cocaine and other illegal drugs (Isralowitz 2002b).

Worldwide, cocaine is the second most common problem drug in terms of treatment demand. It is the most widespread problem drug in the Americas, and the second or third most common problem in several countries throughout Europe. Approximately 13.4 million people, or 0.3 percent of the global population, are affected by cocaine use. About 70 percent of all cocaine used in the Americas and half of the total number of cocaine users worldwide are in North America. Abuse levels in the United States are three times higher than they are in Europe. Cocaine abuse in Eastern Europe and in Asia is relatively low (National Institute on Drug Abuse 2001).

In Europe, details about cocaine use include:

- Although cocaine is less commonly used than amphetamines or Ecstasy, its use is rising.

- Depending on the country, between 1 and 6 percent of those aged sixteen to thirty-four and 1 to 2 percent of schoolchildren have tried cocaine at least once, although some surveys show levels of up to 4 percent among fifteen to sixteen year olds.
- Higher levels of use are found among socially outgoing and employed young adults in urban centers.
- Cocaine tends to be used experimentally or intermittently and is usually sniffed in powder form.
- Many clients treated for heroin use also use cocaine either intravenously or smoked as "crack."
- Severe problems associated with smoking "crack" have been identified, particularly among female sex workers.
- The proportion of clients seeking treatment for cocaine use is increasing in many countries. How much this is linked to heroin use or has developed from heavy recreational use of other drugs is unclear. (European Monitoring Centre for Drugs and Drug Addiction 2000)

After marijuana, cocaine is the second most commonly used illegal substance in the United States. In 2000, 25 million persons, or about 10 percent of the country's population over the age of 12 years, reported cocaine use sometime in their life; approximately 3.3 million reported use in the past year, and 1.2 million reported current use (that is, within the past thirty days). About 2 percent of the population, or 5.3 million persons, used crack cocaine in their lifetime; 721,000 persons used it in the past year; and 265,000 used the substance in the past month. In 2002, an estimated 2 million persons (0.9 percent) were current (within the past thirty days) cocaine users, 567,000 of whom used crack during the same time period (0.2 percent) (Substance Abuse and Mental Health Services Administration 2001; Substance Abuse and Mental Health Services Administration 2003b).

From 1965 to 1967, only 0.1 percent of youths had ever used cocaine, but rates rose throughout the 1970s and 1980s, reaching 2.2 percent in 1987. A period of decline followed in the early 1990s, after which the trend reversed, reaching a peak of 2.7 percent in 2002. Rates of cocaine use show substantial variation by age, with the highest for the young-adult age group (18 to 25 years). The percentage of youths aged 12 to 17 who had ever used cocaine increased slightly from 2001 to 2002 (2.3 to 2.7 percent). The percentage of young adults aged 18 to 25 who had ever used cocaine was less than 1 percent during the mid-1960s, but rose steadily throughout the 1970s and early 1980s, reaching 17.9 percent in 1984. By 1996, the rate had dropped to 10.1 percent but increased to 14.9 percent in 2001 and rose to 15.4 percent in 2002 (Substance Abuse and Mental Health Services Administration 2003b).

Incidence of cocaine use generally rose throughout the 1970s to a peak in 1980 (1.7 million new users) and subsequently declined until 1991 (0.7 million new users). Cocaine initiation steadily increased during the 1990s, reaching 1.2 million in 2001. Age-specific incidence rates have generally mirrored the overall incidence trends, with greater initiation among adults than among youths under 18. Approximately 70 percent of cocaine initiates in 2001 were age 18 or older. Since 1975, males have generally composed the majority of cocaine initiates. In 2001, there were 0.7 million new male users and 0.5 million new female users. The average age of cocaine initiates rose from 18.6 years in 1968 to 23.8 years in 1990 and subsequently declined to approximately 21 years from 1995 to 2001.

Lifetime, past-year, and past-month cocaine use is more common among males than females; when broken down by age, however, gender differences are not always found. Although female cocaine users account for between 17 and 30 percent of the mortality demographics in major cities, males account for the majority of deaths, emergency department mentions, and cocaine treatment admissions in all locations throughout the United States. Overall, and for those aged 12 to 25 and 26 to 34, whites have a higher lifetime use of cocaine than blacks and Hispanics. Also, there appear to be no differences in race/ethnicity for past-year use, but past-month use tends to be higher among blacks and Hispanics than whites. In the total population, past-year and past-month cocaine use tends to be more likely to occur among those with less than a high school education than those who had attended or graduated from college. Unemployed adults use cocaine at higher rates than employed adults.

Based on hospital emergency department data, cocaine/crack cocaine was reported in 29 percent of the drug episodes, compared with 16 percent for heroin/morphine, 16 percent for marijuana/hashish, and 2 percent for methamphetamine/speed. By comparison, mentions of alcohol in combination with other drugs occurred in 34 percent of the ED episodes in 2000. Other information about U.S. cocaine use shows that new youthful cocaine users are not for the most part showing up in standard indicators.

Mortality demographics continue to reflect an older cocaine-using population. Likewise, data continue to suggest an aging cohort of cocaine users with a few exceptions that bear watching.

Throughout the United States, the following routes of cocaine and crack use have been reported. Smoking, typically crack, is the dominant route of administration among primary cocaine treatment admissions. Needle-exchange workers in major cities on the East Coast see some injecting drug users (IDUs) dissolving crack cocaine in vinegar or lemon juice to be used most often in combination with heroin (known as "speedballing"). In Chicago, imposed drug-paraphernalia laws to eliminate the sale of crack pipes have caused crack (rock) users to improvise, using cans or bottles to smoke the drug; smokers commonly use a car antenna and a piece of scouring pad as a screen to smoke rock. The smoking of crack with metal "straight shooters" that are usually car antennas may cause problems with the lungs due to the metal alloys from the antennas. Crack/marijuana combinations are reported in some areas. For example, "bazooka" is crack and tobacco in a joint. Some users dip crack in formaldehyde to produce a more intense high (National Institute on Drug Abuse 1996; National Institute on Drug Abuse 2001).

Illicit-Drug Overviews

Many aspects of the illicit-drug problem warrant attention. The following overviews of disease, terrorism, and youth show the connection between illicit drugs and other problems, including health, crime, security, and social well-being.

Drug Use, Disease, and Ground-Level Zero for the Problems—the Former Soviet Union

In 1984, research groups led by Robert Gallo of the U.S. National Cancer Institute, Luc Montagnier at the Pasteur Institute in Paris, and Jay Levy at the University of California at San Francisco all identified a retrovirus as the cause of AIDS. Today, it is widely acknowledged that the spread of HIV/AIDS as well as hepatitis C and other blood-borne viruses is in part linked to drug use, in particular injection drug use. A cure for these diseases remains elusive; however, considerable efforts through prevention, education, treatment, and rehabilitation are being made to try to curb infection. For illicit-drug users, policies and programs tend to focus on the need for demand-and-supply reduction of drugs, education, and measures that reduce or eliminate the need to share nonsterile injecting equipment.

At the end of 2002, an estimated 42 million people were living with HIV/AIDS. In that year alone, 5 million people became infected with HIV, of which more than 95 percent lived in developing countries. The epidemic has claimed an estimated 3.1 million lives, and 33 percent of the people living with HIV/AIDS are between the ages of fifteen and twenty-four. Although sub-Saharan Africa remains the most affected region, accounting for about 70 percent of people living with HIV/AIDS, considerable attention is being given to the former Soviet Union where the spread of injection drug use is increasing and the fact that injection of a substance directly into the bloodstream is by far the most efficient mode of HIV transmission, much more so than through sexual intercourse. The chances of contracting HIV infection through the injection route increase when injection drug users (IDUs) share contaminated injecting equipment, solutions, pots, or containers (UNAIDS/WHO 2002; UNAIDS 2000).

In the region of Eastern Europe and central Asia, about 1 percent or more of all adults are injecting illicit drugs such as opiates and amphetamines, and many of these people have become infected with HIV. In 2002, there were an estimated 250,000 new infections in that region, most of them IDUs (Dehne et al. 1999; UNAIDS/WHO 2002).

In the Russian Federation, where estimates of the number of IDUs range between 1 million and 2.5 million, the HIV epidemic emerged only in 1996. Approximately 90 percent of the new HIV infections are IDUs, with more than 100,000 infections reported in the course of 2001. Almost 60 percent of HIV infections in Ukraine are related to injection drug use. Until recently, the prevalence of HIV infection has been low in central Asia. Now the problem is evident and growing in Kazakhstan, Azerbaijan, Georgia, Kyrgyzstan, Tajikistan, and Uzbekistan where there has been a considerable increase of injection drug use with cheap opium heroin originating from Afghanistan and its neighboring countries. For example, in Uzbekistan, in the first six months of 2002, new HIV infections nearly equaled the number that had been recorded in the whole of the previous decade. Some recent city-based studies conducted in the Eastern European and central Asian region report that many female IDUs are involved in commercial sex (UNAIDS/WHO 2002).

Both hepatitis C virus (HCV) and hepatitis B virus (HBV) infections are highly prevalent among IDUs. In Europe and the former Soviet Union, it has been reported that depending on location, between 40 and 90 percent of the injecting subpopulations monitored are infected with the virus (World Health Organization 2000a). Data on HBV among IDUs indicate prevalence varying between 20 and 60 percent (World Health Organization 2000b).

HIV and tuberculosis are closely linked. In a joint press release issued in 2001, the United Nations AIDS Program and World Health Organization reported that about 13 million people worldwide are infected with both HIV and TB. Also, up to 50 percent of those people living with HIV can expect to develop TB, which is the most common cause of death in persons with HIV. HIV severely weakens the immune system and makes people highly vulnerable to diseases such as TB (U.S. Information Service 2001).

Among infectious diseases, TB remains the second leading killer in the world, with more than 2 million TB-related deaths each year. Nearly one-third of the entire population of the world is infected with this bacterium that is easily spread through the respiratory route—that is, when it is present in a patient's lungs, it can be passed on to another person through coughing (Centers for Disease Control and Prevention 2002). TB is most prevalent in crowded low-income areas with substandard health conditions, and it is linked to drug users and alcoholics who have a history of crime, imprisonment, and unemployment (Migliori and Ambrosetti 1998). Drug users are two to six times more likely to contract TB than nonusers, and compared to other people with TB, IDUs are more likely to develop the disease in multiple organs and body sites, rather than only in the lungs (National Institute on Drug Abuse 2001).

A serious form of the disease is multidrug-resistant tuberculosis (MDR TB). The American Lung Association reports that "resistance to one or several forms of treatment occurs when the bacteria develops the ability to withstand antibiotic attack and relay that ability to their progeny" (2003). Since that entire strain of bacteria inherits this capacity to resist the effects of various treatments, resistance can spread from one person to another. On an individual basis, however, inadequate treatment or improper use of the antituberculosis medications remains an important cause of drug-resistant tuberculosis. The World Health Organization estimates that up to 50 million persons worldwide may have been infected with drug-resistant strains of tuberculosis in 2001.

In the former Soviet Union, deteriorating conditions, including poverty, unemployment, inadequate hygiene and heath care, and a lack of preventive health education, have provided fertile ground for the rise of injection drug use and the spread of HIV and tuberculosis (Malinowska-Sempruch 2002). Referred to as "Ebola with wings," tuberculosis has increased sharply in Russia and central Asia during the past decade. The occurrence has more than doubled—from 34 per 100,000 in 1992 to 90 per 100,000 in 2000. In contrast, the U.S. rate is 5.8 cases per 100,000. A reason tuberculosis is common among IDUs in the former Soviet Union is that many of them have a history of incarceration in poorly ventilated prisons where inmates fall ill with TB that tends to be resistant to medications.

On April 4, 2003, the World Bank announced that it had approved a $150 million loan to the Russian Federation for its Tuberculosis and AIDS Control Project. According to the World Bank director for Russia, "the rapidly growing number of people infected with TB and HIV pose daunting challenges to the country's social and economic development" (World Bank 2003).

Illicit Drugs and Terrorism: The Connection, Cost, and Need for Change

The distribution of drugs goes hand in hand with terrorism. Terrorism is financed, in large part, by the production and sale of illegal drugs such as opium, heroin, and cocaine. Terrorist organizations need money to operate, and for the most part their interests are fueled through illegal funding sources, particularly those related to the production and trafficking of illicit drugs. As noted earlier in this chapter, drugs are used as a monetary equivalent to pay for weapons and support of terrorist activity—in Afghanistan, the Bekaa Valley in Lebanon, as well as elsewhere throughout the world where cultivators and tribal drug lords working with militias have built up a thriving business generating billions of dollars each year in illegal revenues.

Despite a year-old ban by the Taliban on growing poppy, which may have been a calculated ploy to control the world market prices, September 11, large-scale bombing of the area, and subsequent relief and construction efforts led by the United States, Afghanistan and the region remain the number-one producers of opium and heroin in the world. And the revenues from this activity continue to support terrorist activity.

A new national priority and resolve are sweeping through the United States to address terrorism. It has been pointed out that this mission will not be accomplished quickly—this is not Desert Storm; it will take time, patience, and resources. Such resources will be drawn, in part, by rechanneling governmental support for human services and by staff reduction. New York City alone is facing a potential deficit of $4 billion to $6 billion in a $39 billion budget. As pointed out by Felix Rohatyn, chairman of the New York–based Municipal Corporation from 1975 to 1993, "Is it reasonable, under existing circumstances, to believe that the city and the state can close budget gaps of possibly $6 billion in one fiscal year and maintain the city as a viable economic and social entity? . . . It would be impossible to do so as a practical matter. . . . [L]ayoffs throughout the declining economy, both reducing revenues and increasing costs for state and local governments, will undo many of the positive effects of any federal stimulus program proposed by President Bush" (2001).

Throughout the world, there is a need to address the problem of terrorism, just as there is a need to address the problem of drugs and disease—problems that are intertwined, requiring policy that supports rapid responses and effective results. Reform of present governmental policy and action should not be viewed as an admission of failure in the War on Drugs; rather, it should be considered a much needed step toward responsible decision making to move the United States and other nations forward at a very challenging time. It is hoped that progressive and open-minded leadership will have the courage and steadfastness to make changes that are needed, those that respond to the needs of millions of people rather than the ideological, political, and economic interests of a few (Isralowitz 2002a).

Youths and Illicit-Drug Use in the United States: Attitudes and Behavior

The following examination of illicit-drug use and youth in the United States is drawn from the National Survey on Drug Use and Health (Substance Abuse and Mental Health Services Administration 2003b). It provides an examination of measures related to the prevention of illicit-substance use among youths aged twelve to seventeen. These measures include perceptions of risk, availability of substances (cigarettes, alcohol, and illicit drugs), perceived parental disapproval of substance use, attitudes toward school and religion, participation in youth activities, involvement in delinquent behavior, and exposure to substance abuse–prevention messages and programs.

Perceptions of Risk

Youths were asked how much they thought people risk harming themselves physically and in other ways when they use various substances. Response choices in the survey were "great risk," "moderate risk," "slight risk," or "no risk." Only 32.4 percent of youths indicated that smoking marijuana once a month was a great risk. A higher percentage of youths perceived a great risk in using cocaine once a month (50.5 percent). In contrast, smoking one or more packs of cigarettes per day was cited as a great risk by 63.1 percent of youths. About three-fifths of all youths (62.2 percent) thought that having four or five drinks of an alcoholic beverage nearly every day was a great risk. Youths of different ages reported different patterns of perceived risk from substance use. The percentage of youths who perceived smoking marijuana once a month as a great risk decreased with age. Specifically, 42 percent of youths aged twelve and thirteen and 24.1 percent of youths aged sixteen and seventeen perceived smoking marijuana once a month as a great risk. In contrast, the percentage of youths who perceived using cocaine once a month as a great risk increased with age. Specifically, 42.8 percent of youths aged twelve and thirteen and 59.2 percent of those aged sixteen and seventeen perceived a great risk of using cocaine once a month. Among youths indicating that "smoking marijuana once a month" was a "great risk," only 1.9 percent indicated that they had used marijuana in the past month. However, among youths who indicated "moderate, slight, or no risk," the prevalence rate was 11.3 percent—almost six times larger.

Availability

Approximately one in six youths (16.7 percent) reported that someone selling drugs in the past month had approached them. Those who had been approached reported a much higher rate of past-month use of an illicit drug than those who had not been approached (36.2 and 6.7 percent, respectively). Slightly more than half of youths aged twelve to seventeen indicated that it would be fairly or very easy to obtain marijuana if they wanted some (55 percent). Yet the ease of obtaining marijuana varied greatly by age. Only 26 percent of twelve and thirteen year olds indicated that it would be fairly or very easy to obtain marijuana; 79 percent of those sixteen and seventeen years of age indicated that it would be fairly or very easy to obtain this substance. The percentages of youths reporting that it was fairly or very easy to obtain specific drugs were 25 percent for cocaine, 19.4 percent for LSD, and 15.8 percent for heroin. The percentage of youths who reported that it would be fairly or very easy to obtain marijuana was similar for youths who lived in large metropolitan areas (55.2 percent), small metropolitan areas (55.5 percent), and nonmetropolitan areas (53.6 percent). There were some statistically significant differences across metropolitan and nonmetropolitan areas in the percentages of youths reporting that it would be easy to obtain cocaine, heroin, and LSD; however, these differences were typically quite small.

Parental Disapproval of Substance Use

Youths who perceived that their parents would "strongly disapprove" of their use of illicit substances were much less likely to use those substances than youths who perceived that their parents would only "somewhat disapprove" or "neither approve nor disapprove." For example, among youths who perceived that their parents would strongly disapprove of smoking one or more packs of cigarettes a day (89.5 percent of youths), only 9.4 percent had used cigarettes in the past month compared with 44 percent of youths who perceived that their parents would not strongly disapprove. Most youths (89.1 percent) reported that their parents would strongly disapprove of their trying marijuana once or twice. Among these youths, only 5.5 percent had used marijuana in the past month. However, among youths who perceived that their parents would only somewhat disapprove or neither approve nor disapprove of their trying marijuana, 30.2 percent reported past-month use of marijuana.

Attitudes about School

Youths were asked whether they liked or kind of liked school, whether assigned schoolwork was meaningful and important, whether their courses at school during the past year were very or somewhat interesting, whether the things learned in school during the past year would be important later in life, and whether teachers always or sometimes in the past year let them know that they were doing a good job with schoolwork. Youths who had these types of positive attitudes about their school were less likely to use substances than other students. For example, 78.8 percent of youths reported that they "liked or kind of liked going to school." Among those youths, 9.3 percent had used an illicit drug in the past month; however, among youths who either "didn't like it very much" or "hated it," 20.8 percent had used an illicit drug in the past month.

Delinquent Behavior

Approximately one-fifth (20.6 percent) of youths aged twelve to seventeen reported having gotten into a serious fight at school or work one or more times during the past year. Taking part in a group-against-group fight was reported by 15.9 percent of youths. Other delinquent activities included carrying a handgun (3.3 percent), selling illegal drugs (4.4 percent), stealing (or trying to steal) something worth more than fifty dollars (4.9 percent), and attacking others with the intent to seriously hurt them (7.8 percent). Youths who self-reported delinquent behavior during the past year were more likely to use illicit drugs in the past month than other youths. Specifically, youths reported the following levels of using an illicit drug in the past month depending on whether they had engaged in the delinquent behavior: getting into a serious fight at school or work (20.7 percent versus 9.3 percent); carrying a handgun (34.6 versus 10.8 percent); selling illegal drugs (68.8 percent versus 9 percent); and stealing or trying to steal something worth fifty dollars or more (43.8 versus 9.9 percent).

Participation in Religious and Other Activities

Among youths who attended religious services twenty-five times or more in the past year (33 percent of youths), 7.1 percent had used an illicit drug in the past month. Among youths attending less often or not at all, 13.9 percent reported past-month use. Among youths who agreed or strongly agreed that religious beliefs are a very important part of their life (78.2 percent of all youths), 9.2 percent had used an illicit drug in the past month. In contrast, among youths who "disagreed or strongly disagreed" with the statement, 20.5 percent had used an illicit drug. Among youths who participated in two or more youth activities, such as band, sports, student government, or dance lessons (84.6 percent of youths), only 10.7 percent had used an illicit drug in the past month. On the other hand, among those youths indicating one or no youth activities in the past year, 17.3 percent had used an illicit drug in the past month.

Exposure to Prevention Messages and Programs

In 2002, a majority (83.2 percent) of youths aged twelve to seventeen reported having seen or heard alcohol- or drug-prevention messages outside of school in the past year. Youths who had seen or heard these messages indicated a slightly lower past-month use of an illicit drug (11.3 percent) than youths who had not seen or heard these types of messages (13.2 percent). Among youths aged twelve to seventeen who were enrolled in school during the past twelve months, 78.8 percent reported having seen or heard drug- or alcohol-prevention messages in school during that period. Of those indicating they had seen or heard these messages, the rate of past-month illicit-drug use was 10.9 percent compared with 14.6 percent for the remaining youths. More than half of all youths aged twelve to seventeen (58.1 percent) indicated that they had talked with at least one parent in the past year about the dangers of tobacco, alcohol, or drug use. The prevalence rate for past-month use of an illicit drug was 11.3 percent among this group and 12.1 percent among those who had not had this parental discussion. Youths were asked if they had participated in various special programs dealing with substance use and other related problems in the past year. These programs and the percentage of youths participating were problem-solving, communication-skills, or self-esteem groups (23.5 percent); violence-prevention programs (17.1 percent); alcohol-, tobacco-, or drug-prevention programs outside of school (12.7 percent); pregnancy- or sexually transmitted disease (STD)–prevention programs (13.9 percent); and programs for dealing with alcohol or drug use (5.5 percent).

References

American Lung Association. 2003. "Multidrug-Resistant Tuberculosis Fact Sheet." Available at http://www.lungusa.org/diseases/mdrtbfac.html (accessed April 1, 2003).

Centers for Disease Control and Prevention. 2002. "World TB Day 2002." Available at http://www.cdc.gov/nchstp/tb (accessed March 24, 2003).

Clines, F. 2001. "Fighting Appalachia's Top Cash Crop, Marijuana." *New York Times,* February 28.

Dehne, K., J. Grund, L. Kodakevich, and Y. Kobyshcha. 1999. "The HIV/AIDS Epidemic among Drug Injectors in Eastern Europe: Patterns, Trends and Determinants." *Journal of Drug Issues* 29, no. 4: 393–402.

European Monitoring Centre for Drugs and Drug Addiction. 2000. *Annual Report on the State of the Drug Problem in the European Union*. Lisbon: European Monitoring Centre.

Isralowitz, R. 2002a. "Drugs and Terrorism: The Need for Immediate Policy Change." *Journal of Social Work Practice in the Addictions* 2, no. 2: 97–99.

———. 2002b. *Drug Use, Policy and Management*. Westport, CT: Auburn House.

JTO—Join Together Online. 2001a. "CASA Releases New Study on Drugs in Schools." Boston University School of Public Health. Available at http://www.jointogether.org/sa/news/alerts/reader/0,1854,545651,00. html (accessed September 5, 2001).

———. 2001b. "U.S. Official Says to Expect Costly Columbian Drug War." Boston University School of Public Health. Available at http:// www.jointogether.org/sa/news/reader/0%2C1030%2C267034%2C00.ht ml (accessed April 6, 2001).

Kazancigil, A., and C. Milani. 2002. *Globalisation, Drugs and Criminalisation: Final Research Report on Brazil, China, India and Mexico*. New York: United Nations Office for Drug Control and Crime Prevention.

Malinowska-Sempruch, K. 2002. "From Concern to Action: Harm Reduction as the Key to HIV Prevention and Treatment Efforts in Eastern Europe and the Former Soviet Union." Available at http://www.soros. org/initiatives/ihrd/articles_publications/articles/unaids_20020709 (accessed January 21, 2004).

Migliori, G., and M. Ambrosetti. 1998. "Epidemiology of Tuberculosis in Europe." *Mondali Archives of Chest Diseases* 53, no. 6: 681–687.

National Institute on Drug Abuse (NIDA). 1996. *Epidemiologic Trends in Drug Abuse*. Vol. 1: *Highlights and Executive Summary*. Rockville, MD: National Institutes of Health.

———. 2000. *Epidemiologic Trends in Drug Abuse*. Vol. 1: *Highlights and Executive Summary*. Rockville, MD: National Institutes of Health.

———. 2001. *Epidemiologic Trends in Drug Abuse*. Vol. 1: *Highlights and Executive Summary*. Rockville, MD: National Institutes of Health.

———. 2002. *Epidemiologic Trends in Drug Abuse*. Vol. 1: *Highlights and Executive Summery*. Rockville, MD: National Institutes of Health.

Rohatyn, F. 2001. "Fiscal Disaster the City Can't Face Alone." *New York Times*, October 9, A25.

Schlosser, E. 1997. "More Reefer Madness." *Atlantic Monthly* (April) 4: 90–102.

Substance Abuse and Mental Health Services Administration (SAMHSA). 2001. *Summary of Findings from the 2000 National Household*

Survey on Drug Abuse. Rockville, MD: United States Department of Health and Human Services.

———. 2003a. *Emergency Department Trends From the Drug Abuse Warning Network, Final Estimates 1995–2002.* Rockville, MD: United States Department of Health and Human Services.

———. 2003b. *Results from the 2002 National Survey on Drug Use and Health: National Findings.* Rockville, MD: United States Department of Health and Human Services.

U.S. Department of State, Office of International Information Agency. 1992. *Consequences of Illegal Drug Trade: The Negative Economic, Political, and Social Effects of Cocaine in Latin America.* Washington, DC: U.S. Department of State, Office of International Information Agency.

U.S. Information Service. 2001. "WHO and UNAIDS Emphasize Link between AIDS and TB: Health Agencies Warn of Potential for TB Cases to Double." Available at http://www.wwaegis.com/news/isis/2001/US010406. htm (accessed April 24, 2001).

UNAIDS. 2000. *Report on the Global HIV/AIDS Epidemic.* Geneva: UNAIDS/WHO.

UNAIDS/WHO. 2002. *AIDS Epidemic Update.* Geneva: UNAIDS/WHO.

United Nations Economic and Social Council, Commission on Narcotic Drugs. 2003. *World Situation with Regard to Drug Abuse.* Vienna: Commission on Narcotic Drugs.

United Nations General Assembly Political Declaration. 1998. "Declaration on the Guiding Principles of Drug Demand Reduction." Available at http://www.un.org/ga/20special/demand.htm (accessed January 13, 2004).

United Nations Office for Drug Control and Crime Prevention (ODCCP). 2002. *Global Illicit Drug Trends.* New York: ODCCP Studies on Drugs and Crime.

Willard, J., and C. Schoenborn. 1995. "Relationship between Cigarette Smoking and Other Unhealthy Behaviors among Our Nation's Youth: United States, 1992." In *Advance Data* no. 263. Washington, DC: National Center for Health Statistics, April 24.

World Bank. 2003. "Tackling Tuberculosis and HIV/AIDS in Russia." April 7. Available at http://web.worldbank.org/WBSITE/EXTERNAL/NEWS/0,contentMDK:20102994~menuPK:34457~pagePK:34370~piPK:34424~theSitePK:4607,00.html (accessed January 13, 2004).

World Health Organization. 2000a. "Fact Sheet no. 164: Hepatitis C." Rev. October. Geneva: WHO.

———. 2000b. "Fact Sheet no. 204: Hepatitis B." Rev. October. Geneva: WHO.

4

Tobacco and Alcohol: What Are the Facts and Data?

More illness and death occur from the use and abuse of two legal drugs, tobacco and alcohol, than all illegal substances combined. In this chapter, facts, data, and discussion are presented about these two drugs of mass destruction. Among the issues examined are female and adolescent use of both substances, the role of advertising and big business with tobacco, infant alcohol syndrome, binge drinking, and driving while under the influence of alcohol.

Tobacco

Tobacco is a drug, and cigarettes as well as smokeless tobacco products are delivery systems for nicotine, which is an addictive substance. Nicotine, found in the smoke of cigarettes, cigars, and pipes as well as in smokeless tobacco products, can, through repeated use, result in addiction. Cigarette smoking allows nicotine to be inhaled through the lungs. For smokeless tobacco or environmental tobacco exposure, the nicotine is absorbed through the mucosal lining of the mouth or nose or through the skin. Cigar and pipe smokers do not usually inhale the smoke, so the nicotine is also absorbed through the mucosal membranes of the mouth. After inhalation or absorption, nicotine passes rapidly into the arterial bloodstream and then into the brain (Benowitz 1996).

Tobacco use is considered the most important preventable cause of death and disease in the United States and the world.

Based on U.S. government and World Health Organization (WHO) estimates, tobacco-related disease causes annually 450,000 deaths in the United States, 500,000 deaths in the European Union countries, and about 2 million deaths in other countries throughout the world with a high proportion coming from people living in the poorest areas. The Switzerland Addiction Research Institute (2003) claims that tobacco causes 4.9 million deaths annually. The WHO believes that 10 million people are expected to die each year from smoking-related illnesses by the year 2030, with 70 percent of these deaths coming in developing countries.

The U.S. National Household Survey on Drug Abuse in 1999 shows that 67 million people aged twelve or older were current tobacco users (that is, have used in the past month). This number is about 30 percent of the civilian noninstitutionalized population aged twelve or older. In 2002, an estimated 71.5 million Americans (30.4 percent of the total population aged twelve or older) reported current (past-month) use of tobacco products. About 61.1 million (26 percent) smoked cigarettes, 12.8 million (5.4 percent) smoked cigars, 7.8 million (3.3 percent) used smokeless tobacco, and 1.8 million (0.8 percent) smoked tobacco in pipes (Substance Abuse Mental Health Services Administration 2003).

According to the WHO, there are now 1.1 billion smokers in the world. This is one-third of the world's adult population. In developed countries, 41 percent of men and 21 percent of women regularly smoke. Each person, on average, consumes 2,400 cigarettes a year. In developing countries, 50 percent of men and 8 percent of women smoke an average of 1,400 cigarettes a year. The counties with the highest rates of cigarette use are (listed in order): Poland, Greece, Hungary, Japan, Korea, Switzerland, Iceland, the Netherlands, Yugoslavia (now Serbia and Montenegro), Australia, United States, Spain, Canada, New Zealand, Ireland, Germany, Belgium, Israel, Cuba, Bulgaria, and the United Kingdom.

Female Tobacco Use

The U.S. surgeon general has reported that smoking-related disease among women is an epidemic and that the number of women who die each year from smoking accounts for 39 percent of all smoking-related deaths. For many years, smoking prevalence was more prominent among men; it took nearly twenty-five years before the gap narrowed and smoking became commonplace among women, said the surgeon general. Not only do women share the same health risks as men, but they also face health consequences that are unique to women, including pregnancy complications, problems with menstrual function, and cervical cancer. According to *Women and Smoking: A Report of the Surgeon General* (Centers for Disease Control and Prevention 2001b), there has been a 600 percent increase in women's death from lung cancer since 1950. At least 90 percent of the lung cancer deaths in women are linked to smoking. In the report, eight major findings were cited:

- Despite strong evidence about the health risks associated with smoking, 22 percent of women smoked cigarettes in 1998.
- In 2000, 29.7 percent of female high school seniors said they had smoked within the past thirty days.
- Since 1980, an estimated 3 million women in the United States have died prematurely from smoking-related diseases and burns caused by fires that were started by cigarettes.
- Lung cancer is now the leading cause of cancer death among U.S. women, exceeding breast cancer.
- Exposure to secondhand smoke is a cause of lung cancer and coronary heart disease among women who are lifetime nonsmokers.
- Women who stop smoking greatly reduce their risk of dying prematurely, and quitting smoking at any age is beneficial.
- Smoking during pregnancy remains a major public health problem, despite increased evidence of the adverse health effects.
- Marketing by the tobacco industry is a factor in why girls both in the United States and in other countries start to smoke.

In 2002, 17.3 percent of pregnant women aged fifteen to forty-four smoked cigarettes in the past month, compared with 31.1 percent of nonpregnant women in the same age group.

The WHO recognizes the need to do more to reduce smoking-related diseases in women. In *Women and the Tobacco Epidemic—Challenges for the 21st Century* (2001), it reports that tobacco-related diseases are on the rise among women and points to aggressive tobacco marketing and exposure to secondhand smoke for the increase. The report said that only recently have women in developing countries begun to smoke and that it may be several decades before the full health impact is felt, but devastating health consequences are inevitable unless action is taken now. Also, the report notes that false images of good health, fitness, stress relief, beauty, and being slim are used to appeal to women and that tobacco products are promoted as a means of attaining maturity, gaining confidence, being attractive, and being in control of one's destiny—effectively exploiting the struggle of women everywhere for equality.

Adolescent Tobacco Use

The U.S. Centers for Disease Control (CDC) has reported that every day in the United States more than 6,000 people under the age of 18 try their first cigarette, and more than half of them will become daily smokers. In 2002, an estimated 4.5 million adolescents, or 33.3 percent of that age group, smoked in the United States (University of Michigan News and Information Services 2002). The rate of lifetime daily cigarette use among youths aged twelve to seventeen is 8.2 percent (Substance Abuse Mental Health Services Administration 2003).

Young people grossly underestimate the addictiveness of nicotine. Of daily smokers who think that they will not smoke in five years, nearly 75 percent are still smoking five to six years later. Data show the following:

- Thirty-four point eight percent of high school students are current (used in past thirty days) smokers.
- Fourteen percent of high school males currently use smokeless tobacco.
- Fifteen point five million children are exposed to secondhand smoke at home.
- Youths consume about 900 million packs of cigarettes each year, generating tobacco company revenues of $1.5 billion per year.

The Centers for Disease Control and Prevention (2001a) has stated that among young people, the short-term health consequences of smoking include damage to the respiratory system, addiction to nicotine, and the associated risk of other drug use. According to the 2003 American Legacy Foundation and the National Center on Addiction and Substance Abuse, teenage tobacco users are fourteen times more likely to use marijuana than their nonsmoking peers. Long-term health consequences of youth smoking are reinforced by the fact that most young people who smoke regularly continue to smoke throughout adulthood. Among the effects arethe following:

- Smoking hurts young people's physical fitness in terms of both performance and endurance—even among young people trained in competitive running.
- Smoking among youths can hinder the rate of lung growth and the level of maximum lung function.
- The resting heart rates of young adult smokers are two to three beats per minute faster than nonsmokers.
- The younger people start smoking cigarettes, the more likely they are to become strongly addicted to nicotine.
- Smoking is associated with poor overall health and a variety of short-term adverse health effects in young people and may also be a marker for underlying mental health problems such as depression among adolescents.

Worldwide, 14 percent of the youths aged thirteen to fifteen smoke, and one-quarter of all children who do smoke started by age ten. In June 1995, a group of twenty-two international organizations and individuals met at the Rockefeller Foundation's Bellagio Study and Conference Center in Italy to examine the implications of the current global trend in tobacco production and consumption, especially in developing countries, for sustainable development. Regarding children and youth, it was reported that 300 million will eventually be killed by tobacco use based on current smoking patterns. In a report issued by the WHO focused on Europe, *Hazardous Harmonization in Smoking by European Youth* (2002), it was reported that while there are decreasing rates by adults in some countries, no country has shown a significant decrease in smoking by young people since 1997. Around 30 percent of fifteen to eighteen year olds in Europe are smokers. Since the mid-1990s, smoking among youths in Eastern Europe has risen only slightly, while rates among Western European teenagers have remained stable over the same period. Furthermore, it was reported that there are no significant differences in tobacco consumption among young people between countries and subregions. The following charts, drawn from the WHO report, provide comparisons of youth/adult and regional differences in smoking rates in Europe.

Table 4.1
Geographical Differences in Smoking Rates (% Smokers) among Adults and Young People (Fifteen to Sixteen Year Olds)

Age Group	Eastern Countries	Western Countries	Difference East/West
Young People	13	26	3
Adults	33.5	24	9.5

Source: WHO. 2002. Hazardous Harmonization in Smoking by European Youth. Copenhagen: WHO Regional Office for Europe, 15 February. Press backgrounder EURO/03/02. Available at http://www.who.dk/document/cma/PB032002e.pdf (accessed February 27, 2004).

Table 4.2
Gender Differences in Smoking Rates (% Smokers) among Adults and Young People (Fifteen to Sixteen Year Olds)

Age Group	Male	Female	Difference Male/Female
Young People	29	25	4
Adults	34.5	22	12.5

Source: WHO. 2002. Hazardous Harmonization in Smoking by European Youth. Copenhagen: WHO Regional Office for Europe, 15 February. Press backgrounder EURO/03/02. Available at http://www.who.dk/document/cma/PB032002e.pdf (accessed February 27, 2004).

Table 4.3
Age Group/Gender Differences in Smoking Rates (% Smokers) among Adults and Young People (Fifteen to Sixteen Year Olds), according to Comparable Data from Thirteen Countries

Gender	Young People	Adults	Difference Youth/Adult
Male	29.6	36	–6.5
Female	25.5	21.5	+4

Source: WHO. 2002. Hazardous Harmonization in Smoking by European Youth. Copenhagen: WHO Regional Office for Europe, 15 February. Press backgrounder EURO/03/02. Available at http://www.who.dk/document/cma/PB032002e.pdf (accessed February 27, 2004).

Table 4.4
Smoking Prevalence (%) among Young People in Europe

Country	Boys		Girls		Total Youth	
	1993–1996	1997–2001	1993–1996	1997–2001	1993–1996	1997–2001
Austria†	29	30	31	36	30	33
Bulgaria*		35		38		36
Croatia*	27	31	18	25	23	28
Czech Republic*	30	39	20	34	26	36
Denmark*	22	31	24	32	23	32
Estonia*	36	38	17	18	25	27
Finland*	33	41	36	38	35	39
France‡	22	28	18	20	20	24
Hungary*	32	31	24	25	28	28
Iceland*	27	24	27	26	27	25
Ireland*	36	31	38	36	37	34
Israel†	9	24	9	13	9	19
Italy*	25	22	24	28	25	25
Latvia‡	33	38	14	23	23.5	30
Lithuania*	29	46	12	23	20	35
Malta*	20	20	18	21	19	20
Netherlands‡		27		26		27
Norway*	25	31	25	34	25	33
Poland‡	27	27	13	20	20	24
Portugal*	14	18	12	15	13	17
Russian Fed.*		46		38		42
Spain‡		25.2		35.8		23.5
Slovakia*	26	35	13	26	20	30
Slovenia*	16	25	17	26	16	26
Sweden*	28	26	28	25	28	25
Switzerland†	17	25	18	25	17.5	25
Ukraine*	41	39	18	18	29	29
United Kingdom*	25	24	30	28	27	26

Source: WHO. 2002. Hazardous Harmonization in Smoking by European Youth. Copenhagen: WHO Regional Office for Europe, 15 February. Press backgrounder EURO/03/02. Available at http://www.who.dk/document/cma/PB032002e.pdf (accessed February 27, 2004).

*Data from European School Survey Project conducted in 1995 and 1999.
†Data from WHO Survey of Health Behaviour in School-Aged Children conducted in 1993–1994 and 1997–1998.
‡Data from national or other source.

Advertising

Tobacco has secured its position in many societies by controlling the behavior of its consumers. This has been accomplished through vigorous marketing methods (for example, the introduction of filtered cigarettes in the 1950s, low-tar cigarettes in the 1960s, and then smokeless and perfumed cigarettes) as well as by commanding a special position among governmental policy makers who for years have protected the substance for reasons beyond the "best interests" of the public. The following are among the statements and slogans used by the tobacco industry since the glamour era of cigarette advertising began, soon after World War I:

- In the 1920s, Lucky Strike introduced the slogan "Reach for a Lucky instead of a Sweet," using celebrity endorsers like George M. Cohan, Amelia Earhart, and Helen Hayes to bring the message home.
- Well into the 1950s, cigarette advertisers continued to proclaim the health benefits of their product. "How are your nerves?" an ad for one brand asked and proposed a test. Any man who could not button a vest in twelve seconds probably suffered from frayed nerves and should begin smoking immediately.
- Camels announced that its special Turkish tobacco stimulated the flow of digestive fluids and raised the level of alkalinity in the stomach.
- Kool, in the brand's early days, claimed to offer protection against catching colds. And the tobacco industry used doctors, athletes, movie stars, and newsmakers to promote the use of cigarettes—for example, "More doctors smoke Camels than any other cigarette," one ad proclaimed. In the 1950s, Ronald Reagan, as an actor, lent his magic touch to Chesterfields, a brand endorsed by Joe Lewis in 1947 as "the champ" of cigarettes. (Grimes 1997)

During the past few years, there has been a reversal of tobacco industry fortunes, led by a vigorous campaign against the substance by the Food and Drug Administration (FDA) in the United States and the medical community. Report after report reveal collusion and manipulation by tobacco companies to promote and preserve a market for their product—including special populations such as children and youths, women, and minority people. In a detailed account of the FDA's battle with the tobacco companies, David Kessler, the FDA's former director, provides much information about the issues of tobacco advertising and marketing techniques:

> After researching gender differences in the 1970s, some industry researchers concluded that women found it harder than men to quit smoking. [One industry official theorized that] "Women are more neu-

rotic than men and more likely to need to smoke in stressful situations." . . . The industry recognized the implications of this "neurosis" for product development [thinking that] women were . . . more likely to respond to publicity about the health risks of smoking by switching to "lighter" cigarettes [which have more tar and nicotine than consumers think]. . . . [I]ndustry executives cynically did what they could [through female-oriented cigarettes] to make it harder still to quit smoking. (Kessler 2001, 274)

Although cigarette makers must adhere to advertising restrictions under the 1998 tobacco settlement in the United States, they have still managed to increase their promotional spending activity. According to the U.S. Federal Trade Commission (FTC), cigarette manufacturers increased promotional spending 22.3 percent in 1999. Advertising in magazines rose 25.5 percent to $281.3 million, and direct-mail advertising increased by 63.8 percent to $94.6 million. The FTC reported that the $8.24 billion spent by the tobacco industry on advertising and promotions in 1999 was the most ever reported by the major cigarette manufacturers.

Because of the 1999 ban on billboard advertising, the tobacco industry has shifted its advertising strategy to other areas, such as convenience stores. Additionally, other ways to promote cigarettes have appeared—for example, on clocks, shopping baskets, or display shelving containing tobacco advertising. Philip Morris, the tobacco giant, which according to a poll has one of the worst reputations in U.S. business and recently changed its name to "Altria," which derives from Latin and means "high," donates $60 million a year to charity, and spends another $100 million in advertising to inform the public about its good deeds. It has been reported that each year, Philip Morris holds a desert adventure–sports event in Utah aimed at attracting young smokers to the Marlboro brand. The company sends its Marlboro Adventure Team—a major overseas promotional tool for the brand—to Utah with an entourage of foreign journalists. The journalists cover the annual desert event and bring back footage that is broadcast in Marlboro ad campaigns and as a promotion for future events.

Despite vigorous marketing attempts, cigarette smoking is on the decline in the United States, Western Europe, and other countries as a result of public opinion and politically responsive government. Nevertheless, with people in Western countries already addicted, tobacco industries have focused their efforts on other countries like those in Asia, Eastern Europe, nations of the former Soviet Union, Latin America, and Africa for new profits. Although many governments in Asia have launched antismoking campaigns, their efforts have been overwhelmed by the "Madison Avenue glitz" unleashed by the major cigarette companies. Several Asian nations have banned cigarette advertising on television and radio in recent years, but the tobacco companies often find ways around the bans through indirect promotions that skirt the law, including sports events, glossy advertisements for clothing brands, or travel agencies that bear the name and logo of a cigarette brand.

Here are some additional facts and data about the cigarette-advertising situation:

- The World Health Organization's Framework Convention on Tobacco Control says that banning tobacco advertising and sponsorship is one of the two most effective ways of reducing tobacco use. The other method is increasing prices for tobacco products. The United States, Germany, and Japan strongly oppose an outright ban on advertising. The United States has said such a ban would be a violation of free speech under the U.S. Constitution. Publishers of European newspapers are very much opposed to a European Union ban on tobacco advertising in newspapers and magazines; on radio, the Internet, and television; and at international sports events because it would cripple media companies by reducing advertising revenues as they face economic slowdown. The ban could also cause many small local newspapers to close as a result of lost income from tobacco ads.
- The WHO has accused U.S.-based tobacco companies of encouraging minors to smoke by offering free cigarettes. Although distributing cigarettes to minors is illegal in most countries, it is common to see young girls giving out cigarettes in the streets in many developing nations. Tobacco companies portray cigarettes as a symbol of sophistication, independence, and glamour to attract young smokers.
- Although magazine and billboard advertising has declined, it has been reported that there is an explosion of marketing expenditures at the retail outlet.

According to the U.S. Federal Trade Commission, tobacco companies have increased their in-store promotions by paying retailers for prime shelf space and offering giveaways to sell their products. The U.S. Centers for Disease Control and Prevention has found that cigarette advertising displays in stores where adolescents shop may encourage them to smoke. Among the tobacco promotions were interior and exterior signs placed low enough to be at eye level of young children, self-service cigarette displays, and discounts. Matthew Myers, president of the Campaign for Tobacco-Free Kids, has said that seven out of ten teenagers visit a convenience store at least once a week. The retail outlet is the perfect place to get kids.

- Cigarette advertising can impede parents' efforts to prevent children from smoking. Cigarette ads influence teens to smoke even when parents are highly involved in their lives.

- After reviewing magazine advertisements, researchers at the University of Chicago concluded that tobacco companies continue to direct cigarette ads to school-age children. According to the Massachusetts Tobacco Control Program, the U.S. Smokeless Tobacco Company spends millions of dollars on advertising in magazines where at least 15 percent of the readership is young people. Such a marketing strategy would be in violation of the 1998 Master Settlement Agreement between major U.S. tobacco companies and forty-six states. The agreement specifically bans youth-targeted advertising.

- Women are more likely than men to smoke low-tar cigarettes, a large percentage believing that the products are less damaging than regular cigarettes. The National Cancer Institute shows that "low tar" and "light" cigarettes do not lower a smoker's chance of getting smoking-related diseases. Lawsuits against tobacco companies like Philip Morris claim that that there has been a conscious effort to market low-tar cigarettes as less dangerous than regular cigarettes. Under a European Union directive, a ban on terms such as *low tar* went into effect in September 2003.

- Tobacco advertising remains prominent in many

women's magazines. Such magazines publish on average 4.5 tobacco ads per issue. Cigarette advertising in such magazines is designed to promote the link between glamour and cigarettes.

It's about Money: Tax Revenues and Big Business

The Master Settlement Agreement of 1998 required tobacco companies to pay $246 billion to states and place limits on tobacco advertising. In spite of this agreement, tobacco companies continue to turn a profit. Antismoking advocates thought a crackdown on tobacco ads and an increase in cigarette prices would result in fewer smokers. Tobacco companies, however, continue to recruit new smokers, and according to industry figures it appears that consumers have gotten used to paying more for their addiction and consumption levels appear to be only marginally affected.

Additional data and facts confirm the connection between money, tax revenues, big business, government, and tobacco:

- The tobacco industry spent millions of dollars in direct and soft-money contributions for political elections. According to public records, Philip Morris contributed $2.7 million to Republican causes in a recent election cycle compared with a risk-hedging $538,000 to Democrats. Since Bush was elected, the stock market has pushed up tobacco stocks dramatically, meaning that people think the administration will be doing their bidding. The tobacco industry donated $120,000 in hard and soft money to the Bush campaign for the presidency. Philip Morris donated $100,000 for Bush's inauguration. Since 1989, the company has lavished no less than $14.3 million on its Republican friends. When questioned about its pattern of contributions, a Philip Morris spokesman said that "it is very appropriate for us to be contributing our policy positions and being involved in the political process" (Lazarus 2002). The annual tobacco industry contributions to federal candidates and political parties are more than $5 million. The tobacco industry expenditures lobbying

Congress during 1998 were more than $65 million. The annual tobacco industry advertising and promotion expenditures nationwide are more than $6.8 billion. With all this money spent, current prospects for the tobacco industry have weakened. For example, the tobacco giant R. J. Reynolds announced in September 2003 that it would cut its workforce by 40 percent, eliminating 2,600 jobs as part of a plan to cut $1 billion in costs by 2005. Nevertheless, the company still expects to earn 60 to 90 cents per share on earnings of $170 million to $220 million in 2003. Philip Morris, "Altria," announced in November 2002 that it would spend $350 million on promoting its cigarette brands worldwide, hoping to bolster its earnings and stock market trading price.

- A U.S. federal commission on smoking recommended to the Bush administration that the federal tax on cigarettes be increased from $.39 to $2.39 a pack (February 2003). Health and Human Services Secretary Tommy Thompson said in testimony to the U.S. House of Representatives Budget Committee that "this administration does not raise taxes." Thompson has also been quoted as saying that "the tax question is problematic, politically."

- The U.S. Centers for Disease Control and Prevention reports that increasing the price of cigarettes is an effective way to reduce teen smoking.

- The CDC has calculated the societal costs of smoking. Each pack of cigarettes sold in the United States costs the nation an estimated $7.18 in medical care and lost productivity. That adds up to a total of $150 billion each year, or about $3,391 per smoker per year.

- The Master Settlement Agreement of 1998 contained no requirement that states spend any specific percentage of their settlement money. The economic downturn has forced many states to spend a significant percentage of their tobacco settlement funds for purposes like highway repairs and tax relief rather than drug prevention and education. Using the settlement funds for such purposes has a negative result because credit-rating agencies (such as Standard and Poor's) are likely to lower a state's credit rating if the state fails to convince them that it has a long-term solution for its deficit. The use of tobacco revenue for deficit coverage is a good indicator of the state being under stress. A downgrading of its credit status means that the state has to provide a higher rate of interest for the money it borrows through public bond offerings.

• States are collecting record amounts of revenues from tobacco taxes and the tobacco settlement; however, they are cutting spending on programs to keep children from starting to smoke and help smokers quit. The states in the 2002–2003 budget year collected a record $20.3 billion in tobacco-generated revenues, an increase of 9 percent from the year before. They cut spending for tobacco prevention and cessation programs by $86.2 million, or 11 percent. (Campaign for Tobacco-Free Kids 2003)

More cigarettes are traded than any other single product in the world, with an annual value estimated to be $400 billion. According to the WHO, one-quarter of all cigarettes produced in the world are smuggled, enabling multinational tobacco companies to increase sales by evading local tariffs, maintaining a competitive price with domestic producers, and promoting internationally recognized brands such as Marlboro, Kool, Kent, and others. Additionally, smuggling insulates the tobacco companies from national controls to limit cigarette consumption that the WHO warns will cause millions of deaths over the next thirty years.

The smuggling charge has brought tobacco companies to U.S. courts, where they are being accused of violating the Racketeer Influenced and Corrupt Organizations Act, of defrauding governments of hundreds of millions of dollars in tax revenues, and of hiding and ultimately taking profits back to the United States, which constitutes money laundering. After a six-month investigation by the *Nation,* the Center for Investigative Reporting, and the PBS newsmagazine show *NOW with Bill Moyers,* the complex distribution system of a multibillion-dollar trade in smuggled cigarettes was exposed. The WHO sees smuggling as a major public health issue, asserting that it incapacitates one of the government's best weapons for lowering tobacco consumption—high taxes. The WHO has a simple calculation to describe the challenge.

More smuggling equals cheaper cigarettes equals more smokers, which means more smoking-related illnesses and deaths. According to the World Bank, if the price of cigarettes were to increase just 10 percent—which could be maintained through taxation—an estimated 40 million people would quit smoking worldwide (Schapiro 2002).

Finally, one of the most scathing charges against the U.S. government's relation to tobacco companies can be found in *Smoke & Mirrors: The Canadian Tobacco War:*

> The United States spends billions of dollars in its war on illegal drugs. The American government portrays drug-producing countries such as Colombia, Bolivia and Afghanistan as the root or the problem and is waging an international campaign to combat drug production in the third world. At the same time, U.S. multinationals are busy exporting tobacco addiction all over the globe. They make the same obscene profits as drug producers and traffickers. They all exploit, poison and kill their victims except that tobacco barons cause much more death and misery than foreign drug lords. With over [3] million tobacco deaths in the world every year, the hypocrisy of the American position is astounding.
>
> The United States [attempted] to open up tobacco markets in Taiwan, Thailand, South Korea, and Japan in the 1980s. The tobacco industry was controlled by government monopolies in these countries and American tobacco companies had no access. In 1985 the U.S. government warned that severe trade sanctions would be imposed and waged an intense campaign to open up these markets to American tobacco companies. In 1986 Taiwan and Japan succumbed to the threats and allowed American tobacco products and South Korea followed in 1988 [and Thailand too later complied]. American tobacco companies followed with huge advertising and promotional campaigns to gain market share.
>
> The forced opening of these markets to American [tobacco companies] and subsequent massive campaigns to [cause addiction to] these populations can only be described as gross crimes against humanity. The United States government and American tobacco companies share complicity in this overt attempt to entice foreign peoples into drug addiction for monetary gain. The hypocrisy is that the American government

was waging tough antismoking campaigns at home while vigorously promoting tobacco addiction abroad. At the same time [the American government was] waging a full-scale war against the international drug trade [while] they were the biggest international drug dealers in the world causing much more death and misery abroad than illegal drugs ever did in the United States. (Cunningham 1996, 217–220)

Alcohol

The magnitude of alcohol problems has been overshadowed in recent years by the preoccupation with the widespread use of illicit drugs, including heroin, cocaine, crack, and Ecstasy, and the threat of AIDS. According to the Switzerland Addiction Research Institute, annually 1.8 million deaths worldwide are the result of alcohol use while illegal drugs caused 223,000. The WHO claims more than 55,000 people aged fifteen to twenty-nine across Europe die each year as a result of alcohol-related road accidents, poisoning, suicide, and murders. The American Medical Association believes that alcohol contributes to more than 100,000 deaths annually in the United States from drunk driving, stroke, cancer, cirrhosis of the liver, falls, and other adverse effects. These results lead to the conclusion that if one adds together the deaths from every abused illegal drug, it still does not equal the deaths or costs caused by alcohol alone.

In 1995 in the United States, the cost of alcohol use and alcoholism-related treatment services, medical consequences, lost earnings due to illness, lost earnings due to crime and victimization, crashes, fires, criminal justice, and so on was estimated to be $167 billion. The comparable cost related to illegal drug use for that same year was about $110 billion. The total cost to society of alcohol is on order of thirty times what the United States spends on its treatment—about $6 billion in 1997.

In 2002, alcohol use was targeted as the cause for 41 percent of all driving fatalities (17,419 deaths) in the United States. It is the major factor of adult drowning and has been seriously implicated in millions of injuries and thousands of deaths resulting from industrial accidents, a substantial proportion of general (noncommercial) aviation crashes, and boating accidents. The vast majority of fire fatalities and fire burns involve alcohol use at the time of the accident—cigarette smoking is a major cause of fires, and a direct association exists between drinking and smoking in the general population. Alcohol has been found to be involved in up to 70 percent of all deaths and 63 percent of all injuries from falls. Suicide is a major cause of death in the United States, and about 30 percent of those who commit suicide are alcoholics. Alcoholics are far more likely than nonalcoholics to attempt and commit suicide while drinking, and alcohol's mood-changing properties have been seen as a possible link to suicidal actions. Child abuse, neglect, molestation, and marital violence are prevalent types of aggression in the family, and alcohol use is a precipitating factor of these problems as well.

The U.S. Department of Justice estimates that nearly one-third of the nation's state prison inmates drank heavily before committing rapes, burglaries, and assaults. As many as 45 percent of the country's homeless, estimated to be about 700,000 on any given night, are alcoholics. The Bureau of Justice Statistics reports that offenders in local jails throughout the country charged with or convicted of driving while intoxicated were more than one in every eleven inmates. Among convicted inmates, 86 percent of those serving a sentence for driving while intoxicated (DWI) had been sentenced in the past. Almost one-third of the DWI inmates had served three or more previous sentences in jail or prison. Those persons arrested for driving while impaired are more likely to be serious offenders in terms of the nature of criminal activity. In 1997, roughly 1.7 million drivers were arrested for driving under the influence of alcohol or narcotics (Isralowitz 2002).

The use of alcohol in the United States has risen steadily since the end of Prohibition to 1978. Since the early 1980s, however, there has been a downward trend—a behavior pattern that appears in consonance with the use of most psychoactive substances, including cocaine (see table 4.5). The number of new regular users, defined by the U.S. Public Health Service as people who drink alcohol once a month or more, peaked at 3.4 million in 1977, and since the 1980s the number has remained at more than 2 million new regular drinkers each year. Other factors characterizing the downward trend of alcohol use during the past decade include a decline in sales, self-reported alcohol consumption for all ages, and fewer young people ever drinking. Alcohol-related traffic fatalities dropped from 25,165 in 1982 to 17,858 in 1992, 16,653 in 2001, and 17,970 in 2002. Another important indicator of the drop in excessive alcohol use is cirrhosis (liver disease) deaths (Yoon et al. 2002).

Drinking patterns in the United States show the following facts for lifetime, past-year, and past-month alcohol use:

- Adult males drink more than females.
- An estimated 120 million Americans aged twelve or older (51 percent of the population in this age group) report being current (within the past thirty days) drinkers of alcohol.
- More than one-fifth (22.9 percent, or 54 million) of the persons aged twelve or older participated in binge drinking (five or more drinks on the same occasion) at least once in the past thirty days prior to the survey.
- Those with a high school education or less and those

Table 4.5
Per Capita Ethanol Consumption for the United States, 1850–1999[1]

Year	Beer	Wine	Spirits	Total
1999	1.25	0.32	0.64	2.21
1995	1.25	0.29	0.64	2.17
1990	1.34	0.33	0.78	2.45
1985	1.33	0.38	0.90	2.62
1980	1.26	0.34	1.04	2.76
1975	1.26	0.32	1.11	2.69
1970	1.14	0.27	1.11	2.52
1965	1.04	0.24	0.99	2.27
1960	0.99	0.22	0.86	2.07
1955	1.01	0.22	0.77	2.00
1950	1.04	0.23	0.77	2.04
1945	1.17	0.20	0.88	2.25
1940	0.73	0.16	0.67	1.56
1934	0.61	0.07	0.29	0.97
Prohibition				
1919	1.08	0.12	0.76	1.96
1915	1.48	0.14	0.94	2.56
1910	1.47	0.17	0.96	2.60
1905	1.31	0.13	0.95	2.39
1900	1.19	0.10	0.77	2.06
1890	0.90	0.14	0.95	1.99
1880	0.56	0.14	1.02	1.72
1870	0.44	0.10	1.53	2.07
1860	0.27	0.10	2.16	2.53
1850	0.14	0.08	1.88	2.10

Source: National Institute on Alcohol Abuse and Alcoholism (NIAAA). Available at http://www.niaaa.nih.gov/databases/consum01.htm (accessed January 19, 2004).

1. Numbers may not sum to totals due to rounding.

with some college were more likely than college graduates to report heavy alcohol use.

- White people tend to drink more than black and Hispanic people.
- Adults who graduate from college drink more than those who do not graduate from college. Heavy alcohol use, however, is more prevalent among those without college education.
- People who are employed drink more than those who are unemployed. (Substance Abuse Mental Health Services Administration 1999; Substance Abuse Mental Health Services Administration 2003)

Female Alcohol Use

It is estimated that of the 15 million alcohol-abusing or alcohol-dependent individuals in the United States, approximately 4.6 million, or nearly one-third, are women. According to the National Institute on Alcohol Abuse and Alcoholism in 1997, women tend to drink less alcohol and have fewer alcohol-related problems and dependence symptoms than men. Among the heaviest drinkers, however, women equal or surpass men in the number of problems that result from their drinking. Drinking behavior differs with age, role status, and marital status of women. In general, a woman's drinking resembles that of her husband, siblings, or close friends. Younger women tend to have higher rates of drinking-related problems than do older women; however, the incidence of alcohol dependence is greater among middle-aged women (aged thirty-five to forty-nine). Women who have never been married or who have been divorced or separated are more likely to drink heavily and experience alcohol-related problems than women who are married or widowed. Unmarried women living with a partner are at high risk to engage in heavy drinking and to develop drinking problems.

Female alcoholics may encounter different incentives and obstacles to seeking treatment than those encountered by men. Women are more likely to seek treatment because of family problems, and they are often encouraged by parents or children to pursue therapy. Men are usually encouraged to pursue therapy by their wives. Fewer women than men reach treatment through the criminal justice system or through employee-assistance programs.

Lack of child care is one of the most frequently reported barriers to treatment for alcoholic women.

Additional facts about women and alcohol use include the following:

- Forty-five percent of females aged twelve or older report current (past-month) alcohol use, 8 percent are binge drinkers (defined as five or more drinks on the same occasion at least once in the past month), and 2 percent drink heavily.
- Current alcohol use is heaviest among women aged twenty-six to thirty-four; binge and heavy drinking is highest among eighteen to twenty-five year olds.
- Women may be at higher risk for developing alcohol-related problems at lower levels of consumption than men.
- Nearly 4 million American women aged eighteen and older can be classified as alcoholic or problem drinkers—this is one-third the number for men; of these women, 58 percent are between the ages of eighteen and twenty-nine.
- Compared with men, women with drinking problems are at increased risk for depression, low self-esteem, alcohol-related physical problems, marital discord or divorce, a history of sexual abuse, and drinking in response to life crises.
- Among the personal and environmental factors that increase women's risks for problem drinking are the influence of a husband's or partner's drinking; depression; sexual experience, including alcohol expectancies and reported effects of drinking on sexual behavior, sexual orientation, and sexual dysfunction; and violent victimization, including physical and sexual victimization in childhood as well as in adulthood.
- Never-married, divorced, and separated women generally have the highest rates of heavy drinking and drinking-related problems, widowed women the lowest rates, and married women intermediate rates.
- Alcohol is present in more than one-half of all incidents of domestic violence, with women most likely to be battered when both partners have been drinking. (Collins and Messerschmidt 1993, 96)

Among pregnant women aged fifteen to forty-four, results from the 2002 National Survey on Drug Use and Heath show that 9 percent used alcohol and 3 percent reported binge drinking in the month prior to the survey. These rates were significantly lower than the rates for nonpregnant women of that age (53.4 and 23.4 percent, respectively). Heavy alcohol use was relatively rare (0.7 percent) among pregnant women (Substance Abuse Mental Health Services Administration 2003).

Adolescent and Young-Adult Alcohol Use

Despite the fact that it is illegal for virtually all high school students as well as many college students and young adults, experience and active use with alcoholic beverages are widespread.

Based on national results of adolescent drug use in 2002 (ibid.), about 10.7 million persons aged twelve to twenty reported drinking alcohol in the month prior to the survey. This is about 29 percent of the total age group.[1] Of these youths, nearly 7.2 million (19 percent of the total age group) were binge drinkers, and 2.3 million (6 percent) were heavy drinkers. More males than females aged twelve to twenty reported binge drinking (22 percent versus 17 percent). Among persons in this age group who used alcohol on a monthly basis, whites were far more likely to do so (33 percent) than blacks (19 percent) and Asians (16 percent). Binge drinking was reported by 23 percent of the underage whites, 23 percent of the underage American Indians or Alaska natives, 17 percent of underage Hispanics, 9 percent of underage Asians, and 10 percent of underage blacks. The prevalence of current alcohol use increased with age: 2 percent—age twelve; 7 percent—age thirteen; 13 percent—age fourteen; 20 percent—age fifteen; 29 percent—age sixteen; and 36 percent—age seventeen. Rates of binge drinking were about 1 percent—age twelve; 3 percent—age thirteen; 7 percent—age fourteen; 12 percent—age fifteen; 18 percent—age sixteen; and 25 percent—age seventeen. The rate peaked at age twenty-one (50 percent). The highest prevalence of both binge drinking and heavy drinking in 2002 was for young adults aged eighteen to twenty-five, with the peak rate of the measures occurring at age twenty-one. Heavy alcohol use was reported by 15 percent of persons aged eighteen to twenty-five and by 20 percent of persons aged twenty-one. Binge and heavy alcohol-use rates decreased faster with increasing age than did rates of past-month alcohol use. Overall, the rate of alcohol use is likely to be higher among dropouts, and dropout rates differ among racial and ethnic groups in the United States.

The high prevalence of use among youths aged twelve to seventeen and young adults aged eighteen to twenty suggests that laws prohibiting the purchase, possession, and use of alcohol by young people in this age range may not be very effective. In terms of youths and young adults, including women, the alcohol industry and soft drink companies (for example, Coca-Cola and Pepsi) have been very active promoting a market for new alcohol and alcohol-related products. Like the cigarette industry, effort is being made to address the psychology of these groups in terms of increasing their use of alcohol. Alcoholic beverages mixed with juices and sweet liquids, malt lemonades, and caffeine-loaded "energy" drinks (for instance, Red Bull, KMX, and Adrenaline Rush) are examples of this strategy to enlarge the drinking population and increase sales. Also, it has been reported that binge drinking among college students appears to be the result of marketing and frequent price promotions.

On September 9, 2003, a long-awaited report titled *Reducing Underage Drinking: A Collective Responsibility* was announced by the National Academy of Sciences (NAS). The report called for cooperation among the alcohol industry, health organizations, governments, parents, and others to combat what the authors called the nation's biggest youth drug problem. The press releases issued by the NAS, the Distilled Spirits Council (September 10), and the Beer Institute (September 9) follow.

National Academy of Sciences

More young people drink alcohol than use other drugs or smoke tobacco, and underage drinking costs the nation an estimated $53 billion annually in losses stemming from traffic fatalities, violent crime, and other behaviors that threaten the well-being of America's youth. Curbing underage drinking is an uphill battle because alcohol is legal and readily available to adults. To tackle the problem, a new report from the National Research Council and Institute of Medicine of the National Academies offers a comprehensive strategy that requires a deep, shared commitment from many institutions and individuals, including alcohol manufacturers and retail businesses, the entertainment industry, and parents and other adults in local communities. Federal and state governments should help forge the commitment to curtail alcohol consumption by minors, the report adds. For example, the federal government should do more to educate adults about existing laws and the consequences of underage drinking. Federal and state governments should also provide additional financial assistance and other support to reinforce community-based initiatives, and to research the effectiveness of the proposed strategy itself and related policies. "All segments of U.S. society should address underage drinking in a serious, coordinated, and sustained manner," said Richard J. Bonnie, John S. Battle Professor of Law and director of the Institute of Law, Psychiatry, and Public Policy at the University of Virginia at Charlottesville, and chair of the committee that wrote the report. "We have to find effective ways to protect our nation's youth while we respect the interests of responsible adult consumers of alcohol. The recommendations in this report attempt to strike the right balance." The congressionally mandated study lays out a strategy that includes heightened adult supervision of children's behavior and calls upon the alcohol and entertainment industries to take stronger steps to shield young people from unsuitable messages about alcohol consumption. Taken as a whole, the plan would have a considerable impact, the committee said, adding that the strategy should be subject to ongoing refinement.

To fund the proposed activities and to help reduce underage consumption, Congress and state legislatures should raise excise tax rates on alcohol—particularly on beer, which studies show is the alcoholic beverage that most young people prefer. Alcohol is much cheaper today, after adjusting for inflation, than it was thirty to forty years ago. Higher tax rates should be tied to the consumer price index to keep pace with inflation. Increasing the cost of alcohol has well-documented deterrent effects on underage drinkers, the report points out.

A National Wake-Up Call Most adults express concern about underage drinking and voice support for public policies to curb it. Yet surveys show that youths often obtain alcohol from adults. Studies also show that many parents underestimate both the extent of the problem and their own children's alcohol-consumption habits.

States and localities should use a wide range of educational and enforcement measures to boost compliance with laws that prohibit selling or providing alcohol to children, adolescents, and young adults under the legal drinking age of twenty-one. The aim is to deter adults and youths alike, the report says. Among the recommended steps are increasing the frequency of compliance checks, in which authorities monitor whether businesses are obeying minimum-drinking-age laws and levy fines when necessary, and requiring all sellers and servers of alcohol to complete state-approved training as a condition of employment. Likewise, the federal government should require states to achieve specified rates of retailer compliance with youth-access laws as a condition of receiving federal funds. And states should enhance efforts to prevent and detect the use of false identification (ID) by minors who want to purchase alcohol—for example, by issuing driver's licenses and state ID cards that can be electronically scanned.

In addition, states that allow Internet sales and home delivery of alcohol should adopt regulations that require customers to sign statements verifying their identity and age at the time of delivery. At the local level, police, working with community leaders, should create policies for detecting and shutting down underage drinking parties, the report says.

State and local leaders should develop efforts to reduce underage drinking that are tailored to specific circumstances of the problem in their communities, according to the report. A broad range of public and private organizations and institutions, including the federal government, should encourage and fund community efforts that have a solid scientific base.

Likewise, the federal government should fund and actively support the development of a national media campaign to encourage parents and other adults to take steps in their own households and neighborhoods to discourage underage drinking. Officials should carefully craft this activity to make sure that it would reach a diverse audience, the report advises. All intervention and education programs, the committee stressed, should be rigorously evaluated.

Roles for Alcohol and Entertainment Industries A substantial portion of alcohol advertising reaches an underage audience or is presented in a style that is attractive to youth, the report states. For example, television ads for alcohol often appear during programs when the percentage of underage viewers is greater than their percentage in the overall U.S. population.

The committee recommended that trade associations in the alcohol industry and individual companies strengthen their advertising codes to prohibit placement of commercial messages in venues where a large portion of the audience is underage. These groups should also establish independent, external review boards to investigate complaints about ads and enforce codes. In 1999, the Federal Trade Commission issued similar recommendations urging the industry to toughen its advertising standards for alcoholic beverages. For years, those standards have permitted ad placement in media where adults constitute at least 50 percent of the audience. The industry is expected to soon announce tougher standards that will restrict marketing to audiences with a much larger proportion of adults.

In addition, alcohol companies, advertising firms, and commercial media should refrain from marketing practices—such as certain product designs or promotion techniques—that may appeal to young people, the report cautions.

The alcohol industry should also join with private and public entities to create and fund an independent nonprofit foundation that is focused solely on preventing and reducing underage drinking. The industry currently invests in programs that were established with that stated goal; however, the results of these programs typically are not assessed using rigorous scientific methods.

The entertainment media have key roles to play, too. Officials in the music, television, and film industries should use rating systems and codes to reduce the likelihood that large numbers of young listeners and viewers will be exposed to unsuitable messages about alcohol consumption—even when adults are expected to make up the majority of the audience. The Motion Picture Association of America, for instance, should consider content about alcohol use when rating films and assign mature ratings for movies that portray drinking in a favorable light.

The overall goal of the committee's broad strategy is to promote public awareness of the importance of reducing underage drinking, as well as greater accountability in mass communication. To this end, Congress should provide funding for the U.S. Department of Health and Human Services (HHS) to routinely track youth exposure to alcohol ads by monitoring advertising practices. Likewise, HHS should regularly review representative samples of movies, TV programs, music recordings, and videos offered to audiences that are 15 percent or more underage. Findings from this work should be reported to Congress and the public, the committee said. Moreover, HHS should issue a comprehensive report to Congress each year on trends in underage drinking and progress in reducing the problem.

Larger Governmental Investments Needed   The use of alcohol among adults is deeply rooted in U.S. culture, and beliefs vary widely about alcohol consumption and expectations for young people. But underage drinking is dangerous, the report emphasizes. It is a significant factor in youth traffic fatalities, and associated with suicide, other violence, and academic failure. When people start drinking in childhood or adolescence, they increase their risk of developing alcohol-related problems as adults.

In the 2002 Monitoring the Future survey, a federally sponsored study, about 72 percent of twelfth graders and 39 percent of eighth graders reported that they had consumed some alcohol in the past year. That study also showed that more than one-quarter of high school seniors had consumed five or more drinks in a row in the previous two weeks.

Federal and state excise taxes are potentially important tools for preventing and reducing underage drinking and its harmful consequences, the committee concludes. Extensive research indicates that even small changes in these tax rates can decrease the prevalence of drinking among youths, who tend to have limited discretionary income. Current federal excise tax rates of $2.14 per 750-milliliter bottle of 80-proof spirits, $.33 per six-pack of beer, and $.21 per bottle of wine represent a long downward slide in the value of these taxes. Further, the federal government needs to enhance and better organize research in this area. A federal interagency coordinating committee should be formed, with the secretary of HHS serving as chair, to provide national leadership on the topic. HHS should create a national training and research center on underage drinking and collect more detailed data on the problem—gathering information on regional trends and on brands of alcohol that are popular among young people, for instance. HHS should also issue annual reports on progress in implementing the proposed strategy.

State policy makers should designate an agency to spearhead and coordinate their activities and programs in this area, according to the report. Also, residential colleges and universities, which face serious alcohol-related problems among students under twenty-one, should develop, adopt, and evaluate comprehensive prevention approaches in partnership with local communities.

The report was sponsored by the U.S. Department of Health and Human Services. The National Research Council and the Institute of Medicine are private nonprofit institutions that provide science and health policy advice under a congressional charter. The Research Council is the principal operating arm of the National Academy of Sciences and the National Academy of Engineering. The Web site for the National Research Council and Institute of Medicine Board on Children, Youth, and Families is http://www.nap.edu.

The Distilled Spirits Council

The Distilled Spirits Council released its own report in September 2003, called "Parents and Adults Are the Key to Reducing Underage Drinking: Raising Taxes Is Not the Answer":

The Distilled Spirits Council today said it was pleased the National Academy of Sciences (NAS) underage drinking study "recognized the critical role parents and adults play in further reducing underage drinking" but denounced the call for increased taxes on alcohol saying, "research shows raising taxes would do little to reduce underage drinking and would severely impact the hospitality industry and responsible adult consumers."

Peter H. Cressy, President of the Distilled Spirits Council of the United States said, "We were pleased the NAS report underscored that parents and adults need to be the primary target of any campaign to reduce underage drinking. The distilled spirits industry has long held this view and has been providing educational materials for parents, educators and role models for over a decade." Cressy noted the industry has been implementing and supporting many of the recommendations in the NAS report for decades. He cited as examples the programs of The Century Council, the distilled spirits industry's not-for-profit organization that has spent more than $130 million over the last 12 years on community programs to reduce illegal, underage drinking. The Century Council's award-winning community programs are being used by police departments in more than 42 states, more than 1,200 colleges across the country and all branches of the United States Armed Forces.

Cressy said the industry would not support some recommendations including raising taxes as a means to reduce underage drinking. Cressy pointed to the fact that the NAS' own report states that most youth obtain alcohol from adults, a finding mirrored in yesterday's FTC [Federal Trade Commission] report.

"As both the NAS and FTC reports point out, most youth obtain alcohol from non-commercial outlets," said Peter Cressy. "Therefore it makes no sense to further penalize responsible adult drinkers and the hospitality industry by raising taxes on spirits when more than half the purchase price already goes to taxes."

The Beer Institute

The Beer Institute also released a statement, by its president, Jeff Becker, titled "In Response to the National Academy of Sciences (NAS) Report on Underage Drinking":

The NAS Panel relied on a compilation of existing information, much of which contained erroneous conclusions, as the background for their report. Given this, we are not surprised to see misguided recommendations such as raising beer excise taxes. Experience has shown that the only clear results from increasing beer excise taxes are higher unemployment and higher prices for responsible adults—such measures do nothing to lower teen drinking.

In addition, at a time when both federal and state governments are looking for ways to eliminate bureaucracy and balance budgets, the report's call for the creation of a new federal interagency coordinating committee, a national training and research center, new federal annual reporting requirements, the establishment of a new external review panel, and additional Congressional funding, is woefully misguided. Governments at all levels already spend billions of dollars on programs designed to address illegal underage drinking, alcohol and substance abuse. And the fact of the matter is that underage drinking over the last few years has decreased—not increased.

Further, we note that the NAS report stated that youth usually "obtain alcohol—either directly or indirectly—from adults." If the report plainly states that youth are not buying alcohol—how will higher prices deter them? Even for those who do purchase alcohol, research has shown that for youth—unlike adults— higher prices do not impact underage drinking.

The fact of the matter is that what we know about raising excise taxes is that it means jobs will be lost and responsible adults who enjoy beer will pay higher prices. Taxes borne by beer consumers are already far higher than those of most other products in the U.S. In fact, federal, state, and local taxes are the most expensive ingredient in every beer purchased, making up approximately 44 percent of the cost of every beer. Hardworking adult beer drinkers shouldn't be forced to pay more for beer in order to address an issue that is more effectively addressed through voluntary measures.

At the same time, we are encouraged to see positive attention paid to many of the effective, targeted and

sensible approaches—such as increasing parental involvement, and consistent enforcement of existing underage drinking laws—that the beer industry supports. These approaches have been the focus of the
extensive educational programs to prevent illegal underage drinking the industry has implemented for
twenty years in communities nationwide.

Steady progress has been achieved over the past two
decades in reducing underage drinking, a fact borne out
in several government-funded studies and surveys. In
fact, one of the main indicators cited in the NAS report,
the National Survey on Drug Use and Health, reported
last week most teens—82 percent—do not drink.

Brewers have actively encouraged such approaches
for many years. Millions of copies of educational materials have been distributed free of charge to parents
and educators throughout the nation. Several other
programs supported by the industry or undertaken in
cooperation with state officials are addressed in the
NAS document.

The Beer Institute, established in 1986, is the national
trade association for the brewing industry, representing
both large and small brewers, as well as importers and
industry suppliers. The institute is committed to the
development of sound public policy and to the values
of civic duty and personal responsibility. Their Web site
address is http://www.beerinstitute.com.

Among Americans, it is commonly believed that youths and
young adults drink more frequently and experience more alcohol-related problems than their European counterparts. This perception, in turn, is often used as an argument for change in U.S.
alcohol policies and prevention initiatives, including elimination
of minimum-drinking-age laws and development of programs
that teach responsible drinking to young people. Do European
young people drink less and have fewer problems than their
American counterparts? This question was addressed by a study
of the U.S. Department of Justice, Office of Juvenile Programs
(2001). Figures 4.1, 4.2, and 4.3 compare youths aged fifteen to sixteen in twenty-six European countries to similar-age youths (that
is, tenth graders) in the United States. The drinking patterns were
compared on prevalence of drinking in the past thirty days,
prevalence of drinking five or more drinks in a row, and the

Figure 4.1
Prevalence of Drinking in Past Thirty Days: United States and Europe

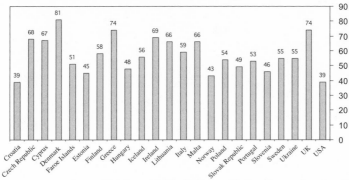

Source: U.S. Department of Justice. 2001. Comparison of Drinking Rates and Problems: European Countries and the United States. Calverton, MD: Pacific Institute of Research and Evaluation.

Figure 4.2
Prevalence of Drinking Five or More Drinks in a Row:
United States and Europe

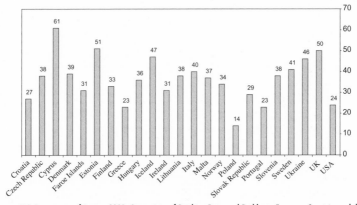

Source: U.S. Department of Justice. 2001. Comparison of Drinking Rates and Problems: European Countries and the United States. Calverton, MD: Pacific Institute of Research and Evaluation.

prevalence of intoxication in the past thirty days. The findings provide no evidence that youths from the United States drink more than their European counterparts.

Infant Alcohol Syndrome

The U.S. National Institute of Alcohol Abuse and Alcoholism (NIAAA) reports that alcohol use during pregnancy is a public

Figure 4.3
Prevalence of Intoxication in Past Thirty Days: United States and Europe

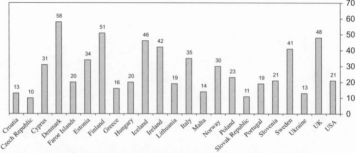

Source: U.S. Department of Justice. 2001. Comparison of Drinking Rates and Problems: European Countries and the United States. Calverton, MD: Pacific Institute of Research and Evaluation.

health problem because it can cause a range of harmful consequences to the developing fetus, resulting in serious birth defects. The most serious condition caused by prenatal alcohol use is fetal alcohol syndrome (FAS). This problem is characterized by deformed facial features, smaller heads, abnormal joints and limbs, growth retardation, and developmental abnormalities in the central nervous system that often include mental retardation as well as poor coordination, learning problems, and short memories. Other FAS characteristics that often exist are mental health problems, disrupted school experience, inappropriate sexual behavior, trouble with the law, alcohol and drug problems, difficulty caring for themselves and their children, and homelessness. In the United States, estimates of FAS range from 0.5 to 2 cases per 1,000 live births. In high-risk populations, reported rates are 9.8 per 1,000 live births (Hankin 2002; Stratton, Howe, and Battaglia 1997; Streissguth and Kanter 1997).

Another perspective of the Fetal Alcohol Syndrome problem calls into question the seriousness of FAS and the fear it has generated. The following is an excerpt from the Internet site of Dr. David Hanson, "Alcohol: Problems and Solutions—Fetal Alcohol Syndrome."

Should Pregnant Women Drink at All?

Is there a safe or acceptable level of alcohol consumption for pregnant women?

- The Royal College of Obstetricians and Gynaecologists recently conducted a large study including 400,000 American women, all of whom had consumed alcohol during pregnancy. Not a single case of fetal alcohol syndrome occurred and no adverse effects on children were found when consumption was under 8.5 drinks per week.

- A recent review of research studies found that fetal alcohol syndrome only occurs among alcoholics. The evidence is clear that there is no apparent risk to a child when the pregnant woman consumes no more than one drink per day.
- A study of moderate drinking during pregnancy found no negative effects. The researchers suggested that one drink per day provides a significant margin of safety, although they did not encourage drinking during pregnancy.

A study of pregnancies in eight European countries found that consuming no more than one drink per day did not appear to have any effect on fetal growth. A follow-up of children at 18 months of age found that those from women who drank during pregnancy, even two drinks per day, scored higher in several areas of development.

- A recent analysis of seven major medical research studies involving over 130,000 pregnancies suggests that consuming two to fourteen drinks per week does not increase the risk of giving birth to a child with either malformations or fetal alcohol syndrome.
- Negative effects appear to be related to relatively higher levels of consumption per occasion, and hence, to higher blood alcohol content levels. Thus, it appears to be very important never to consume more than one drink in any one day while pregnant.

The guidelines of the Royal College of Obstetricians and Gynaecologists recommend "women should be careful about alcohol consumption in pregnancy and limit this to no more than one standard drink per day." These conclusions appear consistent with the research findings of the Institute of Medicine of the National Academy of Sciences, a major science body in the U.S.

The American College of Obstetricians and Gynecologists concludes, "[T]here is no evidence that an occasional drink is harmful. Women who drink heavily throughout pregnancy may have smaller babies with physical and mental handicaps, but women who drink moderately may have babies with no more problems than those women who drink rarely or not at all."

This group of medical specialists points out that "[i]t's hard to determine the amount and timing of alcohol consumption that puts the fetus at risk. One study shows that women who drank only occasionally and moderately (described in this particular study as between one and forty-five drinks spaced out over a month) had babies with no more problems than those women who drank rarely or not at all. There were no differences either in size or number of babies' handicaps between the women who drank moderately and those who abstained or drank lightly."

The Harvard Women's Health Watch advises pregnant women "having more than one alcoholic drink per day puts the fetus at risk for various defects and disabilities." Thus, it suggests that expectant women should limit themselves to one drink per day. The health publication emphasizes that one drink is twelve ounces of beer, five ounces of wine, or 1.5 ounces of spirits or liquor.

But, of course, alcohol consumption might have very subtle or undetectable undesirable effects on children. Therefore, until more is known for certain, pregnant women might well be advised to choose the safest option, that of abstaining during pregnancy.[2]

What Is the Problem?

There is no scientific support for the type of widespread hysteria that permeates public discussion on fetal alcohol syndrome [FAS]. Many people falsely believe that even a single drink during pregnancy can cause FAS. If this were true, the majority of the populations of dozens of countries around the world would suffer the effects of FAS!

Some pregnant women have actually become frantic upon realizing they had inadvertently eaten salad that had wine vinegar dressing, fearing their children would be born suffering from fetal alcohol syndrome. Of course, wine vinegar, being vinegar, contains no alcohol.

In reality, there is absolutely no evidence that light drinking, even on a daily basis, leads to fetal alcohol syndrome. Actually, most women who are light or moderate drinkers choose not to drink during pregnancy. The real problem is found among frequent heavy drinkers, who most often are alcoholics consuming heavily on a daily basis throughout their pregnancies.

Additionally, those who give birth to FAS children characteristically smoke, use illegal drugs, are frequently malnourished, and rarely receive adequate medical care during pregnancy. And drinking during pregnancy has not declined among such women over time. Because of their addiction, these women are virtually immune to our current educational approach. This may also be because so many of these women are poorly educated and often lead marginal lives.

This is the target group to which our efforts and resources need to be directed in a massive drive to get these women the necessary help and treatment. It will not be cheap or easy, but it is essential if we seriously want to reduce the incidence of fetal alcohol syndrome. We need to abandon scare tactics for real solutions.

Binge Drinking

The consumption of five or more drinks in a row on at least one occasion is defined as "binge drinking." Based on the National Institute on Drug Abuse "Monitoring the Future" report (Johnston, O'Malley, and Backman 1999), 12 percent of eighth graders, 22 percent of tenth graders, 29 percent of twelfth graders, and 40 percent of college students reported five or more drinks in a row at least once in the prior two-week period. It has been noted that while there has been a significant decline in the use of other drugs among high school seniors and college-age youths, very little has changed in terms of the pattern of binge drinking over time, according to four studies conducted by the Harvard School of Public Health from 1993 to 2001.

Government publications note that a host of risk factors, including sexual encounters with their inherent chance of pregnancy, sexually transmitted diseases, and HIV exposure, as well as date rape and other violence, can and do occur more frequently while students are consuming large amounts of alcohol by binge drinking.

Binge drinking facts from public information newsletters and Internet sources show the following:

- College students engage in binge drinking more than their noncollege peers.
- Students who binge drink are more likely to damage property, have trouble with authorities, miss classes, have hangovers, and experience injuries than those who do not.
- Binge drinking in high school, especially among males, is strongly predictive of binge drinking in college.
- College presidents agree binge drinking is the most serious problem on campus.
- Students more likely to drink are white, age twenty-three or younger, and are residents of a fraternity or sorority.
- The percentage of students who are binge drinkers is nearly uniform from freshman to senior year, even though students under twenty-one are prohibited from purchasing alcohol.
- More than half of the binge drinkers, almost one in four students, are frequent binge drinkers—they binge three or more times in a two-week period, although one in five students report abstaining from drinking alcohol. (SAMHSA 1999; Alcohol Policies Project 2000; Harvard School of Public Health 1993–2001)

As with fetal alcohol syndrome, a different interpretation of the facts is presented. The following perception is that of Dr. David Hanson.

What Is Binge Drinking?

To most people, binge drinking brings to mind a self-destructive and unrestrained drinking bout lasting for at least a couple of days during which time the heavily intoxicated drinker "drops out" by not working, ignoring responsibilities, squandering money, and engaging in other harmful behaviors such as fighting or risky sex. This view is consistent with that portrayed in dictionary definitions, in literature, in art, and in plays or films such as the classic "Come Back Little Sheeba" and "Lost Weekend" or the recent "Leaving Las Vegas."

It is also consistent with the usage of physicians and other clinicians. As the editor of the *Journal of Studies on Alcohol* emphasizes, binge describes an extended period of time (typically at least two days) during which time a person repeatedly becomes intoxicated and gives up his or her usual activities and obligations in order to become intoxicated. It is the combination of prolonged use and the giving up of usual activities that forms the core of the clinical definition of binge.

Other researchers have explained that it is counterproductive to brand as pathological the consumption of only five drinks over the course of an evening of eating and socializing. It is clearly inappropriate to equate it with a binge.

A recent Swedish study, for example, defines a binge as the consumption of half a bottle of spirits or two bottles of wine on the same occasion. Similarly, a study in Italy found that consuming an average of eight drinks a day was considered normal drinking—clearly not bingeing. In the United Kingdom, bingeing is commonly defined as consuming eleven or more drinks on an occasion. But in the United States, some researchers have defined bingeing as consuming five or more drinks on an occasion (an "occasion" can refer to an entire day). And now some have even expanded the definition to include consuming four or more drinks on an occasion by a woman.

Consider a woman who has two glasses of wine with her leisurely dinner and then sips two more drinks over the course of a four or five hour evening. In the view of most people, such a woman would be acting responsibly. Indeed, her blood alcohol content (BAC) would remain low. It's difficult to imagine that she would even be able to feel the effects of the alcohol. However, some researchers would now define her as a binger!

How useful is such an unrealistic definition? It is very useful if the intent is to inflate the extent of a social problem. And it would please members of the Prohibition Party and the Women's Christian Temperance Union. But it is not very useful if the intent is to accurately describe reality to the average person.

It is highly unrealistic and inappropriate to apply a prohibitionist definition to describe drinking in the United States today. Perhaps we should define binge drinking as any intoxicated drinking that leads to certain harmful or destructive behaviors. Perhaps we should at least require that a person have a certain minimum level of alcohol in the bloodstream as a prerequisite to be considered a binger. Perhaps we could even require that a person be intoxicated before being labeled a "binger." But one thing is certain: the unrealistic definitions being promoted by some researchers are misleading and deceptive at best.

The conclusion is clear: Be very skeptical the next time you hear or read a report about "binge" drinking. Were the people in question really bingeing? By any reasonable definition, most almost certainly were not.

What Is the Extent of "Binge" Drinking?

Although a continuing barrage of newspaper articles, TV shows, and special interest–group reports claim that binge drinking among young people is a growing epidemic, the actual fact is quite to the contrary. Binge drinking among young people is clearly declining and it has been doing so for many years.

"Binge" drinking among high school seniors has declined from 41.2 percent to 31.3 percent between 1980 and 1997. That's a drop of almost one-fourth (24 percent).

Similarly, the proportion of U.S. military personnel who "binge" has also declined significantly, according to six worldwide surveys conducted for the military over a recently ended fifteen-year period.

"Binge" drinking is also down among American college students, and it has clearly been declining for a number of years. This is clear. For example, according to a recent study of college drinking by Dr. Henry Wechsler of Harvard University, "binge" drinking has decreased significantly across the country over the four years since his earlier study. His research also found that the proportion of abstainers jumped nearly 22 percent in that short period of time.

These findings are consistent with data collected for the National Institute on Drug Abuse by the Institute for Social Research (ISR) at the University of Michigan. The ISR research found that college "binge" drinking in the United States recently reached the lowest level of the entire seventeen-year period that its surveys have been conducted. Similarly, it found that the proportion of drinkers has reached an all-time low among college students.

Research conducted at colleges across the United States repeatedly since the early 1980s by Dr. David Hanson (State University of New York) and Dr. Ruth Engs (Indiana University) has found declines over that time both in the proportion of collegians who drink at a high level and in the proportion who drink any alcohol.

So the facts are clear. "Binge" drinking is down and abstinence is up among American college students. Yet, in spite of this and other overwhelming evidence, the false impression persists that drinking is increasing and that "bingeing continues unabated."

So What's the Harm?

This misperception is dangerous because when young people go off to college falsely thinking that "everybody" is drinking and bingeing, they are more likely to drink and to "binge" in order to conform. Correcting this misperception is important because it can empower young people and break the vicious self-fulfilling prophecy that helps perpetuate collegiate alcohol abuse.

Individual students almost always believe that most others on campus drink more heavily than they do, and the disparity between the perceived and the actual behaviors tends to be quite large. By conducting surveys of actual student behavior and publicizing the results, the extent of heavy drinking can be quickly and significantly reduced. The most carefully assessed such abuse prevention project on campus has demonstrated a 35 percent reduction in heavy drinking, a 31 percent reduction in alcohol-related injuries to self, and a 54 percent reduction in alcohol-related injuries to others. And similar results have been demonstrated at colleges across the country with this quick and inexpensive approach.

Too many college students still abuse alcohol. But people who exaggerate the problem and distort its magnitude are actually making the problem worse. If we are to further reduce alcohol abuse and the problems it causes, we have to publicize the actual facts and correct damaging misperceptions. Doing so will empower students to do what they as individuals generally want to do: drink less or not drink at all.

The challenge of correcting dangerous misperceptions about college-student drinking is enormous. Many researchers and others have a vested interest in inflating the extent of "binge" drinking and stories of drinking epidemics make dramatic headlines that sell more publications. But scare tactics are actually counterproductive and it turns out that the most effective way to reduce alcohol abuse is simply to tell the truth and make sure that young people understand the facts.[3]

Licit-Drug Overviews

Many aspects of tobacco and alcohol abuse warrant attention. The following overviews focus on the alcohol issue in particular. Children of alcoholics and impaired driving attract considerable concern because of their impact on individuals, families, and society—their well-being and safety.

Children of Alcoholics

It is estimated that about 7 million children under the age of eighteen live in households in the United States with at least one alcoholic parent. There is a genetic factor associated with vulnerability to alcohol dependence; however, there are other issues of concern, including social and psychological dysfunction, that may result from growing up in an alcoholic home. Among the symptoms that may be exhibited as a result of living in such an environment, as well as other types of dysfunctional families, are depression and anxiety, including crying, bed-wetting, social isolation, fear of school, or nightmares (Center for Substance Abuse Prevention 1994).

The following "Facts for Families," prepared by the American Academy of Child and Adolescent Psychiatry (1999), provides insight of the problem:

> One in five adult Americans lived with an alcoholic while growing up. Child and adolescent psychiatrists know these children are at greater risk for having emotional problems than children whose parents are not alcoholics. Alcoholism runs in families, and children of alcoholics are four times more likely than other children to become alcoholics. Most children of alcoholics have experienced some form of neglect or abuse.

A child in such a family may have a variety of problems:

> Guilt—The child may see himself or herself as the main cause of the mother's or father's drinking.
>
> Anxiety—The child may worry constantly about the situation at home. He or she may fear the alcoholic parent will become sick or injured, and may also fear fights and violence between the parents.
>
> Embarrassment—Parents may give the child the message that there is a terrible secret at home. The ashamed child does not invite friends home and is afraid to ask anyone for help.
>
> Inability to have close relationships—Because the child has been disappointed by the drinking parent many times, he or she often does not trust others.
>
> Confusion—The alcoholic parent will change suddenly from being loving to angry, regardless of the child's behavior. A regular daily schedule, which is very important for a child, does not exist because bedtimes and mealtimes are constantly changing.
>
> Anger—The child feels anger at the alcoholic parent for drinking, and may be angry at the nonalcoholic parent for lack of support and protection.
>
> Depression—The child feels lonely and helpless to change the situation.

Although the child tries to keep the alcoholism a secret, teachers, relatives, other adults, or friends may sense that something is wrong. Child and adolescent psychiatrists advise that the following behaviors may signal a drinking or other problem at home:

- Failure in school; truancy
- Lack of friends; withdrawal from classmates
- Delinquent behavior, such as stealing or violence
- Frequent physical complaints, such as headaches or stomachaches
- Abuse of drugs or alcohol
- Aggression toward other children
- Risk-taking behaviors
- Depression or suicidal thoughts or behavior

Some children of alcoholics may act like responsible "parents" within the family and among friends. They may cope with the alcoholism by becoming controlled, successful "overachievers" throughout school, and at the same time be emotionally isolated from other children and teachers. Their emotional problems may show only when they become adults.

Whether or not their parents are receiving treatment for alcoholism, these children and adolescents can benefit from educational programs and mutual-help groups such as programs for children of alcoholics, Al-Anon, and Alateen. Early professional help is also important in preventing more serious problems for the child, including alcoholism. Child and adolescent psychiatrists help these children with the child's own problems, and also help the child to understand they are not responsible for the drinking problems of their parents.

The treatment program may include group therapy with other youngsters, which reduces the isolation of being a child of an alcoholic. The child and adolescent psychiatrist will often work with the entire family, particularly when the alcoholic parent has stopped drinking, to help them develop healthier ways of relating to one another.

Impaired Driving

A person who operates an automobile or motorcycle while under the influence of alcohol (or other drug) is driving impaired. The following information about impaired driving has been drawn from multiple sources published on the Internet by Mothers

Against Drunk Driving (MADD) and the National Highway Traffic Safety Administration, U.S. Department of Transportation (2002). The facts presented below have been categorized in terms of patterns of use and impaired driving; the consequences, often injury and death; and costs.

Patterns of Use and Impaired Driving

- Impairment is not determined by the type of drink, but rather by the amount of alcohol ingested over a specific period of time.
- The speed of alcohol absorption affects the rate at which one becomes drunk. Unlike foods, alcohol does not have to be slowly digested. As a person drinks faster than the alcohol can be eliminated, the drug accumulates in the body, resulting in higher and higher levels of alcohol in the blood.
- A standard drink is defined as 12 ounces of beer, 5 ounces of wine, or 1.5 ounces of 80-proof distilled spirits, all of which contain the same amount of alcohol.
- The average person metabolizes alcohol at the rate of about one drink per hour. Only time will sober a person up. Drinking strong coffee, exercising, or taking a cold shower will not help. Beer is the drink most commonly consumed by people stopped for alcohol-impaired driving or involved in alcohol-related crashes. Alcohol-related fatalities are caused primarily by the consumption of beer (80 percent), followed by liquor/wine at 20 percent.
- There is evidence that heavier drinkers prefer to drink at bars and other persons' homes, and at multiple locations requiring longer driving distances. Young drivers have been found to prefer drinking at private parties, while older, more educated drivers prefer bars and taverns.
- The rate of alcohol involvement in fatal crashes is more than three times as high at night as during the day (63 percent versus 19 percent).
- For fatal crashes occurring from midnight to 3:00 A.M., 79 percent involved alcohol.
- In 2002, 31 percent of all fatal crashes during the week were alcohol-related, compared to 54 percent on

weekends. For all crashes, the alcohol involvement rate was 4 percent during the week and 11 percent during the weekend.

The Consequences: Injury and Death

- In 2000, the United States experienced the largest percentage increase in alcohol-related traffic deaths on record. Forty percent of all traffic fatalities were deemed to be related to alcohol in 2000, versus 38.3 percent in 1999.
- In 2002, an estimated 17,419 people died in alcohol-related traffic crashes—an average of one every thirty minutes. These deaths constitute 41 percent of the 42,815 total traffic fatalities.
- In 2001, about 1,461 fatalities occurred in crashes involving alcohol-impaired or intoxicated drivers who had at least one previous DWI conviction—about 8.4 percent of all alcohol-related traffic fatalities.
- The intoxication rate (those over 0.08 BAC) for male drivers involved in fatal crashes was 25 percent, compared with 12 percent for female drivers.
- Those drivers twenty-one to twenty-four years old were most likely to be intoxicated (BAC of 0.08 or greater) in fatal crashes in 2002. Thirty-three percent of drivers twenty-one to twenty-four years old involved in fatal crashes were intoxicated, followed by ages twenty-five to thirty-four (28 percent) and thirty-five to forty-four (26 percent).
- Incidence of intoxication for drivers in fatal crashes in 2001 was highest for motorcycle operators (31 percent) and lowest for drivers of large trucks (2 percent).
- About three in every ten Americans will be involved in an alcohol-related crash at some time in their lives.
- In 2001, more than half a million people were injured in crashes where police reported that alcohol was present—an average of one person injured approximately every two minutes.
- Drunk driving is the nation's most frequently committed violent crime.
- In 2000, motor vehicle crashes were the leading cause

of death for people from one to thirty-four years old.

Costs

- Alcohol-related crashes in the United States cost the public an estimated $114.3 billion in 2000, including $51.1 billion in monetary costs and an estimated $63.2 billion in quality-of-life losses. People other than the drinking driver paid $71.6 billion of the alcohol-related crash bill.
- In 2000, alcohol-related crashes accounted for an estimated 18 percent of the $103 billion in U.S. auto insurance payments. Reducing alcohol-related crashes by 10 percent would save $1.8 billion in claims payments and loss-adjustment expenses.
- In 2000, the average alcohol-related fatality in the United States cost $3.5 million. The estimated cost per injured survivor was $99,000.
- In 2000, the societal costs of alcohol-related crashes in the United States averaged $1.00 per drink consumed. People other than the drinking driver paid $0.60 per drink.

Notes

1. Percentages are rounded to the nearest whole number.

2. David Hanson, professor emeritus of sociology, State University of New York, Potsdam, NY. This excerpt was presented with permission. Gratitude is expressed to Professor Hanson for the use of his information, which is available at http://www2.Potsdam.edu/alcohol-info (accessed June 1, 2003). References used by Dr. Hanson for his presentations of FAS and binge drinking may be found at his Web site.

3. Ibid.

References

Alcohol and Drug Information Clearinghouse. 2003. "A Parenting Perspective: Children of Alcoholics." Available at http://www.prevlink.org/getthefacts/facts/coa.html (accessed June 1, 2003).

Alcohol Policies Project, Center for Science in the Public Interest. 2000.

"Fact Sheet: Binge Drinking on College Campuses." Available at http://www.cspinet.org/booze/collfact1.htm (accessed January 21, 2004).

American Academy of Child and Adolescent Psychiatry. 1999. "Children of Alcoholics." AACAP Facts for Families series #17. Available at http://www.aacap.org/publications/factsfam/alcoholic.htm (accessed July 1, 2003).

American Legacy Foundation and the National Center on Addiction and Substance Abuse. 2003. "Reducing Teen Smoking can Cut Marijuana Use Significantly." September 16. Available at http://www.teensarenota disease.com/CASA_smoking_pot_link.htm (accessed March 9, 2004).

Benowitz, N. 1996. "Pharmacology of Nicotine: Addiction and Therapeutics." *Annual Review of Pharmacology and Toxicology* 36: 597–613.

Campaign for Tobacco-Free Kids. 2003. "Health Groups Say Tobacco Prevention Programs Can Save States Money And Cuts Are 'Penny-Wise, Pound-Foolish.'" Press release, January 22. Available at http://tobaccofreekids.org/Script/DisplayPressRelease.php3?Display=591 (accessed January 28, 2004).

Center for Substance Abuse Prevention (CSAP). 1994. *Prevention Primer: An Encyclopedia of Alcohol, Tobacco, and other Prevention Terms.* United States Department of Health and Human Services. Rockville, MD: SAMHSA.

Centers for Disease Control and Prevention (CDC). 2001a. *CDC Fact Book 2000/2001.* Washington, DC: U.S. Public Health Service, Office of the Surgeon General.

———. 2001b. *Women and Smoking: A Report of the Surgeon General.* Washington, DC: U.S. Public Health Service, Office of the Surgeon General.

Collins, J., and P. Messerschmidt. 1993. "Epidemiology of Alcohol-Related Violence." *Alcohol Health and Research World* 17, no. 2: 93–100

Cunningham, R. 1996. *Smoke & Mirrors: The Canadian Tobacco War.* Ottawa: International Development Research Centre.

Distilled Spirits Council. 2003. "Parents and Adults Are the Key to Reducing Underage Drinking: Raising Taxes Is Not the Answer." Press release September 10. Available at http://www.discus.org/mediaroom/2003/release.asp?pressid=114 (accessed January 27, 2004).

Grimes, W. 1997. "The Next to Last Whiff of Smoke and Mirrors." *New York Times,* April 20, 2.

Hankin, J. 2002. "Fetal Alcohol Syndrome Prevention Research." National Institute of Alcohol Abuse and Alcoholism. Available at http://www.niaaa.nih.gov/publications/arh26-1/58-65.htm (accessed January 21, 2004).

Harvard School of Public Health, College of Alcohol Studies Surveys. 1993–2001. Available at http://www.hsph.harvard.edu/cas/Documents/trends/ (accessed January 1, 2004).

Hibell, B., et al. 1997. *The 1995 ESPAD Report: Alcohol and Other Drug Use among Students in 26 European Countries.* Stockholm: Swedish Council for Information on Alcohol and Other Drugs.

Isralowitz, R. 2002. *Drug Use, Policy and Management.* Westport, CT: Auburn House.

Johnston, L., P. O'Malley, and J. Backman. 1999. *The Monitoring the Future National Results on Adolescent Drug Use: Overview of Key Findings.* Bethesda, MD: National Institute on Drug Abuse. Available at http://www.monitoringthefuture.org (accessed June 1, 2003).

Kessler, D. 1995. "Sounding Board: Nicotine Addiction in Young People." *New England Journal of Medicine* 333, no. 3 (July 20): 186–189.

———. 2001. *A Question of Intent.* New York: Public Affairs.

Lazarus, David. 2002. "U.S. Pushed by Philip Morris, Stalling Global Ban on Tobacco Ads." Join Togther On Line, September 22. Available at http://www.jointogether.org/sa/news/features/reader/0,1854,555463,00.html (accessed January 28, 2004).

Mothers Against Drunk Driving (MADD). "Did You Know. . . ." Available at http://www.madd.org/stats/0,1056,1789,00.html (accessed January 1, 2004).

National Council on Alcoholism and Drug Dependence. 1998. "FYI: Binge Drinking." Available at http://www.ncadd.org/facts/fyibinge.html (accessed January 1, 2004).

———. 1999. "Use of Alcohol and Other Drugs Among Women: Consumption Rates, Pattrens and Trends." August. Available at http://www.ncadd.org/facts/women.html (accessed January 28, 2004).

National Highway Traffic Safety Administration (NHTSA), U.S. Department of Transportation. 2002. *Traffic Safety Facts 2000: Alcohol.* Washington, DC: NHTSA. Available at http://www.dol.gov/asp/programs/drugs/party/fact.htm (accessed January 1, 2004).

———. 2003. "DOT Releases Preliminary Estimates of 2002 Highway Fatalities." News Release April 23. Available at http://www.dot.gov/affairs/nhtsa1303.htm (accessed January 13, 2004).

National Institute on Alcohol Abuse and Alcoholism. 1990. "Alcohol and Women." Available at http://alcoholism.about.com/library/blnaa10.htm (accessed January 21, 2004).

Schapiro, M. 2002. "Big Tobacco." *Nation* (May 6). Available at http://www.thenation.com/doc.mhtml?i=20020506&s=schapiro (accessed January 1, 2004).

Stratton, K., C. Howe, and F. Battaglia, eds. 1997. *Fetal Alcohol Syndrome: Diagnosis, Epidemiology, Prevention, and Treatment.* Washington, DC: National Academy Press.

Streissguth, A., and J. Kanter, eds. 1997. *The Challenge of Fetal Alcohol Syndrome.* Seattle: University of Washington Press.

Substance Abuse and Mental Health Services Administration (SAMHSA). 1999. *National Household Survey on Drug Abuse Main Findings.* Rockville, MD: United States Department of Health and Human Services.

———. 2002. *National Household Survey on Drug Abuse.* Rockville, MD: United States Department of Health and Human Services.

———. 2003. *Emergency Department Trends from the Drug Abuse Warning Network, Final Estimates 1995–2002.* Rockville, MD: United States Department of Health and Human Services.

Switzerland Addiction Research Institute. 2003. "Tobacco, Alcohol, Drugs Killing 7 Million a Year." Available at http://www.abc.net.au/science/news/health/HealthRepublish_792982.htm (accessed January 10, 2004).

University of Michigan News and Information Services. 2002. *Teen Smoking Declines Sharply in 2002, More than Offsetting Large Increases in the Early 1990s.* Ann Arbor: University of Michigan News and Information Services. Available at http://www.monitoringthefuture.org (accessed January 1, 2004).

U.S. Department of Health and Human Services and SAMHSA's National Clearinghouse for Alcohol and Drug Information. "Prevention Primer." Available at http://store.health.org (accessed July 1, 2003).

U.S. Department of Justice, Office of Juvenile Programs. 2001. "Comparison of Drinking Rates and Problems: European Countries and the United States." Available at http://www.ncjrs.org/html/ojjdp/compendium/2001/9902NCPC_PIRE.pdf (accessed January 1, 2004).

World Health Organization. 2001. *Women and the Tobacco Epidemic—Challenges for the 21st Century.* Geneva: WHO.

———. 2002. *Hazardous Harmonization in Smoking by European Youth.* Available at http://www.who.dk/document/cma/PB032002e.pdf (accessed January 1, 2004).

Yoon, Y., H. Yi, B. Grant, F. Stinson, and M. Dufor. 2002. *Surveillance Report #60: Liver Cirrhosis Mortality in the United States, 1970–99.* Rockville, MD: National Institute on Alcohol Abuse and Alcoholism, Division of Biometry and Epidemiology.

5

Chronology

This chapter lists significant events, legal decisions, and international agreements that have had an impact on the drug problem in the United States and the policies that have been adopted. Among the examples are those that relate to issues of drug-supply reduction by limiting the cultivation, production, trafficking, and distribution of drugs. Demand-reduction initiatives that seek to prevent the onset of drug use, help drug users break the habit, and provide treatment through rehabilitation and social reintegration are presented as well.

1875– **1890**	California passes the first antiopium law in the United States, declaring it a felony to use laudanum, an opium preparation, or any other narcotic. This attempt fails to control unlawful use of opium in the state.
	In 1881, California passes a law making it a misdemeanor to maintain a place where opium is sold, given away, or smoked. The bill applies only to commercial places, presumably the opium dens commonly frequented by Chinese immigrants. Smoking opium alone, or with friends in a private residence, is not covered by the legislation.
	During the last quarter of the nineteenth century, other western states such as Nevada and the Territory of Oregon pass legislation restricting the sale and use of opium and other substances. Doctors, however, continue to prescribe opium derivatives for a variety

1875–1890 of ailments. Many over-the-counter preparations con-
(cont.) taining quantities of morphine, heroin, and opium are
still available to anyone complaining of an illness
(Casey 1978).

1906 Congress passes the first Pure Food and Drug Act, despite opposition from the patent-medicine interests.
The 1906 act requires that medicines containing opiates and certain other drugs must say so on their la-
bels. Later amendments to the act also require that the
quantity of each drug be truly stated on the label, and
that the drugs meet official standards of identity and
purity (Brecher et al. 1972; Brecher 1972).

1909 First international meeting on drugs is held in Shanghai, China, to discuss opium. President Theodore Roo-
sevelt convenes the meeting in an effort to help China
deal with the problem of opium addiction among its
inhabitants. He hopes that in return China will reopen
its market to imported U.S. manufactured goods. This
market was closed in response to restraints placed on
Chinese immigration to the United States under the
Chinese Exclusion Act. The United States is in support
of a total ban on opium. Britain, fearing the loss of its
valuable trade, opposes the plan. Thirteen nations at-
tend, but no international treaty comes out of the conference.

The U.S. Congress passes the Act to Prohibit the Importation and Smoking of Opium and the Opium Exclusion Act, making it criminal to buy and sell opium
for nonmedicinal purposes (Drug Policy Alliance
1998).

1912 The 1909 Shanghai conference did not produce an international treaty; however, another international
drug conference is held in 1912. At the 1912 International Opuim Conference in the Hague, some forty-six
nations discuss morphine, cocaine, cannabis, heroin,
as well as opium. The outcome of the conference is the
Hague Convention for the Suppression of Opium and

Other Drugs. It requires the production, sale, and use of opium, heroin, morphine, and cocaine be limited to medical and other legitimate purposes. Both the United States and Italy want cannabis included in the convention, but they are unsuccessful (Yao 1958).

1913   Congress passes the Harrison Act that is considered to be a cornerstone of U.S. drug policy, including the criminalization of drugs and the War on Drugs.

Prior to the act, narcotic use in the United States had been declining; there was no black market in drugs, no organized crime drug structure with its associated violence and pervasive corruption of governmental officials, and drug users were not stigmatized as predatory criminals. After passage of the law, many physicians were arrested, and some were convicted and imprisoned for supplying narcotics to addicts even on a physician's prescription.

On May 15, 1915, just six weeks after the effective date of the Harrison Act, an editorial in the *New York Medical Journal* declared:

> As was expected . . .the immediate effects of the Harrison antinarcotic law were seen in the flocking of drug habitues to hospitals and sanatoriums. Sporadic crimes of violence were reported too, due usually to desperate efforts by addicts to obtain drugs, but occasionally to a delirious state induced by sudden withdrawal. . . .The really serious results of this legislation, however, will only appear gradually and will not always be recognized as such. These will be the failures of promising careers, the disrupting of happy families, the commission of crimes that will never be traced to their real cause, and the influx into hospitals to the mentally disordered of many who would otherwise live socially competent lives.

1913
(cont.)

In 1918, after three years of the Harrison Act, the secretary of the treasury appoints a committee to look into the problem. The chairman of the committee is Congressman Homer T. Rainey; members include a professor of pharmacology from Harvard, a former deputy commissioner of internal revenue responsible for law enforcement, and Dr. A. G. Du Mez, secretary of the United States Public Health Service. Among its findings are the following:

- Opium and other narcotic drugs (including cocaine, which Congress had erroneously labeled as a narcotic in 1914) are being used by about 1 million people. (This was almost certainly an overestimate.)
- The "underground" traffic in narcotic drugs is about equal to the legitimate medical traffic.
- The "dope peddlers" appear to have established a national organization, smuggling the drugs in through seaports or across the Canadian or Mexican borders—especially the Canadian border.
- The wrongful use of narcotic drugs has increased since passage of the Harrison Act. Twenty cities, including New York and San Francisco, report such increases.

To stem the rising tide of drug problems, the 1918 committee calls for sterner law enforcement. It recommends more state laws patterned after the Harrison Act.

Congress responds by tightening the Harrison Act. In 1924, for example, a law is enacted prohibiting the importation of heroin altogether, even for medicinal use. This legislation grows out of the widespread misapprehension that, because of the deteriorating health, behavior, and status of addicts following passage of the Harrison Act and the subsequent conversion of addicts from morphine to heroin, heroin must be a much more damaging drug than opium or morphine.

In 1925, Dr. Lawrence Kolb reports that "If there is any difference in the deteriorating effects of morphine and heroin on addicts, it is too slight to be determined clinically" (Kolb 1925). On the contrary, heroin ousts morphine almost completely from the black market after the law is passed.

An editorial in the *Illinois Medical Journal* for June 1926, after eleven years of federal law enforcement, concludes: "The Harrison Narcotic law should never have been placed upon the Statute books of the United States. It is to be granted that the well-meaning blunderers who put it there had in mind only the idea of making it impossible for addicts to secure their supply of 'dope' and to prevent unprincipled people from making fortunes, and fattening upon the infirmities of their fellow men" (McNamara 2002; Brecher et al. 1972).

1916   *United States v. Coca Cola Company of Atlanta* is brought before the Supreme Court, alleging that "Coca-Cola" is adulterated and misbranded. The allegation of adulteration is that the product contains an added poisonous or added deleterious ingredient, caffeine, which might render the product injurious to health. It is alleged to be misbranded in that the name "Coca-Cola" is a representation of the presence of the substances coca and cola; that the product contained no coca and little if any cola and thus was an "imitation" of these substances and was offered for sale under their "distinctive name." The Court rules in favor of the company, declaring that "Coca-Cola" is the "distinctive name" of the product under which it has been known and sold for more than twenty years as an article of food and not in violation of the Food and Drugs Act provisions.

1919   The U.S. Supreme Court hears the Harrison Act in *United States v. Doremus* and upholds the Harrison Act as a valid exercise of the taxing power only by a 5–4 margin.

1920   The Volstead Act (Prohibition) becomes the Eigh-
        teenth Amendment to the U.S. Constitution
        (1920–1933). It legislates abstinence from alcohol. The
        act prohibits the manufacture, sale, transport, import,
        or export of alcoholic beverages. Upon ratification of
        the amendment by the states, Congress votes its ap-
        proval in October 1919, and enacts it into law as the
        National Prohibition Act of 1920.

        The law puts legal brewers out of business and opens
        the nation's door to unintended consequences: boot-
        legging, gambling, prostitution, rackets, gangsters,
        and organized crime (Minnesota Historical Society
        2003).

1922   The Narcotics Drugs Import and Export Act (also
        known as the Jones-Miller Act) is passed to eliminate
        use of narcotics except for legitimate medicinal use.
        Also, the legislation establishes the Federal Narcotics
        Control Board (in the Treasury Department). Specifi-
        cally, the act provides fines of up to $5,000 and prison
        sentences of up to ten years for any individual found
        guilty of being party to the unlawful importation of
        narcotics. The legislation has little influence upon the
        illicit-drug marketplace except to increase the price of
        heroin and cocaine.

1925   In the landmark case *Linder v. United States*, the U.S.
        Supreme Court rules unanimously, 9–0, that narcotic
        agents have no legal right to interfere in the medical
        prescription of narcotics—even if the prescription is
        solely intended to maintain the narcotic addict on
        their drug of choice. This is a major legal setback to
        the supporters of the narcotic laws who want to stop
        narcotic maintenance as a moral issue. In response,
        the narcotic agents get around the ruling by indicting
        15,000 people in the following years (by their own
        records) but do not bring any of them to trial simply
        because they know they would lose in court. The in-
        dictments, however, are sufficient to instill enough
        fear to permanently stop all medical attempts at nar-

cotic maintenance in the United States (Schaffer Library of Drug Policy, Historical Research on Drug Policy; *Linder v. United States*).

1926   In *United States v. Daugherty,* the defendant is convicted of three separate offenses of sale of cocaine, and receives three consecutive five-year sentences. The court rules that it is legal to treat all three offenses as separate offenses for sentencing but states: "We deem it proper to add that the sentence of fifteen years imposed upon respondent seems extremely harsh."

1929   Legislation (the Narcotics Control Act and the Narcotics Farm–Porter Act) authorizes the construction of two hospitals for drug addicts and the creation of the Public Health Service (PHS) Narcotics Division. The first of two facilities is built in Lexington, Kentucky, in 1935, and the second facility opens in Fort Worth, Texas, in 1938. These facilities are in fact prisons modified to provide medical and psychiatric services.

1930   The Federal Bureau of Narcotics (FBN) is created in the Treasury Department under a commissioner of narcotics. The bureau is an enforcement structure under the direction of Commissioner Harry Anslinger who serves in the position as the bureau's first commissioner for more than thirty-two years. The Federal Bureau of Narcotics is one of the current Drug Enforcement Agency's predecessor agencies.

1932   Congress passes the Uniform State Narcotic Act to encourage state governments to control the rising use of marijuana and to research the connection between marijuana use and crime. Endorsed by the Federal Bureau of Narcotics as an alternative to federal laws, by 1937 every state prohibits marijuana use.

1936   The government releases *Reefer Madness,* a docudrama about the dangers of marijuana. The movie is still a cult classic.

1937   The Marijuana Tax Act imposes special taxes on persons engaged in marijuana-related activities. Passage of the act makes nonmedical use of marijuana illegal. Only the birdseed industry, which argues that hemp seeds give birds' feathers a particularly shiny gloss, is exempted from the act, and to this day birdseed producers are allowed to use imported hemp seeds treated so they do not sprout.

The Marijuana Tax Act effectively bans recreational and medicinal use of cannabis in the United States. The fines for violating the provisions of the act that calls for the purchase of a Treasury Department tax stamp are excessive—five years' imprisonment, a $2,000 fine, or both for noncompliance. Also, the act authorizes the secretary of the treasury to grant the commissioner (then Harry Anslinger) and agents of the Treasury Department's Bureau of Narcotics absolute administrative regulatory and police powers in the enforcement of the law (Bonnie and Whitebread 1970; Stack 2002; Musto 1972; Woodward 1937a; Solomon). In testimony to Congress, Anslinger states, "Marihuana is an addictive drug which produces in its users insanity, criminality, and death."

The American Medical Association goes on record stating:

> There is no evidence . . . that the medicinal use of [cannabis and its preparations and derivatives] has caused or is causing cannabis addiction. As remedial agents, they are used to an inconsiderable extent, and the obvious purpose and effect of this bill is to impose so many restrictions on their use as to prevent such use altogether. Since the medicinal use of cannabis has not caused and is not causing addiction, the prevention of the use of the drug for medicinal purposes can accomplish no good

end whatsoever. . . . The American Medical Association has no objection to any reasonable regulation of the medicinal use of cannabis and its preparations and derivatives. It does protest, however, against being called upon to pay a special tax, to use special order forms in order to procure the drug, to keep special records concerning its professional use and to make special returns to the Treasury Department officials, as a condition precedent to the use of cannabis in the practice of medicine. (Woodward 1937b)

1942   The Opium Poppy Act passes, prohibiting the cultivation of the opium poppy except under license in the United States.

1944   The New York Academy of Medicine publishes the *La-Guardia Report* that examines the social, medicinal, and legal aspects of marijuana. The report concludes, among other things, that marijuana does not lead to addiction.

1946   The Narcotics Act gives the Federal Bureau of Narcotics authority over synthetic narcotics that could be demonstrated as being addictive (U.S. Drug Enforcement Agency).

1951   The Boggs Act is the first major drug legislation passed since the 1937 Marijuana Tax Act. In response to an apparent increase in illicit-drug use among minority populations in many northern cities, the act calls for mandatory minimum federal sentences for drug offenders, who face two to five years for a first offense, five to ten for the second, and ten to twenty for the third, with no possibility of parole or probation after the first conviction ("On the Flip Side").

1956   The Narcotics Control Act is put into effect, imposing harsher penalties than before. All drug violations are now punishable by two to ten years for a first offense; five to twenty years for a second offense; ten to forty years for a third offense; a $20,000 fine; five to twenty-five years on a first-time conviction for sales or smuggling, ten to forty years thereafter; ten to forty years for sale by an eighteen year or older person to a minor; and ten years to life imprisonment for heroin sale to a minor with a possible death sentence. Other provisions of the act rescind the ability to suspend a sentence or grant probation except in cases of simple probation. Narcotics agents are given permission to make arrests without warrants, and drug users, drug addicts, and drug offenders are made to register at the border when entering or leaving the country (King 1974).

1960   The Manufacturing Act tightens controls and restrictions over legally manufactured narcotic drugs. A system of licensing manufacturers and setting quotas for classes of drugs, both natural and synthetic, is set in place.

The Single Convention on Narcotic Drugs creates a legal framework for combating trafficking in narcotic drugs and drug abuse, including the early identification, treatment, education, after-care, rehabilitation, and social reintegration of the persons involved. The convention does not specify what those measures should be, leaving this to the individual signatories to define. The convention proposes to outlaw cannabis use and cannabis cultivation worldwide and eradicate cannabis smoking within thirty years (by 1991). The U.S. representative to the convention is Harry Anslinger (European Legal Database on Drugs 2003).

President Kennedy appoints the "Prettyman Commission" (Advisory Commission on Narcotic and Drug Abuse). Among its recommendations are to decrease the use of minimum mandatory sentences, increase appropriations for research, and transfer the Federal Bureau of Narcotics to the Department of Health, Education, and Welfare.

1961   Soon after his inauguration, President Kennedy initiates action to have Harry Anslinger retire or removed from his leadership role with the Federal Bureau of Narcotics.

1962   California has a law against being an addict; Larry Robinson is convicted based on the testimony of two policemen who say that he had needle marks and admitted addiction. Robinson and his defense attorneys say the conviction is unconstitutional. In *Robinson v. California,* the state supreme court agrees, stating that one's "status" does not constitute a crime.

1963   The Community Mental Health Centers Act promotes the establishment of community-based treatment centers. It is one of the first legislative acts to focus attention on drug treatment.

1965   The Drug Abuse Control Amendment puts control of nonnarcotic drugs such as amphetamines, barbiturates, and hallucinogenic substances under the purview of the federal government.

1966   The Narcotic Addict Rehabilitation Act specifies narcotic addiction as a "mental illness" and initiates a federally sponsored national program for long-term treatment and rehabilitation of narcotic addicts.

1968   The Alcoholic and Narcotic Addict Rehabilitation Amendments authorize grants for the construction of narcotic treatment facilities in the states, and for specialized training programs and materials for prevention and treatment of narcotic addiction.

1969   Dr. Timothy Leary is charged with possession of marijuana. He argues that the Marijuana Tax Act is unconstitutional on the grounds that it requires self-incrimination in order to comply with the law. The U.S. Supreme Court agrees with Dr. Leary, in *Leary v. United States,* and overturns the Marijuana Tax Act on constitutional grounds.

1970   The Comprehensive Drug Abuse and Prevention and Control Act expands the national drug-abuse program by extending the services of federally funded community treatment centers to nonnarcotic drug abusers as well as addicts.

President Richard Nixon creates the National Commission on Marijuana and Drug Abuse to review national drug policy.

Congress passes the Racketeer Influenced and Corrupt Organizations law and the Continuing Criminal Enterprise (CCE) statute. Both laws address the forfeiture of ill-gotten gain and the removal of the rights of drug traffickers to any personal assets or property, including real estate, cash, automobiles, and jewelry obtained by or used in a criminal enterprise or undertaking (Harrison, Backenheimer, and Inciardi 1995).

1972   The 1970 National Commission on Marijuana and Drug Abuse report "Marijuana: A Signal of Misunderstanding" is released. The report recommends the elimination of criminal penalties for possession of small amounts of marijuana. Noting that half the nation's young people admit using marijuana, the commission argues that relying on the criminal justice system to reduce drug use is neither practical nor effective. Ten states adopt decriminalization laws, and Alaska makes marijuana possession legal.

1974   The National Institute on Drug Abuse is established as part of the Alcohol, Drug Abuse, and Mental Health Administration (ADAMHA). It serves as the lead federal agency for conducting basic, clinical, and epidemiological research to improve the understanding, treatment, and prevention of drug abuse and addiction and the health consequences of these behaviors. NIDA is mandated to be responsible for the Drug Abuse Warning Network and the National Household Survey on Drug Abuse. The Addiction Research Center in Lexington, Kentucky, becomes NIDA's intramural research program.

1978   Testifying before the Select Committee on Narcotics Abuse and Control, two high-ranking Carter officials state: (1) the federal government does not have a specific treatment program for marijuana, and in fact, the administrator of the federal Alcohol, Drug Abuse, and Mental Health Agency says, "There is no treatment required for the use of marijuana as such" (U.S. House of Representatives 1978b, 9); (2) "[W]e have talked about the propriety of decriminalizing the possession of small amounts of marijuana for personal use, under Federal statute only. This would, in effect, merely codify what is already occurring, since Federal law enforcement efforts should not be directed at people who possess small amounts of any drug, particularly marijuana" (U.S. House of Representatives 1978b, 8); and (3) the federal position under the Carter administration is that the move toward decriminalization is a state-by-state choice and should not be mandated by the federal establishment (ibid.; Harrison, Backenheimer, and Inciardi 1995).

1980   The National Organization for the Reform of Marijuana Laws (NORML) asks the Supreme Court to overturn the Controlled Substances Act prohibition on private possession of marijuana. The Court declares in *NORML v. Bell* that it is its responsibility "to construe and enforce the Constitution and laws of the land as they are and not to legislate social policy on the basis of . . . personal inclinations or other nonlegal considerations. . . . The legislative system may not always work efficiently, or fairly, but we have staked our fortunes on it, and our history would support the wisdom of our forefathers' judgment. . . . NORML's efforts have seared the conscience of many representatives. Eleven states have decriminalized possession of marijuana and efforts to decriminalize are continuing in many others. The legislative branch, and not the judicial, is the proper battleground for the fight to decriminalize the possession of marijuana. The people, and not the courts, must decide whether the battle will be won or lost" (*The National Organization for the Reform of Marijuana Laws (NORML) v. Griffin B. Bell* 1980).

1984   The Comprehensive Crime Control Act broadens criminal and civil asset-forfeiture laws and increases federal criminal sanctions for drug offenses.

1986   President Reagan signs the Anti–Drug Abuse Act that mandates sentences for drug-related crimes. In conjunction with the Comprehensive Crime Control Act of 1984, the new law raises federal penalties for marijuana possession and dealing, basing the penalties on the amount of the drug involved. Possession of 100 marijuana plants receives the same penalty as possession of 100 grams of heroin. The act establishes mandatory six- and ten-year prison terms for drug dealing, as well as the now-famous 100-to-1 crack-to-cocaine ratio, in which possession of 5 grams of crack cocaine triggers the same prison sentence as possession of 500 grams of powder cocaine. A life sentence now requires the sale of just 3.3 pounds of crack. A later amendment to this act establishes a "three strikes and you're out" policy, requiring life sentences for repeat drug offenders, and providing for the death penalty for "drug kingpins" (PBS 1998).

1988   The Anti–Drug Abuse Amendment Act raises federal penalties for marijuana possession, cultivation, and trafficking. Sentences are to be determined by the quantity of the drug involved; "conspiracies" and "attempts" are to be punished as severely as completed acts.

          The UN International Conference on Drug Abuse and Illicit Trafficking recognizes that drug abuse is a global phenomenon affecting almost every country, although its extent and characteristics differ from region to region. At the time of the convention, the most widely consumed drug worldwide is cannabis. Three-quarters of all countries report abuse of heroin, and two-thirds report abuse of cocaine. Drug-related problems include increased rates of crime and violence, susceptibility to HIV/AIDS and hepatitis, demand for treatment and emergency room visits, and a breakdown in social behavior.

At the 1988 UN General Assembly special session on the world drug problem, member states recognize that reducing the demand for drugs is an essential pillar in the stepped-up global effort to fight drug abuse and trafficking. They commit themselves to reduce significantly both the supply of and the demand for drugs by 2008.

1990   The Supreme Court rules on two workers who were fired by a private drug-rehabilitation organization because they ingested peyote, a hallucinogenic drug, for sacramental purposes at a ceremony of their Native American church. Their applications for unemployment compensation are denied by the State of Oregon under a state law disqualifying employees discharged for work-related "misconduct."

The Supreme Court, in *Smith v. Oregon*, upholds the Oregon decision, stating that the First Amendment protection of religious freedom applies only to laws that specifically target religious behavior and that an individual's religious beliefs do not excuse one from complying with statutes (that is, the use of banned substances such as peyote) that indirectly infringe on their religious rights.

1992   Drug Enforcement Agency administrator John Lawn officially denies the petition of the National Organization for Reform of Marijuana Laws to reschedule marijuana from Schedule I to Schedule II of the Controlled Substances Act in 1989. On appeal, the decision is reviewed, and the judicial decision is made that marijuana has no currently accepted medical use.

The Drug Enforcement Agency initiates the "Kingpin Strategy" to attack drug organizations at vulnerable areas—the chemicals needed to process the drugs and their finances, transportation, communications, and leadership infrastructure in the United States. The kingpin program essentially controls investigations from DEA headquarters and selects a finite number of targets for intensive investigative activity.

1992   Manuel Noriega, the de facto leader of Panama and
(cont.)   one-time operative for the Central Intelligence
              Agency, is captured and brought to the United States
              to stand trial. He is convicted on charges of racketeer-
              ing, money laundering, and drug trafficking, and sen-
              tenced to forty years in prison.

1996   Voters in California approve legislation, the Compas-
              sionate Use Act, Proposition 215, allowing sick and
              dying patients to use marijuana for medicinal pur-
              poses.

1997   The Drug Free Communities Act becomes a catalyst
              for increased citizen participation in efforts to reduce
              substance abuse among youths and provide commu-
              nity antidrug coalitions with funds to carry out their
              missions. The act requires grants be made to coalitions
              of representatives of youths; parents; businesses; the
              media; schools; youth organizations; law enforce-
              ment; religious or fraternal organizations; civic
              groups; health care professionals; state, local, or tribal
              governmental agencies; and other organizations. Also,
              the act requires the Office of National Drug Control
              Policy to provide technical assistance and training,
              data collection, and dissemination of information on
              practices determined to be effective in reducing sub-
              stance abuse.

1998   The National Youth Anti-Drug Media Campaign is
              created as a government-funded initiative to reduce
              and prevent drug use among young people. Through
              the use of television, radio, and other advertising,
              complemented by public relations efforts including
              community outreach and institutional partnerships,
              the campaign addresses youths directly and indirectly
              as well as encourages their parents and other adults to
              take actions known to affect drug use.

              The largest legal settlement in the United States is
              reached between states and the tobacco industry.
              Hundreds of billions of dollars (in total $246 billion)
              are needed to resolve the settlement.

1999   The Children's Health Act authorizes expanded research and services for a variety of childhood health
problems, reauthorizes programs of the Substance
Abuse and Mental Health Services Administration,
and addresses the problem of youth substance abuse
and the violence associated with it among other provisions.

In terms of reauthorizing the Substance Abuse and
Mental Health Services Administration, the act includes critical provisions to curb drug and alcohol
use, especially among youth. The act authorizes grant
programs targeted at youth drug treatment and early
intervention. Other provisions include support for
law enforcement to combat dangerous drugs such as
methamphetamine and Ecstasy, investigative training
on clandestine methamphetamine laboratories, and
additional resources for high-intensity drug-
trafficking areas, and strengthens punishment for
meth lab operators and amphetamine and Ecstasy
traffickers. The legislation also creates the Methamphetamine and Amphetamine Treatment Initiative at
the Center for Substance Abuse Treatment, provides
for additional research to treat addiction to these dangerous drugs, and establishes prevention grants to
teach children about the dangers of meth, Ecstasy, and
inhalants. This legislation expands the Clinton administration's National Methamphetamine Strategy as
well as efforts to reduce drug abuse through the Youth
Anti-Drug Media Campaign.

2000   The U.S. Supreme Court rules in *Food and Drug Administration (FDA) et al. v. Brown & Williamson Tobacco
Corp. et al.* by a vote of 5–4 that the FDA does not have
jurisdiction to regulate tobacco products or cigarette
company marketing practices under existing law. The
Supreme Court's ruling renders invalid the FDA's
1996 Regulations Restricting the Sale and Distribution of Cigarettes and Smokeless Tobacco to Protect
Children and Adolescents (the FDA's 1996 Tobacco
Regulations). Those portions of the FDA's 1996
Tobacco Regulations that had been in effect—the

2000
(cont.)
provisions that set eighteen as the nationwide minimum legal-sale age for tobacco and required that retailers check photo identification before selling cigarettes to persons who appear younger than twenty-seven years of age—are declared no longer operative.

2001
President Bush signs legislation, the Drug Free Communities Act, to reduce the demand for illegal drugs through education, prevention, and treatment.

2002
Canada and England take legislative measures to lower penalties for cannabis use. A Canadian government Senate committee issues a white-paper report recommending cannabis legislation.

2003
The U.S. Government Accounting Office and other independent evaluators declare major antidrug programs such as the Drug Abuse Resistance Program, the National Youth Anti-Drug Media Campaign, and the Drug Enforcement Agency are failing to achieve measurable success objectives.

Representatives of 142 countries at the forty-sixth session of the UN Commission on Narcotic Drugs in Vienna say they will stick to the strict policies established at a UN antidrug summit five years ago, despite critics' allegations the program is ineffective. Participants in a UN Commission on Narcotic Drugs meeting say in a statement they remain committed to the campaign to curb cultivation, trafficking, and consumption by 2008.

In his State of the Union address, President Bush announces a three-year $600 million plan to help addicts receive treatment. The program will use vouchers that give addicts a way to pay for treatment services, including those provided by faith-based organizations.

Ed Rosenthal, a popular authority on marijuana, is arrested in Oakland, California, by the DEA for distribution of marijuana for medical purposes under state law. Rosenthal is found guilty; however, he is sentenced to one day and released. This arrest sets the stage for further judicial review regarding state and federal marijuana laws, jurisdiction, and enforcement (Harrison 2003).

The Illicit Drug Anti-Proliferation Act (formerly known as the RAVE Act) becomes law. This legislation makes it easier for prosecutors to charge, convict, and imprison property owners, business owners, and managers who fail to prevent drug-related offenses committed by customers, employees, tenants, or other persons on their property. Also, the law authorizes funds to educate parents and children on the dangers of Ecstasy and other "predatory" drugs, and it directs the U.S. Sentencing Commission to consider increasing sentencing penalties for offenses involving GHB, a drug used in sexual assaults.

References

Bonnie, R., and C. Whitebread. 1970. "The Forbidden Fruit and the Tree of Knowledge: An Inquiry into the Legal History of American Marijuana Prohibition." *Virginia Law Review* 56, no. 6 (October). Available at http://www.drugtext.org/library/reports/vlr/vlr4.htm (accessed January 13, 2004).

Brecher, E. 1972. *Licit and Illicit Drugs.* Boston: Little, Brown.

Brecher, E., and the editors of *Consumer Reports Magazine*. 1972. *The Consumers Union Report on Licit and Illicit Drugs, Schaffer Library of Drug Policy.* Available at http://www.druglibrary.org/schaffer/Library/studies/cu/cu8.html (accessed January 13, 2004).

Casey, E. 1978. "History of Drug Use U.S." *Facts About Drugs Abuse* Available at http://www.a1b2c3.com/drugs/gen003.htm (accessed, January 13, 2004).

Drug Policy Alliance. 1998. "Regulating Cannabis: Cannabis Landmarks." Available at http://www.drugpolicy.org/events/archive/conferences/cannabis/landmarks (accessed January 13, 2004).

European Legal Database on Drugs. 2003. "Legal Status of Cannabis." Available at http://eldd.emcdda.org/trends/trends_cannabis.shtml (accessed January 13, 2004).

Harrison, A. 2003. "The Trial of Ed Rosenthal." Available at http://www.alternet.org/story.html?StoryID=14973 (accessed January 13, 2004).

Harrison, L., M. Backenheimer, and J. Inciardi. 1995. "Cannabis Use in the United States: Implications for Policy." In *Cannabisbeleid in Duitsland, Frankrijk En De Verenigde Staten,* edited by Peter Cohen and Arjan Sas, 237–247. Amsterdam: Centrum voor Drugsonderzoek, Universiteit van Amsterdam. Available at http://www.cedro-uva.org/lib/harrison.cannabis.05.html (accessed January 13, 2004).

King, Rufus. 1972. "Narcotics Control Act of 1956." *In The Drug Hang-Up: America's Fifty Year Folly.* Available at http://www.druglibrary.org/special/king/dhu/dhu16.htm (accessed January 13, 2004).

———. 1974. *"The American Legal System": Legal Sanctions to Repress Drug Use. In Drugs and the Criminal Justice System,* edited by James A. Indardi and Carl D. Chambers. Available at http://www.druglibrary.org/special/king/king3.htm (accessed March 9, 2004).

Kolb, Lawrence. 1925. "Pleasure and Deterioraion from Narcotic Addiction." *Mental Hygiene* 9: 699–724.

McNamara, Joseph. 2002. "Testimony for the Little Hoover Commission, Hoover Institution, Stanford University, Stanford, CA." September 26. Available at http://www.bsa.ca.gov/lhcdir/drug/McNamaraSep26.pdf (accessed January 13, 2004).

Minnesota Historical Society. 2003. "Prohibition & the Volstead Act." Available at http://www.mnhs.org/library/tips/history_topics/103prohibition.html (accessed January 13, 2004).

Musto, D. 1972. "The 1937 Marihuana Tax Act." *Archives of General Psychiatry* 26: 101–108.

The National Organization for the Reform of Marijuana Laws (NORML) v. Griffin B. Bell. Civ. A. No. 1897-73 (1980). Available at http://www.druglibrary.org/schaffer/legal/l1980/bell.htm (accessed January 13, 2004).

"On the Flip Side." Available at http://twist.lib.uiowa.edu/beat/Beat-Drugs/SQUARE%7E1.HTM (accessed January 13, 2004).

PBS. 1998. *Busted: America's War on Marijuana.* Available at http://www.pbs.org/wgbh/pages/frontline/shows/dope/etc/cron.html (accessed January 13, 2004).

Schaffer Library of Drug Policy. "Historical Research on Drug Policy." Available at http://www.druglibrary.org/schaffer/history/1920.htm (accessed January 13, 2004).

Solomon, D. "The Marihuana Tax Act of 1937." Schaffer Library of Drug Policy. Available at http://www.druglibrary.org/schaffer/hemp/taxact/mjtaxact.htm (accessed January 13, 2004).

Stack, P. 2002. *Medical Marijuana: A History.* Vol. 16019. Available at http://www.time.com/time/covers/1101021104/history.html (accessed January 13, 2004).

U.S. Drug Enforcement Agency. "The Diversion of Drugs and Chemicals." Available at http://www.deadiversion.usdoj.gov/pubs/program/activities/background.htm (accessed January 13, 2004).

U.S. House of Representatives, Select Committee on Narcotics Abuse and Control, Drug Abuse. 1978a. "Demand Reduction in the United States and Abroad." SCNAC-95-2-1. Washington, DC: U.S. Government Printing Office.

————. 1978b. "Drug Abuse Treatment: Part 1." SCNAC-95-2-12. Washington, DC: U.S. Government Printing Office.

Woodward, W. 1937a. "American Medical Association Opposes the Marijuana Tax Act of 1937." Available at http://www.pdxnorml.org/AMA_opposes_1937.html (accessed January 13, 2004).

————. 1937b. Legal Council, Bureau of Legal Medicine and Legislation, American Medical Association submitted a letter on July 10 to the Hon. Pat Harrison, chairman, Committee on Finance, United States Senate, Washington, DC, regarding the position of the AMA to the Marijuana Tax Act of 1937.

Yao, Y. 1958. "The Single Convention on Narcotic Drugs and the Prevention of Drug Addiction." Available at http://www.undcp.org/odccp/bulletin/bulletin_195801_1_page002.html (accessed January 13, 2004).

6

Biographical Sketches

Many individuals have had a significant influence on drug policy, research, and treatment in the United States during the past hundred years or so. Some have been in the public arena in positions as elected officials or appointed officials. Others are best known for their legislative initiatives. A number have gained public attention because of their organization, litigation, and advocacy efforts. Several in academia and research have attracted media attention for their work or studies of importance. Those presented in this chapter are but a few of the many who have shaped the drug-use "state of affairs"—for better or worse. Internet resources have been used for this chapter.

Harry J. Anslinger (1892–1975)

Known as the "Father of the Drug War," Harry Anslinger was the first U.S. commissioner of narcotics. He held the position for thirty-two years and was U.S. representative on the UN Commission on Narcotics. According to biographer John McWilliams, Anslinger was a cross between William Jennings Bryan and the Reverend Jerry Falwell. He brought to the position a puritanical conviction that Prohibition could succeed if there was enough law enforcement. Anslinger has been likened to J. Edgar Hoover in terms of having conservative, staunchly anticommunist law-and-order values and idiosyncrasies that were strongly imposed on their federal bureaucracies and personnel. And in his book *Outsiders,* Howard S. Becker describes how the Federal Bureau of Narcotics under Anslinger created the marijuana problem in the 1930s to cause the public to demand legislation.

Anslinger had a major role in deriding the LaGuardia Committee and its blue ribbon–panel report published by the prestigious New York Academy of Medicine. The committee found no justification for Anslinger's catastrophic claims of marijuana. It found marijuana use did not lead to addiction in the medical sense, nor was it a gateway to harder drugs; it was not widespread in school yards or being used by children; and there was no relationship between marijuana and juvenile delinquency.

What, then, was behind Anslinger's propaganda that set in motion decades of legislation, prosecution, and punishment against the use of the substance? There seems to be no simple answer; however, conspiracy theorists link Anslinger to William Randolph Hearst, the DuPont Corporation, and Andrew Mellon. First, Hearst—the media giant and industrialist—stood to forfeit a fortune to hemp (that is, the cannabis plant). With the end of the Civil War, the cheaper wood-pulp sulfide process displaced labor-intensive hemp production. By the mid-1930s, however, a new invention, the "Decorticator," threatened to make hemp paper actually cheaper than wood pulp. With his vast holdings in timber, pulp, and paper mills, Hearst was poised to take a substantial financial loss. The Hearst media campaign against hemp was a biased effort to sway public opinion and have the substance banned. At the same time, DuPont (holders of the patent for a sulfuric-acid wood-pulping process) had developed the synthetic fibers rayon and nylon—direct competitors of natural hemp cloth and rope. Finally, there was Andrew Mellon, chairman of the Mellon Bank, which was a main source of finance for DuPont. Mellon was the U.S. treasury secretary responsible for appointing Anslinger as commissioner of the Federal Bureau of Narcotics. Anslinger was married to Mellon's niece (Hartsell 1994).

Another interesting note about Anslinger was reported in the *Atlantic Monthly* in a 1997 article titled "More Reefer Madness." According to the author of the article, E. Schlosser, Anslinger in his memoir, *The Murderers* (1961), confessed to having arranged a regular supply of morphine for "one of the influential members of Congress" who had become an addict. Anslinger's biographer believes that addict was Senator Joseph R. McCarthy.

Len Bias (1963–1986)

A gifted college basketball player, Len Bias died at the age of twenty-two of what was believed to be the use of crack cocaine (according to autopsy reports, the cause was powder cocaine), two days after being selected as the first-round draft pick of the Boston Celtics. Shortly before his death, he had signed a million-dollar endorsement contract with Reebok. The death of Bias reinforced the idea that the country was under assault by drugs. The outrage was especially great in Boston, the home of congressional House Speaker Tip O'Neill. A nonpartisan congressional coalition, along with President Reagan and his wife, Nancy, moved forward a crusade against drugs. Within the period of a few months and without congressional hearings that are usually held for significant legislative actions, the $1.7 billion Anti–Drug Abuse Act was sent to the president for signature, funding drug-treatment programs, interdiction efforts at the U.S. borders, and, perhaps most important, mandatory minimum sentences for certain federal drug offenses. In essence, the message to the public was that drugs, especially crack cocaine, are a menace to society, and those involved with its sale and use need to be put in prison. At the time the act was passed, NBC News labeled crack as "America's drug of choice," and drug czar William Bennett predicted it would invade every home in the United States. *Newsweek* compared crack to the bubonic plague and called it "the most addictive drug known to man."

Prior to the law, federal judges had sentencing discretion. The new statues now dictated mandatory minimum sentences with a primary focus on crack cocaine—cocaine processed so that it can be smoked. Possessing five grams of crack was made a felony with an automatic five-year prison term, while five grams of the same drug in powder form is a misdemeanor likely to carry no jail time. Because a large proportion of crack users are black, the Anti–Drug Abuse Act of 1986 has been considered a racially biased effort targeted against them. According to a senior scientist at ABT Associates, a research think tank based outside of Boston, the problem of disproportion of blacks being sent to prison would disappear if the law treated the powder and crack forms of cocaine equally.

Joseph Califano Jr. (1931–)

Secretary of health, education, and welfare for two years (1977–1979) under President Jimmy Carter, Joseph Califano Jr. mounted major health-promotion and disease-prevention programs targeted against cigarette smoking and alcohol use. Since 1990, he has had a leadership role with the Center on Addiction and Substance Abuse at Columbia University, a think tank addressing substance abuse from a prohibition perspective. Califano has been critical of drug use, claiming it is the principal and direct cause of crime, health problems, declining worker productivity, homelessness, and a range of other problems.

During the Carter administration, Califano became a vigorous critic of smoking. Among other actions, he asked cigarette companies to devote 10 percent of their advertising to a campaign to discourage children and teenagers from smoking, an idea rejected by the companies on the grounds that "the mothers and fathers of this nation, whether smokers or nonsmokers, should continue to have freedom of choice in the education and training of their children." In 1979, Califano was fired as secretary of health, education, and welfare in part because his crusade against tobacco was a considerable political liability to President Carter. Before his dismissal, he pressed Carter to lend clout to the anti-smoking crusade. Once converted to the cause, Carter planned if reelected in 1980 to support a major increase in federal tobacco taxes to two dollars per pack, believing the action would save hundreds of thousands of lives while simultaneously raising billions for health care reform and deficit reduction. In 1997, prior to the massive tobacco settlement with states, Califano expressed his belief again to President Bill Clinton that a two-dollar per-pack tax increase on cigarettes was needed to reduce teen smoking and protect the public health

Sigmund Freud (1856–1939)

Born in what is now the Czech Republic, Sigmund Freud is best known for his development of psychoanalysis for the treatment of psychological and emotional disorders. In 1883, German physician Theodor Aschenbrandt administered cocaine to members of the Bavarian army. It was found that the drug enhanced their endurance on maneuvers. Freud, who was at the time a young neurologist, read the report and experimented with the substance. He played a significant role in the development of the Western cocaine industry, reporting, "I take very small doses of it regularly and against depression and against indigestion, and with the most brilliant success."

Drug giants Merck and Parke Davis (now Pfizer) paid Freud to endorse their rival brands. He wrote several enthusiastic papers on cocaine, most notably *Uber Coca (About Cocaine)* in 1884, reporting "exhilaration and lasting euphoria, which in no way differs from the normal euphoria of the healthy person. . . . You perceive an increase of self-control and possess more vitality and capacity for work. . . . In other words, you are simply normal, and it is soon hard to believe you are under the influence of any drug. . . . Long intensive physical work is performed without any fatigue. . . . This result is enjoyed without any of the unpleasant after-effects that follow exhilaration brought about by alcohol. . . . Absolutely no craving for the further use of cocaine appears after the first, or even after repeated taking of the drug." Freud concluded the paper by recommending cocaine pharmacotherapy for seven conditions: as a mental stimulant, possible treatment for digestive disorders, appetite stimulant in case of diseases such as cancer, treatment for morphine and alcohol addiction, treatment for asthma, aphrodisiac, and local anesthetic. Cocaine was, at that time, neither illegal nor prescribed.

Freud had envisioned taking cocaine in an oral solution that was less likely to be addictive than when administered intravenously. Euphoric effects are delayed and less intense. In the 1880s, however, hypodermic needles started becoming more widely available, and morphine addicts found that subcutaneous injections of cocaine yielded a quick, potent, and addictive high. Before long, many users became hooked on both substances. By 1887, Freud had changed his position about cocaine and reported that it was more dangerous for public health than morphine (Grinspoon and Bakalar).

Francis Harrison (1873–1957)

In 1913, New York representative Francis Harrison introduced two bills into Congress. One was to prohibit use and importation of opium, and the other was to regulate the manufacturing of smoking opium within the United States. Introduced as revenue legislation, there was no real intention of producing revenue. A few months after being introduced, President Wilson signed the bills, which took effect on March 1, 1914. Eventually, the Harrison Act caused more drug use than it prevented. A committee was formed to investigate this problem, which found that illicit use of narcotics had increased dramatically while the act had been in effect. Instead of improving the act, stiffer penalties were imposed.

David Kessler (1951–)

Appointed by President Bush in 1990 as the commissioner for the Food and Drug Administration, David Kessler took a number of steps to make the FDA more consumer-oriented and continued his work with that federal agency until 1997. During his seven years, under two presidents, Kessler took on the tobacco industry in order to tighten regulation.

Under his leadership, the FDA asked whether nicotine was a drug, using the definition "an article other than food intended to affect the structure or function of the body." This set off a long investigation to prove the tobacco industry's "intent." Informants provided internal documents showing that tobacco companies understood the addictive nature of nicotine in the 1960s, and sought to manipulate levels of nicotine in their cigarettes. Patents indicated that the companies devised ways to add nicotine to filters and wrapping paper. Also, an informant provided information about genetically engineered tobacco with high nicotine content that was being imported from Brazil.

The FDA, under Kessler, also discovered documents indicating that the industry had been actively marketing its cigarettes to teenagers. That discovery, Kessler said, changed the dynamic of ongoing court cases and of the industry's fight against regulation. "We were aiming at the heart of the industry," he explained. Juries were much less inclined to accept grounds of choice and personal responsibility when they realized that children were being targeted.

The Supreme Court subsequently ruled against FDA regulation of tobacco, and Congress did not pass significant antitobacco legislation. Nevertheless, Kessler (and C. Everett Koop) has been in the vanguard advocating change of tobacco use in the United States. Kessler's book *A Question of Intent*, published in 2001 by PublicAffairs Press, details his efforts and those of others targeted against the tobacco industry. David Kessler is now dean of Yale University Medical School (Brown University 2001).

C. Everett Koop (1916–)

After establishing a distinguished record as a pioneer in the field of pediatric surgery, C. Everett Koop was appointed by President Reagan in 1981 as deputy assistant secretary for health with the promise that he would be nominated as surgeon general. He was officially sworn in as surgeon general on January 21, 1982.

Koop has been an outspoken advocate of public health issues. The problem of tobacco was one he attacked, calling for "A Smoke-Free Society by the Year 2000." Although the Public Health Service had been calling attention to the dangers of tobacco use since the 1964 surgeon general's report (see Luther Terry) on smoking and health, its antitobacco campaign was relatively low-key until Koop began speaking out on the problem. In 1982, he issued a report on the problems of secondhand smoke that soon led to restrictions on smoking in public buildings and facilities. In 1987, smoking was forbidden on domestic air trips, and by 1990 the ban was made applicable to all flights. Koop was the ideal exponent of the antismokers' message. "A grandfatherly figure with an 'Old Testament' presence, he exuded absolute integrity and a fearless devotion to health. He was the Platonic version of the Surgeon General. Many still think he is the Surgeon General" (Verkiul 1998). The 1986 surgeon general's report on the dangers of passive smoking was also an important milestone in the fight against smoking.

In response to questions about his position to a major settlement between state governments and the tobacco industry, Koop said on the ABC television network show *Nightline* that he was open to some sort of deal; however, he noted that many antismoking activists "want to see the culprit, the tobacco industry, flogged in public, and I understand how they feel. I feel that way myself. They are very guilty. But flogging a company in public, if it does not produce something for the health of the American public, is a futile gesture." When testifying before a Senate committee, he urged lawmakers to "face the scourge of tobacco for what it is and legislate a tobacco policy that holds the industry accountable" (ibid.).

Timothy Leary (1920–1996)

A psychologist, Timothy Leary was a leading advocate for the use of LSD as well as other psychoactive drugs. Leary explored the cultural and philosophical implications of psychedelic drugs. He believed that the experience of using such drugs should be introduced to the general public, particularly the young. His books and papers as a psychologist helped launch the "humanistic psychology" movement with an emphasis on interpersonal relationships, multilevel personality assessments, group therapy, body/mind interaction, and a libertarian redefinition of the doctor-patient relationship.

Experimenting on himself and with friends, as well as on volunteer graduate students, Leary studied the emotional, physical, and social effects of psychedelics at the Harvard University Department of Psychology where he was employed. Before any meaningful results were attained, LSD was labeled as a dangerous new drug and made illegal. Considered too controversial, Leary's experiments were shut down, and he was forced to pursue his LSD research with private funding in Millbrook, New York. Leary continued to publicly promote the benefits of LSD use, and in the 1960s he was cast into the role of an "LSD guru" by the media. As the drug gained popularity with the counterculture, he provided instruction manuals for safe usage. He encouraged respect for the drug and urged the practice of "set and timing" as a safeguard against "bad trips." During this time, he coined the phrase "turn on, tune in, drop out," and published books with titles like *The Psychedelic Experience* (1964). Cultural conservatives saw Leary as a corrosive influence on society— President Nixon called him "the most dangerous man in America"—and many researchers felt Leary delegitimated the serious study of psychedelic drugs.

After arrests in 1965 and 1968 for the possession of marijuana and a prolonged legal battle, Leary was incarcerated in 1970 and soon escaped. Living as a fugitive for more than two years until being recaptured in Afghanistan, he was freed in 1976 and settled in southern California where he died of natural causes (Erowid 2004).

Alfred Lindesmith (1905–1991)

Known for his confrontation with the drug-control establishment, Alfred Lindesmith was a sociologist at the University of Indiana. Lindesmith believed legal prohibition of addictive drugs was futile and wrote on the threat to democracy inherent in such a policy. The career of Lindesmith began during the 1930s and developed in relation to the drug prohibition efforts in the early and mid-twentieth century. Lindesmith was an advocate for rational and humane drug laws that responded to the needs of an addict, including medical treatment. His views were diametrically opposed to those of Harry Anslinger and the Federal Bureau of Narcotics.

The first attack on Lindesmith came in 1939 as a result of his publications that presented his professional beliefs as a dissenter to the prevailing policy of the Bureau of Narcotics—a.k.a. Harry Anslinger. A bureau agent was sent to the University of Indiana to meet with the Board of Trustees and president of that university, informing them that Lindesmith was involved with a criminal organization. The organization was the World Narcotics Research Foundation then being organized by Dr. E. H. Williams. Williams was a nationally known writer on the narcotics problem who operated a narcotics clinic at the behest of the Los Angeles Medical Association and municipal health officials. Related to his humanitarian efforts, he was sought out by federal drug agents and convicted of a technical violation of the narcotic laws in a much criticized trial.

The following year, Lindesmith published an article titled "Dope Fiend Mythology." The bureau responded with a twenty-seven-page answer written by a San Francisco judge, Twain Michelson, titled "Lindesmith's Mythology." Reproduced for mass circulation by the Treasury Department, the government document was disseminated for years in an effort to discredit Lindesmith and as an authoritative statement of bureau policy. In 1948, Lindesmith published an article in the journal *Federal Probation* describing a case in which the bureau allowed two affluent addicts to receive opiates for more than twenty years, in contravention of the bureau's avowed organizational mandate. This outraged the bureau, which demanded a "correction" by that journal and pursued ways of discrediting Lindesmith for decades.

Lindesmith did not have much support in the academic community for his approach to the federal government's drug policy. "For over two decades most prominent academicians either ignored Lindesmith's work or criticized it methodologically or substantively. . . . For his perspective on drugs, Lindesmith endured three decades of harassment by Anslinger and the Federal Bureau of Narcotics, while he was largely ignored in reputable academic circles. By the 1960s, the academic community had finally caught up with Lindesmith's ideas. Unfortunately, by this time dedraconian control policies had become institutionalized. Since the 1960s, few criminologists or criminal law professors have supported government drug policies" (Galliher, Keys, and Elsner 1998).

Richard M. Nixon (1913–1994)

The thirty-seventh president of the United States, Richard M. Nixon succeeded in ending U.S. fighting in Vietnam and improving relations with the former Soviet Union and China. The Watergate scandal, however, brought fresh divisions to the country, leading to his resignation. During Richard Nixon's presidency, many drug-related challenges were addressed. A law-and-order president, Nixon unveiled a drug program that addressed drug abuse as a sickness, not a crime. For the first time in the history of U.S. drug policy, treatment supplanted law enforcement in terms of attention and allocation of funding. Nixon had started with a strategy of trying to reduce demand rather than shut off supply and punish consumers. As the 1972 election approached, the White House moved away from a treatment-oriented strategy to one of getting tough on drugs and anyone who uses them. In an interview with Nixon's domestic policy adviser, John Ehrlichman, it was acknowledged, "We knew we were lying about the health effects of marijuana. We knew we were lying about the relationship between heroin and crime. But this is what we were doing to win the election. And it worked." (Wink 1999).

The Nixon period appears to be marked with two significant drug issues, marijuana and methadone. To control demand, the Nixon administration proposed a dramatic centralization of all federally sponsored efforts in drug treatment, rehabilitation, education, prevention, training, and research in a new White House agency, the Special Action Office for Drug Abuse Prevention (SAODAP). Also, the new organization was designed to counter bureaucratic "foot-dragging" seen by the White House as centered in the National Institute of Mental Health (NIMH), which normally would have funded and overseen the administration's effort to promote methadone maintenance programs. The White House saw NIMH officials as being cautious of government sanctioning one addiction (methadone) in order to reduce the burden caused by another addiction (heroin). The administration's effort to move methadone treatment forward was reflected by the president's designation of Dr. Jerome Jaffe—a prominent supporter of methadone use in treatment—as his special consultant for narcotics and dangerous drugs until SAODAP could be legally constituted by Congress. When Jaffe assumed leadership responsibilities in 1971, there were 135 federally funded drug-treatment programs; eighteen months later, with an increased treatment budget, the number had tripled to 394. Treatment for heroin addiction was prioritized, and the number of methadone treatment programs increased considerably. With a high rate of addiction among Vietnam soldiers and veterans, Dr. Jaffe and his team established new programs to expand the Veterans Administration capability to provide drug treatment. Additionally, the Defense Department initiated a massive urinalysis of all servicemen before they left Southeast Asia. Soldiers using opium-based products including heroin were to be detained for treatment and rehabilitation. President Nixon informed Congress, "We will be requesting legislation to permit the military services to retain for treatment any individual due for discharge who is a narcotic addict. All of our servicemen must be accorded the right of rehabilitation." Shortly after Dr. Jaffe assumed responsibilities, the number of clients in funded treatment programs was estimated at just over 20,000 in October 1971. By December 1972, the figure was more than 60,000. As the methadone problem became more pronounced in urban areas or at least received unfavorable publicity, the White House began to distance itself from the SAODAP. Dr. Jaffe, who has been promised direct access to the president, was cut off from the White House staff. Jaffe resigned in June 1973.

A second issue that Nixon had to face was marijuana. During his presidency, the National Commission on Marijuana and Drug Abuse, after conducting an exhaustive study of marijuana, concluded in 1972 that it was virtually harmless and that people should not go to jail for smoking it. Nixon disagreed with his commission (Psychedelic Library 2004). Based on the Nixon tapes from 1971 to 1972, it has been pointed out that the foundation of the modern war on marijuana was the president's prejudice as well as a cultural war and misinformation. According to the president of Common Sense for Drug Policy, Kevin Zeese, "At a critical juncture when the United States decided how it would handle marijuana, President Nixon's prejudices did more to dominate policy than the thoughtful and extensive review of his own Blue Ribbon Commission. . . . If we had followed the advice of the experts rather than Nixon's prejudices we would have less marijuana use, be spending less money on marijuana enforcement and many million less people would have been arrested."

The following statements by President Nixon reflect his prejudices (Common Sense for Drug Policy 2002; Cockburn and St. Clair 1998):

- Marijuana compared to alcohol: Marijuana consumers smoke "to get high while a person drinks to have fun." Nixon also saw marijuana leading to a loss of motivation and discipline but claimed: "At least with liquor I don't lose motivation."
- Marijuana and political dissent: "radical demonstrators that were here . . . two weeks ago. . . . They're all on drugs, virtually all."
- Jews and marijuana: "I see another thing in the news summary this morning about it. That's a funny thing, every one of the bastards that are out for legalizing marijuana is Jewish. What the Christ is the matter with the Jews, Bob, what is the matter with them? I suppose it's because most of them are psychiatrists."
- Marijuana and the cultural wars: "You see, homosexuality, dope, immorality in general. These are the enemies of strong societies. That's why the Communists and the left-wingers are pushing the stuff, they're trying to destroy us."
- Drug education: "Enforce the law, you've got to scare them."
- Prior to launching the war on Drugs in 1969, H. R. Halderman recorded in his diary a briefing by the president: "[Nixon] emphasized that you have to face the fact that the whole problem is really the blacks. The key is to devise a system that recognizes this while not appearing to."

After the departure of Jerome Jaffe, Robert DuPont was appointed by President Nixon to direct the White House Special Action Office for Drug Abuse Prevention, a position he held until the office terminated in 1975. DuPont, a critic of making drugs more available, has expressed the belief that "[w]hen it comes to getting well from addiction, the best, the most reliable and the most effective path is through active participation in the 12 steps programs, including Alcoholics Anonymous and Narcotics Anonymous" (DuPont 1997).

Benjamin Rush (1745–1813)

A prominent physician and professor of chemistry, Benjamin Rush served as surgeon general of the Continental army. He was one of the signers of the Declaration of Independence in 1776 and an ardent abolitionist. Rush's major contribution to medicine lay with his work with the mentally ill. He believed that all mental illness, including alcoholism, was due to physical causes. In his famous *Inquiry into the Effects of Ardent Spirits upon the Human Body and Mind* published in 1785, Rush enumerated the diseases of the body and mind that plagued the drinker of distilled liquors. He described drunkenness as a disease resembling certain hereditary, family, and contagious diseases. His theories on the problem of alcoholism would eventually become the seeds of alcohol-addiction treatment in the United States.

During the colonial period, most people were not concerned with drunkenness; it was neither troublesome nor stigmatized behavior. Although Rush had no concern with wine and beer, he felt that the consumption of distilled liquor over time could be lethal, and he was the first American to call chronic drunkenness a distinct disease. Later generations of temperance workers would come to refer to Benjamin Rush as the "father of the temperance movement" (University of Waterloo 2001).

George Soros (1930–)

Born in Budapest, George Soros survived Nazi occupation and left Communist Hungry in 1947 for England, where he graduated from the London School of Economics in 1952. In 1956, Soros moved to the United States where he began to accumulate a large fortune through an international investment fund he founded and managed. Soros has been active as a philanthropist since 1979. He has provided support for the establishment of the Drug Policy Alliance (previously the Lindesmith Center), a leading drug-policy and research institute created in 1994 and directed by Ethan Nadelmannn, who has been described by *Rolling Stone* magazine as the point man for drug policy–reform efforts. Soros has also helped finance marijuana referenda in California and Arizona, among other related activities.

Soros became involved in the drug issue because of a commitment to the concept of open society. The open society is based on the recognition that "we act on the basis of imperfect understanding and our actions have unintended consequences. . . . An open society that recognizes fallibility is a superior form of social organization to a closed society that claims to have found all the

answers." In an article that he wrote for the *Washington Post,*
Soros (1997) stated:

> I have devoted much of my energies and resources
> over the past two decades to promoting the concept of
> open society in formerly communist countries. I have
> started to pay more attention to my adopted country,
> the United States, because I feel that the relatively
> open society we enjoy here is in danger. There is noth-
> ing new about this peril; it is a characteristic of open
> societies that they are always endangered.
>
> Our drug policies offer a prime example of adverse,
> unintended consequences. There is perhaps no other
> field where our public policies have produced an out-
> come so profoundly at odds with what was intended.
> But those who are waging a 'war on drugs' refuse to
> recognize this fact. They consider all criticism subver-
> sive. To suggest the possibility that the war on drugs
> may be self-defeating is tantamount to treason in their
> eyes. This was confirmed by their reaction to the ap-
> proval of the drug policy ballot initiatives in California
> and Arizona.

Soros believes "a drug free America is a utopian dream.
Some form of drug addiction or substance abuse is endemic in
most societies. Insisting on total eradication of drug use can only
lead to failure and disappointment. The war on drugs cannot be
won; but, like the Vietnam War, it has polarized our society"
(ibid.).

Luther Terry (1911–1985)

A physician with preventive medicine and public health experi-
ence, Luther Terry came to public prominence when President
Kennedy selected him as surgeon general of the Public Health
Service in 1961.

In 1962, the Royal College of Physicians in Britain published
a report linking cigarette smoking to lung cancer, bronchitis, and
probably cardiovascular disease. Shortly, after the release of this
report, Terry established the Surgeon General's Advisory Committee on Smoking and Health to produce a similar report for the
United States. "Smoking and Health: Report of the Advisory

Committee to the Surgeon General of the United States" was released on January 11, 1964. The report concluded that cigarette
smoking causes lung cancer and chronic bronchitis. The report
also noted that there was suggestive evidence, if not definite
proof, that smoking was linked to emphysema, cardiovascular
disease, and various types of cancer. The committee concluded
that cigarette smoking was a health hazard of sufficient importance to warrant appropriate remedial action.

The landmark surgeon general's report on smoking and health
stimulated a greatly increased concern about tobacco on the part of
the American public and government policy makers. Also, it led to
a broad-based antismoking campaign. At the time, 46 percent of all
Americans smoked; smoking was accepted in offices, airplanes,
and elevators, and TV programs were sponsored by cigarette
brands. Within three months of Terry's report, cigarette consumption had dropped 20 percent but was soon to climb back. The report was also responsible for the passage of the Cigarette Labeling
and Advertising Act of 1965, which, among other things, mandated
the surgeon general's health warnings on cigarette packages.

Andrew Volstead (1860–1947)

The son of Norwegian immigrants, Andrew Volstead was a member of the Republican Party and elected to Congress in 1903 as a
representative from Minnesota. A strong supporter of the civil
rights movement and one of the few politicians in Congress will-
ing to argue for federal legislation against lynching, he was concerned about the growing consumption of alcohol. In 1919, his
National Prohibition Act (also known as the Volstead Act) was
passed by Congress. The law prohibited the manufacture, transportation, and sale of beverages containing more than 0.5 percent
alcohol. At the time of its passage, Senator Morris Sheppard from
Texas said, "There is as much chance of repealing the Eighteenth
Amendment [of the Constitution] as there is for a hummingbird
to fly to the planet Mars with the Washington Monument tied to
its tail." The act was condemned by a large number of the American population who considered it a violation of their constitutional rights. Volstead was defeated in the election of 1922 and re-
turned to Minnesota, where he worked as a lawyer. In 1933,
Prohibition was declared a failure and was repealed ("Volstead,
Andrew Joseph" 2001).

William "Bill" Wilson (1895–1971)

Time magazine identified Wilson as one of the twenty people in United States "who articulate the longings of the last 100 years, exemplifying courage, selflessness, exuberance, superhuman ability and amazing grace." He overcame alcoholism and founded the twelve-step program that has helped millions of others do the same. In writing to Carl Jung in 1962, Wilson said, "In the wake of my spiritual experience there came a vision of a society of alcoholics." The following details have been excerpted from "Bill Wilson," written by Susan Cheever for *Time*. Incarcerated for the fourth time at Manhattan's Towns Hospital in 1934, Wilson had a spiritual awakening that led to the founding of Alcoholics Anonymous and his revolutionary twelve-step program, the successful remedy for alcoholism. The twelve steps have also generated successful programs for eating disorders, gambling, narcotics, debting, sex addiction, and people affected by others' addictions. Aldous Huxley called him "the greatest social architect of our century."

Convinced that by helping another alcoholic he could save himself, Wilson found Dr. Robert Smith, a drunk whose family persuaded him to give Wilson fifteen minutes. Their meeting lasted for hours. A month later, Dr. Bob had his last drink, and that date, June 10, 1935, is the official birth date of AA, which is based on the idea that only an alcoholic can help another alcoholic. "Because of our kinship in suffering," Bill wrote, "our channels of contact have always been charged with the language of the heart."

After years of struggling to promote his mission of help to other alcoholics, the *Saturday Evening Post*, in March 1941, published an article on AA, and suddenly thousands of letters and requests poured in. Attendance at meetings doubled and tripled. Wilson had reached his audience. In "Twelve Traditions," Wilson set down the suggested bylaws of Alcoholics Anonymous. In them, he created an enduring blueprint for an organization with a maximum of individual freedom and no accumulation of power or money. Public anonymity ensured humility. No contributions were required; no member could contribute more than $1,000 (now the limit is $2,000).

Today more than 2 million AA members in 150 countries hold meetings in church basements, hospital conference rooms, and school gyms, following Wilson's informal structure. Members identify themselves as alcoholics and share their stories; there are no rules or entry requirements, and many members use only first names.

Wilson believed the key to sobriety was a change of heart. The suggested twelve steps include an admission of powerlessness, a moral inventory, restitution for harm done, a call to service, and surrender to some personal God. Influenced by AA, the American Medical Association has redefined alcoholism as a chronic disease, not a failure of willpower (Cheever 2003).

References

Brown University. 2001. "Former DEA head David Kessler to Discuss Confronting 'Big Tobacco.'" Available at http://www.brown.edu/Administration/News_Bureau/2000-01/00-098.html (accessed January 14, 2004).

Cheever, Susan. 1999. "Bill Wilson." *Time* (June 14). Available at http://www.time.com/time/time100/heroes/profile/wilson01.html (accessed January 14, 2004).

Cockburn, A., and J. St. Clair. 1998. "Race and the Drug War." Available at http://www.counterpunch.org/drugwar.html (accessed January 14, 2004).

Common Sense for Drug Policy. 2002. "Nixon Tapes Reveal Twisted Roots of Marijuana Prohibition." Available at http://www.csdp.org/news/news/nixon.htm (accessed January 14, 2004).

DuPont, R. 1997. "Violence and Drugs." *Journal of Psychoactive Drugs* 29, no. 4 (October–December): 303–305.

Erowid. 2004. "Timothy Leary." Available at http://www.erowid.org/culture/characters/leary_timothy/leary_timothy.shtml (accessed January 14, 2004).

Galliher, John F., David P. Keys, and Michael Elsner. 1998. "*Lindesmith v. Anslinger:* An Early Government Victory in the Failed War on Drugs." *Journal of Criminal Law & Criminology* 88, no. 2 (winter): 661–682. Available at http://www.druglibrary.org/schaffer/History/anslingerlindesmith.htm (accessed January 15, 2004).

Grinspoon, L., and J. Bakalar. "Medical Uses of Illicit Drugs." Schaffer Library of Drug Policy. Available at http://www.druglibrary.org/schaffer/hemp/medical/meduse.htm (accessed January 14, 2004).

Hartsell, D. 1994. "Reefer Madness?" Available at http://www.erowid.org/plants/cannabis/hemp/hemp_media6.shtml (accessed January 14, 2004).

Psychedelic Library Web site. 2004. Available at http://www.psychedelic-library.org (accessed January 14, 2004).

Schlosser, E. 1997. "More Reefer Madness." *Atlantic Monthly* 279, no. 4 (April): 90–120.

Soros, G. 1997. "The Drug War Debate; The Drug War 'Cannot Be Won'; It's Time to Just Say No To Self-Destructive Prohibition." *Washington Post* (February 2). Available at http://www.mega.nu:8080/ampp/drugwar/j79.html (accessed January 15, 2004).

Verkiul, P. 1998. "A Leadership Case of Tobacco and Its Regulation." Available at http://www.upenn.edu/pnc/ptverkuil.html (accessed January 14, 2004).

"Volstead, Andrew Joseph." 2001. *The Columbia Encyclopedia*. 6th ed. Available at http://www.bartleby.com/65/vo/Volstead.html (accessed January 19, 2004).

University of Waterloo. 2001. "Extracts from Benjamin Rush's Inquiry into the Effects of Ardent Spirits upon the Human Body and Mind." Seagram Museum Library Collections. Available at http://www.lib.uwaterloo.ca/seagrams/temper/sea2.html (accessed January 14, 2004).

Wink, W. 1999. "The Fix We're In." Christian Century Foundation. Available at http://www.religion-online.org/cgi-bin/relsearchd.dll/showarticle?item_id=504 (accessed January 14, 2004).

7

Directory of Organizations, Associations, and Agencies

This chapter provides information about organizations, associations, and agencies that address drug issues from supply-and-demand control to legislation reform, prevention education, treatment, and research. The chapter includes details about significant nongovernmental organizations, university-based research centers, and governmental organizations based in the United States and elsewhere. Information for this chapter has been taken from Internet sources accessed in June and July 2003.

Nongovernmental Organizations

Most of the organizations listed below are voluntary groups that draw support and membership from the general public and professionals. Some have a single national office, while others have chapters in various cities. Most of these organizations provide educational materials through their Web sites. Some raise and distribute funds for research; others conduct educational programs for the public and encourage and develop local support groups. A few maintain extensive library resources that may be accessed on-line (for example, Drug Reform Coordination Network [DRC-Net] maintains the Schaffer Library of Drug Policy at http://www.druglibrary.org; the Drug Policy Alliance maintains the Lindesmith Library database at http://library.soros.org; and

Common Sense for Drug Policy provides information through Drug War Facts, http://www.drugwarfacts.org). The following organizations are a few of the many that address drug issues.

Action on Smoking and Health (ASH)
John F. Banzhaf III, Executive Officer
2013 H Street NW
Washington, DC 20006
(202) 659-4310
Web site: http://www.ash.org

Action on Smoking and Health (ASH) is a nonprofit tax-exempt legal-action antismoking organization based in the United States that has been solely devoted to the problems of smoking for more than thirty-five years. Its main activity is to serve as the legal-action arm of the nonsmoking community, bringing or joining in legal actions concerning smoking, and ensuring that the voice of the nonsmoker is heard. It also serves as an advocate of the nonsmokers' rights movement. ASH's executive director, John F. Banzhaf III, has been called the "Ralph Nader of the Tobacco Industry," "Mr. Anti-Smoking," and the "Man behind the Ban on Cigarette Commercials."

Alcoholics Anonymous (AA)
Grand Central Station
P.O. Box 459
New York, NY 10163
(212) 870-3400
Web site: http://www.alcoholics-anonymous.org

Alcoholics Anonymous (AA) is a voluntary worldwide organization of men and women who meet together to attain and maintain sobriety. The only requirement for membership is a desire to stop drinking. There are no dues or fees for AA membership. It is estimated that there are more than 100,000 groups and more than 2 million members in 150 countries. The AA fellowship is not affiliated with any other organization addressing alcoholism, has no opinion on issues outside AA, and neither endorses nor opposes any causes. Alcoholics Anonymous is self-supporting, accepts contributions limited to $2,000 a year from its members, and does not accept contributions from nonmembers. AA is a program of total abstinence; sobriety is maintained through sharing experience and mutual support provided at group meetings.

Anonymity is an essential characteristic of the organization, and the identity of its members is not disclosed.

American Council for Drug Education (ACDE)
William F. Current, Executive Director
204 Monroe Street, Suite 110
Rockville, MD 20850
(800) 488-3784
E-mail: acde@phoenixhouse.org
Web site: http://www.drughelp.org

The American Council for Drug Education (ACDE) was created in 1977 in response to the substance-abuse problem in the United States. Its purpose is to provide the public with access to scientifically based prevention programs and materials. Information on illegal drugs and their effects is made available to people through its publications, broadcast media, films, educational programs, storybooks, and services. ACDE information and education programs are designed for teens, parents, employers, educators, health care providers, policy makers, and others. In 1995, ACDE became an affiliate of the Phoenix House Foundation, the largest private nonprofit drug-abuse service agency in the country.

Association for Medical Education and Research in Substance Abuse (AMERSA)
Isabel Vieira and Doreen MacLane-Baeder, Codirectors
125 Whipple Street, Third Floor
Providence, RI 02908
(401) 349-000 or (877) 418-8769
E-mail: isabel@amersa.org; doreen@amersa.org
Web site: http://www.amersa.org

The Association for Medical Education and Research in Substance Abuse (AMERSA) was founded in 1976 as a multidisciplinary organization of health care professionals dedicated to improving education in the care of individuals with substance-abuse problems. AMERSA provides leadership and training for all health care professionals in the management of alcohol, tobacco, and other drug problems; it disseminates scientific information about substance-abuse education and research through its national conference and journal, *Substance Abuse;* and it works toward promoting a national network of substance-abuse experts who can advise local, national, and international organizations on health professional substance-abuse education through representation at national forums, among other initiatives.

College on Problems of Drug Dependence (CPDD)
Martin W. Adler, Executive Officer
3420 North Broad Street
Philadelphia, PA 19140
(215) 707-3242
Fax: (215) 707-1904
E-mail: baldeagl@temple.edu
Web site: http://www.cpdd.vcu.edu

The College on Problems of Drug Dependence (CPDD), formerly the Committee on Problems of Drug Dependence, has been in existence since 1929. It is the longest-standing organization in the United States addressing problems of drug dependence and abuse. CPDD functions as an independent body affiliated with other scientific and professional societies representing various disciplines concerned with problems of drug dependence and abuse. It maintains cooperation with governmental, industrial, and academic communities as well as educational, treatment, and prevention facilities in the drug-abuse field, including the World Health Organization.

Common Sense for Drug Policy
Melvin Allen, Director
3220 N Street NW, #141
Washington, DC 20007
(202) 299-9780
Fax: (202) 518-4028
E-mail: info@csdp.org
Web site: http://www.csdp.org

Common Sense for Drug Policy is a nonprofit organization with offices in Washington, D.C.; Lancaster, Pa.; and Los Angeles that addresses issues about drug policy, existing laws, and alternatives to current policies. This organization provides advice and technical assistance to individuals and organizations working to reform current policies, promotes coalition building, disseminates research, hosts public forums, provides pro bono legal assistance to those adversely affected by current drug policy, and maintains an extensive and accessible information data bank—Drug War Facts (http://www.drugwarfacts.org).

Community Anti-Drug Coalitions of America (CADCA)
9001 North Pitt Street, Suite 300
Alexandria, VA 22314
(800) 54-CADCA
E-mail: webmaster@cadca.org or info@cadca.org
Web site: http://www.cadca.org

The Community Anti-Drug Coalitions of America (CADCA) promotes development of drug-free communities throughout the United States. This organization draws support and membership for coalitions from multiple sectors of the community, including businesses, parents, media, law enforcement, schools, faith organizations, health providers, social service agencies, and the government. Through its coalition-building efforts, partners organize and develop plans and programs to coordinate their anti-drug efforts.

Drug Abuse Resistance Education (DARE)
Glenn Levant, Executive Director
P.O. Box 512090
Los Angeles, CA 90051-0090
(919) 676-1031
(800) 223-DARE
Fax: (310) 215-0180
E-mail: anita.bryan@dare.com (DARE America educator)

Founded in 1983, Drug Abuse Resistance Education (DARE) is a program that teaches children from kindergarten through twelfth grade how to resist peer pressure and live in a drug-free environment. "Prior to entering the D.A.R.E. program, officers undergo 80 hours of special training in areas such as child development, classroom management, teaching techniques, and communication skills. An additional 40 hours of training are provided to D.A.R.E. instructors to prepare them to teach the high school curriculum." The DARE program is found throughout the United States and other countries.

Drug Policy Alliance
Ethan Nadelmann, Executive Director
925 Fifteenth Street NW, Second Floor
Washington, DC 20005
(202) 216-0035
Fax: (202) 216-0803

E-mail: dc@drugpolicy.org
Web site: http://www.drugpolicy.org/contact/

The Drug Policy Alliance is a major organization addressing drug-policy reform and promoting "alternatives to the war on drugs based on science, compassion, public health and human rights." The alliance was established in 2000 with the objective of building a national drug policy–reform movement. It has offices in New York, San Francisco, and elsewhere throughout the United States. It is the result of a merger of the Lindesmith Center and the Drug Policy Foundation. The guiding principle of the alliance is harm reduction, an alternative approach to drug policy and treatment that focuses on minimizing the adverse effects of both drug use and drug prohibition. The alliance and its affiliated organizations promote education about alternatives to current drug policies on issues ranging from marijuana and adolescent drug use to illicit-drug addiction, the spread of infectious diseases, policing drug markets, and alternatives to incarceration.

Drug Reform Coordination Network (DRCNet)
David Borden, Executive Director
1623 Connecticut Avenue NW, Third Floor
Washington, DC 20009
(202) 293-8340
Fax: (202) 293-8344
E-mail: drcnet@drcnet.org
Web site: http://www.drcnet.org/aboutdrc/

The Drug Reform Coordination Network (DRCNet) was founded in 1993. This national organization promotes drug-policy reform from a variety of perspectives, including harm reduction, reform of sentencing and forfeiture laws, medical use of current Schedule I drugs, and promotion of an open debate on drug prohibition. DRCNet has a well-developed information-gathering and -distribution capability. It maintains the Schaffer Library of Drug Policy at http://www.druglibrary.org, a major source of information about the history of drug policy, and provides regular information about drug-policy issues though an Internet newsletter.

Drug Strategies
Marie Dyak, Executive Director
1150 Connecticut Avenue NW, Suite 100
Washington, DC 20036

(202) 289-9070
E-mail: dspolicy@aol.com
Web site: http://www.drugstrategies.org

Drug Strategies promotes effective approaches to the nation's drug problems and supports private and public efforts to reduce the demand for drugs through prevention, education, treatment, law enforcement, and community initiatives. Among its efforts, Drug Strategies conducts an annual review of federal drug-control spending, and its "Keeping Score" initiative has become a major resource for improving understanding of the impact of federal drug policy. Drug Strategies is developing a new interactive Web site that helps teenagers connect to counseling and treatment within their own communities.

Drug Watch International
Sandra S. Bennett, President
P.O. Box 45218
Omaha, NE 68145-0218
(402) 384-9212
Web site: http://www.drugwatch.org

Drug Watch International is a network of experts and community volunteers from a wide range of professions whose mission is to prevent drug use. This is accomplished by promoting sound drug policies based on scientific research and opposing efforts to legalize or decriminalize drugs. The purpose of Drug Watch International is to provide policy makers, the media, and the public with current information, factual research, and expert resources, and to counter drug-advocacy propaganda.

Hazelden Foundation
Ellen L. Breyer, President and CEO
P.O. Box 11-CO3
Center City, MN 55012-0011
(800) 257-7810
E-mail: info@hazelden.org
Web site: http://www.hazelden.org/visit_us.dbm

Founded in 1949, the Hazelden Foundation has been a pioneer in the treatment of alcoholism and other drug dependency. It has successfully helped thousands of men, women, and young people with their substance-abuse problems. Hazelden Foundation programs have served as models for many other successful treatment centers all over the world. Its intensive program integrates sound professional practices, which include individualized planning by a multidisciplinary team, with the principles of Alcoholics Anonymous.

Join Together
David Rosenbloom, Director
1 Appleton Street, Fourth Floor
Boston, MA 02116-5223
(617) 437-1500
Fax: (617) 437-9394
E-mail: info@jointogether.org
Web site: http://www.jointogether.org/

Join Together, founded in 1991, supports community-based efforts to reduce, prevent, and treat substance abuse across the nation. This organization is primarily supported by a grant from the Robert Wood Johnson Foundation at the Boston University School of Public Health. Through its Web sites and services, its partnerships with twenty-nine cities, and its alliances with key cosponsors, it helps communities develop and implement strategies designed to improve drug-treatment services. Join Together maintains Join Together Online (JTO), which publishes a daily newsletter on drug and violence information, including current events, professional publications, and government reports. JTO is a major information source recommended for keeping informed of drug-related issues.

Mothers Against Drunk Driving (MADD)
Dean Wilkerson, National Executive Director
511 East John Carpenter Freeway, #700
Irving, TX 75062
(214) 744-6233, ext. 218
Fax: (972) 869-2206
E-mail: heard@madd.org
Web site: http://madd.org

Mothers Against Drunk Driving (MADD) is a nonprofit grassroots organization with more than 600 chapters nationwide. It was founded by a small group of California women in 1980 after a hit-and-run driver killed a thirteen-year-old girl. The focus of MADD is to look for effective solutions to drunk driving and underage drinking problems, while supporting those who have already experienced the pain of these "senseless crimes."

National Association for Children of Alcoholics (NACoA)
Sis Wenger, Executive Director
11426 Rockville Pike, Suite 100
Rockville, MD 20852
(888) 554-COAS
Fax: (301) 468-0985
E-mail: nacoa@nacoa.org
Web site: http://www.nacoa.org/aboutnacoa.htm

The National Association for Children of Alcoholics (NACoA), founded in 1983, is the national nonprofit membership organization working on behalf of children of alcohol- and drug-dependent parents. The mission of NACoA is to advocate for children and families affected by alcoholism and other drug dependencies. This organization raises public awareness; provides leadership in public policy at the national, state, and local levels; advocates appropriate, effective, and accessible education and prevention services; and promotes professional knowledge and understanding.

National Council on Alcoholism and Drug Dependence (NCADD)
Stacia Murphy, Executive Director
20 Exchange Place, Suite 2902
New York, NY 10005
(212) 269-7797
Fax: (212) 269-7510
E-mail: national@ncadd.org
Web site: http://www.ncadd.org

Founded in 1944 by Marty Mann, the first woman to find long-term sobriety in Alcoholics Anonymous, the National Council on Alcoholism and Drug Dependence (NCADD) provides education, information, help, and hope to the public. It advocates prevention, intervention, and treatment through offices in New York and Washington, D.C., and a nationwide network of affiliates.

National Organization of Reform for Marijuana Laws (NORML)
R. Keith Stroup, Executive Director
1600 K Street NW, Suite 501
Washington, DC 20006-2832
(202) 483-5500

Fax: (202) 483-0057
E-mail: norml@norml.org
Web site: http://www.norml.org

The National Organization of Reform for Marijuana Laws (NORML) was founded in 1970 as a nonprofit public-interest advocacy group representing the interests of Americans who smoke marijuana responsibly. NORML leads the fight to reform state and federal marijuana laws, whether by voter initiative or through the elected legislatures. This organization serves as an informational resource to the national media on marijuana-related stories. It lobbies state and federal legislators in support of reform legislation; publishes a regular newsletter; hosts, along with the NORML Foundation, an informative Web site and an annual conference; and serves as the umbrella group for a national network of citizen-activists committed to ending marijuana prohibition and legalizing marijuana.

Partnership for a Drug-Free America (PDFA)
405 Lexington Avenue, Suite 1601
New York, NY 10174
(212) 922-1560
Fax: (212) 922-1570
Web site: http://www.drugfreeamerica.org

The Partnership for a Drug-Free America (PDFA), established in 1986, is a nonprofit coalition of professionals from the communications industry. Through its national drug-education advertising campaign and other forms of media communication, the partnership helps kids and teens reject substance abuse. With roots in the advertising industry, the partnership is composed of a small staff and hundreds of volunteers who create and disseminate the partnership's work. PDFA receives major funding from the Robert Wood Johnson Foundation and support from more than 200 corporations and companies.

The Robert Wood Johnson Foundation—Substance Abuse Policy Research Program
David Altman, National Program Director
Substance Abuse Policy Research Program
Center for Creative Leadership
One Leadership Place
P.O. Box 26300

Greensboro, NC 27438-6300
(336) 286-4418
Fax: (336) 286-4434
Web site: http://www.phs.bgsm.edu/sshp/rwj

The Robert Wood Johnson Foundation seeks to improve the health and health care of all Americans. Among the goals of the foundation is reducing the personal, social, and economic harm caused by substance abuse—tobacco, alcohol, and illicit drugs. To accomplish this objective, the foundation supports training, education, research (excluding biomedical research), and projects that demonstrate the effective delivery of health care services.

University-Based Drug Research and Policy Centers

Monitoring the Future Study, University of Michigan (MFT)
Lloyd D. Johnston, Ph.D., Program Director
University of Michigan
Ann Arbor, MI 48109
E-mail: MTFinfo@isr.umich.edu
Web site: http://monitoringthefuture.org/

The Monitoring the Future (MFT) project, begun in 1975, has many purposes. Among them is to study changes in the beliefs, attitudes, and behavior of young people in the United States. This study focuses on youths from the eighth to the twelfth grades. Approximately 50,000 students in about 420 public and private secondary schools nationwide are surveyed annually.

National Center on Addiction and Substance Abuse at Columbia University (CASA)
Joseph Califano Jr., President and Chairman
633 Third Avenue, Nineteenth Floor
New York, NY 10017-6706
(212) 841-5200
Web site: http://www.casacolumbia.org

The National Center on Addiction and Substance Abuse at Columbia University (CASA) is an organization that brings together multiple professional disciplines to address drug-policy issues through research, education, and related activities. CASA efforts address all substances—alcohol, tobacco, and illegal drugs. Through its Web site, CASA provides useful information about organizations that address drug problems.

Rutgers University, Center of Alcohol Studies (CAS)
Robert J. Pandina, Director
607 Allison Road
Piscataway, NJ 08854-8001
(732) 445-2190
Fax: (732) 445-3500
E-mail: rpandina@rci.rutgers.edu
Web site: http://www.rci.rutgers.edu/~cas2

The Center of Alcohol Studies (CAS) evolved in the late 1930s and 1940s at the Yale University Laboratory of Applied Physiology and relocated in 1962 to Rutgers University. The center has research programs and pre- and postdoctoral training in biochemistry, clinical and experimental psychology, neuropharmacology, sociology, public health, education, and prevention.

University of California, Integrated Substance Abuse Programs (ISAP)
Walter Ling, Director
11075 Santa Monica Boulevard, Suite 200
Los Angeles, CA 90025
(310) 312-0500, ext. 317
E-mail: darc@ucla.edu
Web site: http://www.uclaisap.org

The UCLA Integrated Substance Abuse Programs (ISAP) coordinates substance-abuse research and treatment within the Department of Psychiatry and Biobehavioral Sciences at the UCLA School of Medicine. ISAP is one of the largest substance-abuse research groups in the United States. It maintains an extensive program of substance-abuse research, education, training, and information transfer on national and international levels.

University of Kentucky, Center on Drug and Alcohol Research (CDAR)
Carl Leukefeld, Director
643 Maxwelton Court
Lexington, KY 40506-0350
(859) 257-2355

Fax: (859) 323-1193
E-mail: krieger@uky.edu
Web site: http://www.uky.edu/RGS/CDAR/index.html

The Center on Drug and Alcohol Research (CDAR) at the University of Kentucky, established in 1990, builds on addiction research that began more than five decades ago in Lexington. Presently, it conducts research, teaching, and service related to the biological, psychological, sociocultural, and clinical aspects of substance use, abuse, and dependency. The center brings together faculty from various universities and colleges with interests in drug and alcohol addiction.

University of Maryland, Center for Substance Abuse Research (CESAR)
Eric Wish, Director
4321 Hartwick Road, Suite 501
College Park, MD 20740
(301) 403-8329
Fax: (301) 403-8342
E-mail: cesar@cesar.umd.edu
Web site: http://www.cesar.umd.edu

The Center for Substance Abuse Research (CESAR) at the University of Maryland was established in 1990. CESAR provides information to policy makers, practitioners, and the general public about substance abuse—its nature and scope, its prevention and treatment, and its relation to other problems. The center conducts research and evaluation studies, disseminates information, and provides training and technical assistance to agencies and organizations working in substance abuse–related fields.

Governmental Organizations

Center for Substance Abuse Prevention (CSAP)
Beverly Watts Davis, Director
Substance Abuse and Mental Health Services Administration
Rm 12-105 Parklawn Building
5600 Fishers Lane
Rockville, MD 20857
(301) 443-8956
(800) WORKPLACE

E-mail: info@samhsa.gov
Web site: http://prevention.samhsa.gov

The Center for Substance Abuse Prevention (CSAP) provides national leadership in the development of policies, programs, and services to prevent the onset of illegal-drug use and underage alcohol and tobacco use, and to reduce the negative consequences of using substances. CSAP promotes a comprehensive prevention-system approach that includes community involvement and partnership among all sectors of society.

Center for Substance Abuse Treatment (CSAT)
Westley Clark, Director
Substance Abuse and Mental Health Services Administration
Rm 12-105 Parklawn Building
5600 Fishers Lane
Rockville, MD 20857
(301) 443-8956
(800) 662-HELP
E-mail: info@samhsa.gov
Web site: http://www.samhsa.gov

The Center for Substance Abuse Treatment (CSAT) is responsible for expanding the availability of effective treatment and recovery services for alcohol and drug problems. CSAT supports the nation's effort to provide multiple treatment modalities, evaluate treatment effectiveness, and use evaluation results to enhance treatment and recovery approaches.

National Clearinghouse for Alcohol and Drug Information (NCADI)
John Noble, Director
P.O. Box 2345
Rockville, MD 20847-2345
(301) 729-6686
(800) 729-6686
Fax: (301) 468-6433
E-mail: webmaster@health.org
Web site: http://ncadi.samhsa.gov/

The National Clearinghouse for Alcohol and Drug Information (NCADI) is the information service of the Center for Substance Abuse Prevention (CSAP). NCADI is the world's largest resource for current information and materials concerning substance abuse. NCADI services include: (1) information available in English and Spanish and for the deaf; (2) the distribution of free or low-cost ATOD materials, including fact sheets, brochures, pamphlets, monographs, posters, and videotapes; (3) culturally diverse prevention, intervention, and treatment resources tailored for use by parents, teachers, youths, communities, and prevention/treatment professionals; (4) customized searches in the form of annotated bibliographies from alcohol and drug databases; (5) access to the Prevention Materials Database, including more than 8,000 prevention-related materials and the Treatment Resources Database available to the public in electronic form; and (6) rapid dissemination of federal grant announcements for alcohol and drug prevention, treatment, and research funding opportunities.

National Institute on Alcohol Abuse and Alcoholism (NIAAA)
Ting-kai Li, Director
Willco Building
6000 Executive Boulevard
Bethesda, MD 20892-7003
Web site: http://www.niaaa.nih.gov

The National Institute on Alcohol Abuse and Alcoholism (NIAAA) provides leadership in the national effort to reduce alcohol-related problems by (1) conducting and supporting research in a wide range of scientific areas; (2) coordinating and collaborating with other research institutes and federal programs on alcohol-related issues; (3) collaborating with international, national, state, and local institutions, organizations, agencies, and programs engaged in alcohol-related work; and (4) translating and disseminating research findings to health care providers, researchers, policy makers, and the public.

National Institute on Drug Abuse (NIDA)
Nora Volkow, Director
National Institutes of Health
6001 Executive Boulevard, Room 5213
Bethesda, MD 20892-9561
(301) 443-1124
E-mail: information@lists.nida.nih.gov
Web site: http://www.drugabuse.gov/about/AboutNIDA.html

The National Institute on Drug Abuse (NIDA), part of the National Institutes of Health, Department of Health and Human Services, focuses on key issues about drug abuse, ranging from the molecule to managed care, and from DNA to community-outreach research. NIDA supports more than 85 percent of the world's research on the health aspects of drug abuse and addiction.

National Youth Anti-Drug Campaign
(800) 788-2800
Web site: http://www.mediacampaign.org

The National Youth Anti-Drug Campaign is a program of the White House Office of National Drug Control Policy. The media campaign is designed to educate and empower youths to reject illicit drugs. The campaign uses a variety of media to reach parents and youths, including TV ads, educational materials, Web sites, and publications.

Regional Alcohol and Drug Awareness Resource (RADAR) Network (NCADI/SAMHSA)
M. Cornelius Pierce
Manager RADAR Network Center Development
P.O. Box 2345
Rockville, Maryland 20847-2345
(800) 729-6686, Ext. 5111
Web site: http://ncadi.samsha.gov

The Regional Alcohol and Drug Awareness Resource (RADAR) Network was formed in partnership with state governments and national constituency groups to provide information to prevention practitioners and other community members interested in addressing alcohol, tobacco, and other drug problems. RADAR Network centers are located in every state and U.S. territory. In addition to state RADAR Network centers designated by state governments, the network includes specialty RADAR Network centers that operate at the national level, associate members that work at the community level, and international organizations.

Substance Abuse and Mental Health Services Administration (SAMHSA)
Charles G. Curie, Administrator

Parklawn Building, Room 12-105
5600 Fishers Lane
Rockville, MD 20857
(301) 443-4795
Fax: (301) 443-0284
E-mail: info@samhsa.gov
Web site: http://www.samhsa.gov

The Substance Abuse and Mental Health Services Administration (SAMHSA) was established to provide prevention, diagnosis, and treatment services for substance abuse and mental illnesses. SAMHSA serves as the umbrella under which substance-abuse and mental health–service centers are housed, including the Center for Mental Health Services (CMHS), the Center for Substance Abuse Prevention (CSAP), and the Center for Substance Abuse Treatment (CSAT). SAMHSA also houses the Office of the Administrator, the Office of Applied Studies, and the Office of Program Services.

White House Office of National Drug Control Policy (ONDCP)
John Walters, Director
Drug Policy Information Clearinghouse
P.O. Box 6000
Rockville, MD 20849-6000
1-800-666-3332
Fax: 301-519-5212
E-mail: ondcp@ncjrs.org
Web site: http://www.whitehousedrugpolicy.gov

The White House Office of National Drug Control Policy (ONDCP), established in 1988, is a component of the executive office of the president. The principal purpose of ONDCP is to establish policies, priorities, and objectives for the nation's drug-control program related to the reduction of illicit-drug use, manufacturing, and trafficking; drug-related crime and violence; and drug-related health consequences. By law, the director of ONDCP evaluates, coordinates, and oversees both the international and domestic antidrug efforts of executive-branch agencies and ensures that such efforts sustain and complement state and local antidrug activities.

International Organizations

Canadian Centre on Substance Abuse (CCSA)
Michel Perron, Chief Executive Officer
75 Albert Street, Suite 300
Ottawa, Ontario K1P 5E7
Canada
(613) 235-4048
Fax: (613) 235-8101
E-mail: info@ccsa.ca
Web site: http://www.ccsa.ca

The Canadian Centre on Substance Abuse (CCSA) is a national agency established in 1988. The center promotes debate on substance-abuse issues; disseminates information on the nature, extent, and consequences of substance abuse; and supports and assists organizations involved in substance-abuse treatment, prevention, and educational programming.

Centre for Drug Research, University of Amsterdam, the Netherlands (CEDRO)
Faculty of Social and Behavioural Sciences
SCO-Kohnstamm Instituut
Wibautstraat 4, 1091 GM
Amsterdam
The Netherlands
P.O. Box 94208, 1090 GE
Amsterdam
The Netherlands
31-20-525-4278
Fax: 31-20-525-4317
E-mail: info@cedro-uva.org
Web site: http://www.cedro-uva.org/about.html

The Centre for Drug Research (CEDRO) was established in 1996. Its goal is to conduct social research in the fields of drug use, drug policy, and drug distribution; disseminate information; and promote international communication about various aspects of the drug problem from a social perspective.

Drugtext and the Foundation on Drug Policy and Human Rights

Mario Louis Sylvester Lap, Director
Koninginneweg 189
1075 CP Amsterdam
The Netherlands
31-20-664-4086
E-mail: mario@drugtext.org
Web site: http://www.drugtext.org

The purpose of both Drugtext and the Foundation on Drug Policy and Human Rights is to promote the development and dissemination of knowledge, research, education, scholarship, and international jurisprudence in the area of drug policy and human rights. Drugtext is a nonprofit foundation under Dutch law providing Internet services for the International Harm Reduction Association, the International Foundation on Drug Policy & Human Rights, and the Foundation on Drug Policy and Human Rights.

European Working Group on Drugs Oriented Research (EWODOR)

Rowdy Yates, Director
Department of Applied Social Science
Cottrell Building, Room 4B48
University of Stirling
Stirling, FK9 4LA
Scotland
44-(0)-1786-467695
Fax: 44-(0)-1786-466299
E-mail: p.r.yates@stir.ac.uk
Web site: http://www.stir.ac.uk/Departments/HumanSciences/
AppSocSci/DRUGS/ewodor.htm

The European Working Group on Drugs Oriented Research (EWODOR) was founded in 1986 to provide a forum enabling researchers in the field of drug/alcohol treatment, prevention, and policy to share research experience and expertise; compare procedures, methods, and results; and subject their work to peer examination. EWODOR provides (1) an annual symposium for the presentation of current/recent research in the drug/alcohol field,

(2) an on-line discussion site for the exchange of information, and (3) the archiving of research findings in the drug/alcohol field as a means by which researchers can communicate.

United Nations Office on Drugs and Crime (UNODC)
Antonio Maria Costa, Executive Director
Vienna International Centre
P.O. Box 500
A-1400 Vienna
Austria
43 1 26060 0
Fax: 43 1 26060 5866
E-mail: odccp@odccp.org
Web site: http://www.unodc.org/odccp.html

The United Nations Office on Drugs and Crime (UNODC) is a global leader in the fight against illicit drugs and international crime. Established in 1997, UNODC consists of the Drug Programme and the Crime Programme. Its headquarters are in Vienna with offices in New York and Brussels. UNODC publishes reports about drug use on a region-by-region basis in English, Spanish, French, Arabic, Russian, and Chinese.

World Health Organization (WHO)
Gro Harlem Brundtland, Director General
Avenue Appia 20
1211 Geneva 27
Switzerland
41 22 791 21 11
Fax: 41-22-791-31-11
E-mail: info@who.int
Web site: http://www.who.int/about/contacthq/en/

The World Health Organization (WHO), the UN specialized agency for health, was established on April 7, 1948. WHO conducts and supports research, provides technical assistance, advocates health care policy, and has an extensive library of information resources on health-related issues, including tobacco, alcohol, and illicit drugs, that may be accessed at: http://www. who.int/library/reference/tutorials/wholis/index.en.shtml.

8

Print and Nonprint Resources

Literally thousands of books, journals, articles, news stories, and research studies have been written on the drug problem. Each substance (that is, tobacco, alcohol, marijuana, heroin, and cocaine), as well as each aspect of the problem, such as prevention and treatment, generates vast amounts of information. The goal of this chapter is to identify key resources that are accessible and offer a variety of views of the drug problem. A few choice books are included because of content. Key journal articles are not provided; however, the major outlets for scientific publications and newsletters are listed with contact information. The chapter also supplies addresses to nongovernmental and governmental Web sites that provide access to keyword search information. The resources in this chapter should equip the reader with an adequate amount of contact information for reference and research purposes. The final section of the chapter is a comprehensive listing of the sources used to compile this reference handbook.

Books

Barr, Andrew. 1999. *Drink: A Social History of America.* New York: Carroll & Graff.

In this cultural history of drink in the United States, the author considers the significance of alcohol, historically and socially, symbolic and real, in the evolution of a nation born of a rebel

215

spirit and intoxicated by liberty. Barr examines not only the social influences that determine what, where, with whom, and why we choose to drink but also the scapegoating of alcohol by moral alarmists, the medical establishment, and platform politicians who have more often produced dubious cures than they have accomplished social good.

Falkowski, Carol L. 2003. *Dangerous Drugs: An Easy to Use Reference for Parents and Professionals.* 2d ed. Center City, MN: Hazelden.

This authoritative, up-to-date reference guide describes the latest drugs to hit the community: what they look like, where they come from, and why they are dangerous. Featuring a color photo section, the second edition of *Dangerous Drugs* is an effective reference tool for parents and professionals alike. Easy-to-understand profiles of common legal and illegal drugs include information about how the substance affects the mind, body, and behavior; its addictive and overdose potential; and symptoms and signs of abuse.

Goode, Erich. 1998. *Drugs in American Society.* New York: McGraw-Hill.

This well-respected text probes the drug phenomenon in all its social, cultural, and legal complexity. It covers the full range of psychoactive drug use—from legal medical and prescription use to criminal and recreational use, from casual use to addiction. As in previous editions, Goode remains unique in his emphasis on the sociological perspective, explaining the drug phenomenon using sociological concepts supported by recent data from a wide range of sources. *Drugs in American Society* provides a balanced and up-to-date investigation of drug use.

Gray, Mike. 2000. *Drug Crazy: How We Got into This Mess and How We Can Get Out.* New York: Routledge.

Arguing that the federal government's $300 billion campaign to eradicate drug use over the past fifteen years has been a total failure, Gray calls for legalization of drugs and governmental regulation of their sale, with doctors writing prescriptions to addicts. Although there is a lack of specifics about how this would work and the potential consequences, his argument for decriminalization is strengthened by a revealing history of drug use in the United States.

Isralowitz, R., M. Afifi, and R. Rawson, eds. 2002. *Drug Problems: Cross-Cultural Policy and Program Development.* Westport, CT: Auburn House.

This edited book is the first to be published on the drug problem that exists among people in the Middle East, particularly Israelis and Palestinians. Prepared with support provided by the U.S. Agency for International Development, Regional Middle East Co-operation Program, the book has been referred to as what could be accomplished if "nations not lift up swords any more . . .and beat them into plowshares." This book offers chapters on drug use among Palestinians as well as Israeli Arab and Jewish people, bedouin Arabs, and Russian immigrants. The Israeli and Palestinian authors are equally and well represented throughout this book, joined by their colleagues from the World Health Organization and the United States.

Kessler, David A. 2001. *A Question of Intent: A Great American Battle with a Deadly Industry.* New York: PublicAffairs.

This is the David-and-Goliath story of how an American bureaucrat took on the tobacco industry and helped change its methods of operation. This is a story of power politics and how David Kessler, head of the Food and Drug Administration for seven years under Presidents Bush and Clinton, and his team of lawyers, scientists, advocates, and others were instrumental in forcing tobacco companies to admit that nicotine is addictive and cigarettes cause cancer, and in bringing about a sea change in the industry's legal and popular standing.

Marlatt, Alan G., David C. Lewis, and David B. Abrams, eds. 1998. *Harm Reduction: Pragmatic Strategies for Managing High-Risk Behaviors.* New York: Guilford.

Harm-reduction principles and strategies are designed to minimize the destructive consequences of illicit-drug use and other behaviors that may pose serious health risks. Rather than insisting on abstinence as a prerequisite to continued treatment, proponents of the harm-reduction approach aim to meet drug users "where they're at" with community-based services that empower diverse clients to set and meet their own treatment goals. The first major harm-reduction text, this provocative and timely volume examines a wide range of current applications—from needle exchange and methadone maintenance programs to alternative alcohol interventions and AIDS-prevention campaigns. Insight is also offered into the often contentious philosophical and policy-related debates surrounding this growing movement.

Massing, Michael. 2000. *The Fix.* Berkeley: University of California Press.

Michael Massing exposes the political and ideological narrow-mindedness that has made national drug policy a failure, and demonstrates convincingly why we should reinstate the policy that worked. Drawing on scores of interviews with federal officials charged with directing the drug war and on years of on-the-street reporting, Massing offers a fresh new way of looking at the drug problem. The heart of that problem lies not with recreational users of marijuana, as many politicians and journalists maintain, but with hard-core users of heroin, crack, and cocaine.

Ray, Oakley S., and Charles Ksir. 2004. *Drugs, Society, and Human Behavior.* 10th ed. New York: McGraw-Hill.

The long-time market leader, this book examines drugs from all perspectives, including behavioral, pharmacological, historical, social, legal, and clinical. The book is well designed, providing current facts and information. It is a primary resource for information about the use and abuse drugs.

Schuckit, Mark. 1997. *Drug and Alcohol Abuse: A Clinical Guide to Diagnosis and Treatment.* 4th ed. New York: Plenum.

This book provides an overview of drug mechanisms and drug classification, and covers pharmacology and mental and physical symptoms of depressants, alcohol, stimulants, opiates, cannabis, hallucinogens, caffeine, and nicotine as well as over-the-counter and prescription drugs. The book includes sections on emergency conditions and rehabilitation as well information on comorbid, or dual-diagnosis, issues and new pharmacological treatments.

Straussner, L., and S. Brown, eds. 2000. *The Handbook of Addiction Treatment for Women.* San Francisco: Jossey-Bass.

This edited book addresses the special needs of women who are addicted to drugs, alcohol, and other self-destructive behaviors. Chapters consider the reasons underlying women's additive behavior and addictive thinking, the history of women and addiction, the challenges of the female addict, and issues of diagnosis and treatment. Particular attention is given to differences of age, ethnicity, and circumstance.

Journals and Newsletters

The following list includes journals and newsletters devoted to substance-abuse topics. For most titles, the journal/newsletter's scope, author guidelines, contents, and subscription information are presented at the URL listed. A few journals provide the full-text articles on-line. These references have been drawn from information prepared by the Alcohol & Drug Abuse Institute Library (Nancy Sutherland), University of Washington for the Substance Abuse Librarians and Information Specialists (SALIS): An International Organization, http://salis.org/resources/journals.htm, updated June 19, 2002.

ABMRF Journal. Abstracting and news journal of the Alcohol Beverage Medical Research Foundation. http://www.abmrf.org/journal.htm

Addiction. Contents, subscription information, and instructions for contributors. http://www.addictionjournal.org

Addiction Abstracts. Contents and subscription information. http://www.tandf.co.uk/addiction-abs

Addiction Biology. Contents, subscription information, and instructions for contributors. http://www.tandf.co.uk/journals/titles/13556215.html

Addiction Research and Theory. Aims and scope, instructions for authors, and subscription information. http://www.tandf.co.uk/journals/titles/16066359.html

Addiction Treatment Forum. Newsletter; full text. http://www.atforum.com

Addictions Newsletter. From the American Psychological Association. http://www.kumc.edu/addictions_newsletter

Addictive Behaviors. Contents, guide for authors, and order information. http://www.elsevier.nl/inca/publications/store/4/7/1/

Adicciones. Published by *Socidrogalcohol*, a quarterly journal on alcohol and other drug problems, widely distributed in Spanish-speaking countries; on-line abstracts in Spanish and English. http://www.adicciones.org

Alcohol. "An International Biomedical Journal," published by Elsevier. Contents, order information, and guide for authors. http://www.elsevier.nl/locate/alcohol

Alcohol Alerts. From NIAAA. Full text. http://www.niaaa.nih.gov/publications/alalerts.htm

Alcohol and Alcoholism. Subscription information and instructions for authors. http://alcalc.oupjournals.org/

Alcohol Research & Health. NIAAA's quarterly journal (with abstracts); formerly *Alcohol Health & Research World*. http://www.niaaa.nih.gov/publications/aharw.htm

Alcohol, Tobacco, and Other Drugs Section Newsletter. Newsletter of American Public Health Association. ATOD section. http://www.apha.org/sections/newsletterintro.htm

Alcoholis. On-line newsletter of the Medical Council on Alcoholism (UK). http://www.medicouncilalcol.demon.co.uk/news.htm

Alcoholism Treatment Quarterly. Contents, subscription information, and author instructions. http://www.haworthpressinc.com

Alcoholism: Clinical & Experimental Research. Official journal of the Research Society on Alcoholism. Editorial scope, contents with abstracts, author guide, and subscription information. http://www.alcoholism-cer.com/

American Indian & Alaska Native Mental Health Research. Journal of the National Center for American Indian and Alaska Native Mental Health Research, University of Colorado. http://www.uchsc.edu/ai/ncaianmhr/journal/

American Journal of Drug and Alcohol Abuse. Contents with abstracts, author guidelines, editorial scope, and order information. http://www.dekker.com/servlet/product/productid/ADA

American Journal on Addictions. American Psychiatric Association. Contents, author instructions, and order information. http://www.tandf.co.uk/journals/titles/10550496.html

Drug and Alcohol Dependence. Official journal of the College on Problems of Drug Dependence. Contents, abstracts, order information, and author guidelines. http://www.elsevier.nl/inca/publications/store/5/0/6/0/5/2/

Drug and Alcohol Review. Contents, subscription information, and instructions for contributors. http://www.apsad.org.au

Drug Dependence, Alcohol Abuse, and Alcoholism: Exerpta Medica Abstract Journal. Scope and order information. http://www.elsevier.com/locate/drug

Drug Policy Analysis Bulletin. Newsletter of the American Federation of Scientists. http://www.fas.org

Drugs: Education, Prevention & Policy. Contents, subscription information, and instructions for contributors. http://www.tandf.co.uk/journals/titles/09687637.html

EGambling: Electronic Journal of Gambling Issues (Centre for Addiction & Mental Health). Peer-reviewed; author guidelines. http://www.camh.net/egambling

Employee Assistance Quarterly. Contents, subscription information, and author instructions. http://www.haworthpressinc.com/web/EAQ/

European Addiction Research. Contents, author instructions, and subscription information. http://www.karger.com/ear

International Journal of Drug Policy. Official journal of the International Harm Reduction Association. Contents, abstracts, order information, and author guidelines. Full text of vols. 1–8 made available by Drugtext. http://www.medwebplus. com/obj/25742

International Journal of Drug Testing. On-line journal, full text. http://www.criminology.fsu.edu/journal

The Journal of Addiction and Mental Health. Centre for Addiction and Mental Health. Full text; order information. Published by the Addiction Research Foundation. http://www.camh.net

Journal of Addictions and Offender Counseling. Official journal of the International Association of Addictions and Offender Counselors. Author guidelines. http://www.counseling. org/publications/journals.htm

Journal of Addictions Nursing. Official journal of the National Nurses Society on Addictions. Selected contents, instructions to authors, and subscription information. http://www. liebertpub. com

Journal of Addictive Diseases. Official journal of the American Society on Addiction Medicine (ASAM). Contents, abstracts, and instructions for authors. http://www.asam.org/jol/journal.htm

Journal of Alcohol and Drug Education. Contents and author guidelines. http://www.unomaha.edu/~healthed/JADE.html

Journal of Chemical Dependency Treatment. Official journal of the National Association of Addiction Treatment Professionals. Contents, subscription information, and author guidelines. Search for title at publisher site: http://www.haworthpressinc. com/web/JCDT/

Journal of Child & Adolescent Substance Abuse. Contents, subscription information, and author guidelines. Search for title at publisher site: http://www.haworthpressinc.com/web/JCASA/

Journal of Drug Education. Selected articles, author instructions, and subscription information. Search for title at publisher site: http://www.novapublishers.com/journal

Journal of Drug Issues. Contents, author instructions, and subscription information. http://www2.criminology.fsu.edu/~jdi

Journal of Ethnicity in Substance Abuse. Formerly *Drugs & Society.* Contents, subscription information, and author guidelines. Search for title at publisher site: http://www.haworthpressinc. com/web/JESA/

Journal of Maintenance in the Addictions: Innovations in Research, Theory and Practice. Contents, subscription information, and author guidelines. Search for title at publisher site: http://www.haworthpressinc.com/web/JMA/

Journal of Ministry in Addiction and Recovery. Contents, subscription information, and author guidelines. Search for title at publisher site: http://www.haworthpressinc.com/web/JMAR/

Journal of Psychoactive Drugs. Subscription information. http://www.hafci.org/journal

Journal of Social Work Practice in the Addictions. Contents, subscription information, author guidelines. Search for title at publisher site: http://www.haworthpressinc.com/web/JSWPA/

Journal of Studies on Alcohol. Editorial and subscription information. http://www.rci.rutgers.edu/~cas2/journal

Journal of Substance Abuse Treatment. Contents, author instructions, and order information. http://www.elsevier.com/locate /jsat

Journal of Substance Use. Formerly *Journal of Substance Misuse for Nursing, Health and Social Care.* Contents and scope. http:// www.tandf.co.uk/journals/titles/14659891.html

Morbidity and Mortality Weekly Report (MMWR). Centers of Disease Control. http://www.cdc.gov/mmwr

NIAAA Surveillance Reports. From Alcohol Epidemiologic Data System, on per capita alcohol consumption, liver cirrhosis mortality, alcohol-related traffic crashes, and alcohol-related morbidity based on hospital discharges. PDF format. http:// www.cdc.gov/mmwr/

Nicotine & Tobacco Research. Journal of Society for Research on Nicotine and Tobacco. Contents and author instructions. http://www.tandf.co.uk

NIDA Notes. National Institute on Drug Abuse. Full text. http://www.drugabuse.gov/NIDA_Notes/NNIndex.html

Prevention File: Alcohol, Tobacco, and Other Drugs. Subscription information; some issues full text. http://www.adp. cahwnet.gov/TA/TA_PF.shtml

Prevention Pipeline. Center for Substance Abuse Prevention (CSAP). http://www.health.org/pubs/prevpipe

Prevention Researcher. Newsletter published by Integrated Research Services. http://www.health.org/govpubs/MS510/Articles.htm

Psychology of Addictive Behaviors. Contents, abstracts, and author instructions. http://www.apa.org/journals/adb.html

Pulse Check. U.S. Office of National Drug Control Policy publication, index for this and other ONDCP publications. http://www. whitehousedrugpolicy.gov/publications/drugfact/ pulsechk/f

RANES Report. Roizen's Alcohol News & Editorial Service. Ron Roizen, editor and publisher. http://www.roizen.com

Self-Help Magazine. Full text. http://www.shpm.com

Smoking and Tobacco Control Monograph Series. National Cancer Institute. Full text. http://cancercontrol.cancer.gov/tcrb/ monographs/

Social History of Alcohol Review. Scholarly magazine published by Alcohol and History Temperance Group. http://www. athg.org/

Substance Abuse. Official journal of AMERSA. Editorial scope and subscription information. http://www.amersa.org/Amersa/ameWeb.nsf/Pages/Substance+Abuse

Substance Misuse Bulletin. Centre for Addiction Studies, London. http://www.sghms.ac.uk/depts/addictive-behaviour/ infores/smb.htm

Substance Use & Misuse. Contents with abstracts, author guidelines, and order information. http://www.dekker.com /servlet/product/productid/JA

Tobacco Control Update. On-line newsletter covering tobacco control in Massachusetts. http://www.tobacco.neu.edu/tcu/

Tobacco Control. Full-text, searchable archive; free full text of articles more than twelve months old. http://www.tobacco-control.org/tcrc_Web_Site/Pages_tcrc/Links/International_Links.htm

Web Resources

Information Sources and Databases

The following information has been drawn from governmental publications and other resources in the public domain.

Center for Substance Abuse Treatment (CSAT) (Substance Abuse and Mental Health Services Administration, U.S. Department of Health and Human Services). CSAT information includes information about treatment improvement protocols, technical assistance publications, and other CSAT publications. Information may be accessed from the following Web site: http://samsha.gov/csat/csat.htm

ERIC. The world's largest source of education information, with more than 1 million abstracts of documents and journal articles on education research and practice. Coverage: 1966–present. http://ericir.syr.edu/Eric

Information on Drugs and Alcohol (IDA). IDA contains scientific literature relating to alcohol- and substance-abuse prevention and sociological literature. Provides abstracts and bibliographic records. http://idasearch.health.org/compass

MEDLINE. PubMed, a service of the National Library of Medicine, provides access to more than 12 million MEDLINE citations back to the mid-1960s and additional life-science journals. PubMed includes links to many sites providing full-text articles and other related resources. http://www.ncbi.nlm.nih.gov/entrez/query.fcgi?db=PubMed

MEDLINEplus. MEDLINEplus, a gold mine of good health information from the world's largest medical library, the National Library of Medicine. http://www.nlm.nih.gov/medlineplus

National Clearinghouse for Alcohol and Drug Information (NCADI) Prevline. Prevline is the database portal to the resources of the National Clearinghouse for Alcohol and Drug Information. NCADI is the world's largest resource for current information and materials concerning substance-abuse prevention. http://www.health.org

National Criminal Justice Reference Service (NCJRS) Abstracts Database. The NCJRS Abstracts Database contains summaries of more than 170,000 criminal justice publications, including federal, state, and local government reports, books, research reports, journal articles, and unpublished research. http://abstractsdb.ncjrs.org/content/AbtractsD

National Institute on Alcohol Abuse and Alcoholism—ETOH database. This database contains more than 100,000 records on alcohol abuse and alcoholism. ETOH is updated monthly and contains research findings from the late 1960s to the present, as well as historical research literature. A thesaurus is available for searching alcohol and other drug terms, including a subset index of language used in the ETOH database. http://www.niaaa.nih.gov/databases/databases.htm

National Institute on Drug Abuse (NIDA) Publications Catalog. This semiannually updated catalog provides a listing of research monographs, clinical reports, surveys, brochures, prevention packets, booklets, and posters. Videos are also available. http://www.drugabuse.gov

National Organization for the Reform of Marijuana Laws (NORML). NORML provides information resources about the right of adults to use marijuana responsibly, whether for medical or personal purposes. http://www.norml.org

National Substance Abuse Web Index (NSAWI). This is a search engine that indexes twenty-six authoritative, public interest, and U.S. government sites on the Internet for locating reliable information on prevention, treatment, alcohol, tobacco, and illicit drugs. Use NSAWI to search through every document on prominent sites in the prevention world. Sites are reindexed every two weeks. http://nsawi.health.org

PsycINFO., Made up of more than 1 million searchable records, PsycINFO is an abstract (not full text) database of psychological literature from the 1800s to the present. http://www. apa.org/psycinfo

Schaffer Library of Drug Policy. The Schaffer Library is the largest Internet source addressing issues related to major studies of drugs and drug policy, history of drugs and drug laws, medical marijuana research, government publications on drugs and drug policy, charts and graphs of drug-war statistics, and information on specific drugs. http://www.druglibrary.org/schaffer/index.htm

SMOKING. Items in this database focus on the scientific, medical, technical, policy, behavioral, legal, and historical literature related to smoking and tobacco use and its effect on health. http://www.cdc.gov/tobacco/search

Substance Abuse Information Database (SAID). This database provides summaries and full text of materials relating to workplace substance-abuse issues. http://www.dol.gov/asp/programs/drugs/said.htm

Treatment Resource Database. The Treatment Resource Database provides bibliographic citations to alcohol- and substance-abuse treatment materials with a focus on intervention, recovery, treatment, and relapse prevention. http://sadatabase.health.org/trd

National Statistics

Bureau of Justice Statistics: Sourcebook of Criminal Justice Statistics Online. Data from more than one hundred sources about all aspects of criminal justice in the United States. http://www. albany.edu/sourcebook

Federal Bureau of Investigation: Uniform Crime Reports (UCR). Statistics for crime in the United States. http:// www.fbi.gov/ucr/ucr.htm

National Center for Health Statistics (FASTSTATS). National health data and statistics. http://www.cdc.gov/nchs/fastats/ default.htm

National Highway and Traffic Safety Administration—FARS: Fatality Analysis Reporting System. FARS contains data on all fatal traffic crashes within the fifty states, the District of Columbia, and Puerto Rico. http://www-fars.nhtsa.dot.gov

National Institute on Alcohol Abuse and Alcoholism (NIAAA)—Quick Facts. Provides tables presenting data on alcohol topics, including amounts and patterns of alcohol consumption, alcohol dependence or abuse, consequences of alcohol consumption, and other alcohol-related topics. http://www. niaaa.nih.gov/databases/qf.htm

Substance Abuse and Mental Health Services Administration (SAMHSA), Office of Applied Studies (OAS). The most recent national data on alcohol, tobacco, and other drugs from OAS surveys are found here. http://www.drugabusestatistics. samhsa. gov

Other Web Sites

Web sites with useful links to other substance-abuse resources are marked with an asterisk. The information presented is drawn from material prepared by Substance Abuse Librarians and Information Specialists (SALIS): An International Organization. http://salis.org/resources

Alcohol Advisory Council of New Zealand, New Zealand. http://www.alcohol.org.nz

Alcohol and Drug Abuse Institute Links, University of Washington. http://depts.washington.edu/adai/links/links.htm*

Alcohol Problems and Solutions. http://2.potsdam.edu/alcohol-info*

Alcohol Research Group. http://www.arg.org

Alcoholics Anonymous. http://www.alcoholics-anonymous. org

American Library Association (ALA). http://www.ala.org

Association for Medical Education and Research in Substance Abuse (AMERSA). http://www.amersa.org

Association of Mental Health Librarians. http://www. mhlib.org

Campaign for Tobacco Free Kids. http://tobaccofreekids.org*

Canadian Centre on Substance Abuse, Canada. http:// www.ccsa.ca*

Center for Alcohol and Addiction Studies, Brown University. http://center.butler.brown.edu

Center for Disease Control Tobacco Page. http://www. cdc.gov/tobacco

Center for Substance Abuse Research, University of Maryland. http://www.cesar.umd.edu

Center of Alcohol Studies. http://www.rci.rutgers.edu/~cas2

Centre for Addiction and Mental Health, Canada. http:// www.camh.net

Centre for Drug Research, University of Amsterdam. http://www.cedro-uva.org

Centre for Education and Information on Drugs and Alcohol,

Australia. http://www.ceida.net.au

Common Sense for Drug Policy. http://www.csdp.org.htm*

Daily Dose. http://www.dailydose.net/index.htm*

Drug Policy Alliance (formerly Lindesmith Center- Drug Policy Foundation). http://www.drugpolicy.org*

European Association of Libraries and Information Services on Alcohol and Other Drugs (ELISAD), European Union. http://www.elisad.org

European Monitoring Centre for Drugs and Drug Addiction (EMCDDA), European Union. http://www.emcdda.org

Google (Internet Search Engine). http://google.com*

Hazelden Foundation. http://www.hazelden.org*

Hazelden Foundation Resource Center. http://www.hazelden.org/resource_center.DBM*

Health Web Substance Abuse, University of Minnesota Biomedical Library. http://healthweb.org/browse.cfm?subjectid=88*

Historical Resources on Alcohol Use in America, Rutgers University. http://www.rci.rutgers.edu/~cas2/histsites.htm

Indiana Prevention Resource Center. http://www.drugs.indiana.edu*

Institute of Alcohol Studies, United Kingdom. http://www.ias.org.uk*

International Council on Alcohol, Drugs, and Traffic Safety, Australia. http://raru.adelaide.edu.au/icadts

Join Together Online. http://www.jointogether.org*

Marin Institute. http://www.marininstitute.org

Medical Library Association, Mental Health SIG. http://www.miami.edu/mhsig

Medline. http://www.ncbi.nlm.nih.gov/entrez/query.fcgi?db=PubMed*

Minnesota Institute of Public Health Links. http://www.miph.org/links.html

National Center on Addiction and Substance Abuse, Columbia University. http://www.casacolumbia.org*

National Clearinghouse for Alcohol and Drug Information (NCADI). http://www.health.gov (including Tips for Teens Series)*

National Clearinghouse on Tobacco and Health, Canada. http://www.ncth.ca/NCTHweb.nsf*

National Institute on Alcohol Abuse and Alcoholism (NIAAA). http://www.niaaa.nih.gov*

National Institute on Drug Abuse (NIDA). http://www.nida.nih.gov*

Office of National Drug Control Policy (ONDCP). http://www.whitehousedrugpolicy.gov*

Regional Alcohol and Drug Awareness Resource—RADAR Network (SAMHSA). http:ncadi.samsha.gov*

Research Institute on Addictions, University at Buffalo. http://www.ria.buffalo.edu

Schaffer Library of Drug Policy. http://www.druglibrary.org/schaffer/index.htm*

Special Libraries Association (SLA). http://www.sla.org

Substance Abuse & Mental Health Services Administration (SAMHSA). http://www.samhsa.gov*

Substance Abuse Librarians and Information Specialists (SALIS): An International Organization. http://salis.org/resources*

UN International Drug Control Programme. http://www undcp.org

U.S. Information Agency, Narcotics and Substance Abuse. http://usinfo.state.gov/topical/global/drugs

U.S. National Institute on Alcohol Abuse and Alcoholism. http://www.niaaa.nih.gov*

University of California, Integrated Substance Abuse Programs (ISAP). http://www.uclaisap.org*

Virtual Clearinghouse on Alcohol Tobacco and Other Drugs, International (in English, French, and Spanish). http://www.atod.org*

Web of Addictions. http://www.well.com/user/woa*

Bibliography

Reference information including books, articles, government publications, and other reports appear at the end of most chapters in this book and are listed below.

Books

American Psychiatric Association. 2000. *Diagnostic and Statistical Manual of Mental Disorders.* 4th ed. Washington, DC: American Psychiatric Association.

Cunningham, R. 1996. *Smoke & Mirrors: The Canadian Tobacco War.* Ottawa, Ontario: International Development Research Centre.

Falkowski, C. 2000. *Dangerous Drugs.* Center City, MN: Hazelden.

Goode, E. 1989. *Drugs in American Society.* New York: McGraw-Hill.

Isralowitz, R. 2002. *Drug Use, Policy and Management.* Westport, CT: Auburn House.

Ray, E., and Ksir, C. 1990. *Drugs, Society and Human Behavior.* St. Louis: Times Mirror/Mosby.

Journals

Benowitz, N. 1996. **"Pharmacology of Nicotine: Addiction and Therapeutics."** *Annual Review of Pharmacology and Toxicology* 36: 597–613.

Buckley, W. 1996. **"400 Readers Give Their Views."** *National Review* (July 1): 32.

Buckley, W., E. Nadelman, K. Schmoke, J. McNamara, R. Sweet, T. Szasz, and S. Duke. 1996. **"The War on Drugs is Lost."** *National Review* 12 (February): 35–48.

Dehne, K., J. Grund, L. Kodakevich, and Y. Kobyshcha. 1999. **"The HIV/AIDS Epidemic among Drug Injectors in Eastern Europe: Patterns, Trends and Determinants."** *Journal of Drug Issues* 29, no. 4: 393–402.

Kessler, D. 1995. **"Sounding Board: Nicotine Addiction in Young People."** *New England Journal of Medicine* 333, no. 3: 186.

Migliori, G. and M. Ambrosetti. 1998. **"Epidemiology of Tuberculosis in Europe."** *Mondali Archives of Chest Diseases* 53, no. 6: 681–687.

Nadelman, E. 1993. **"Should We Legalize Drugs? History Answers."** *American Heritage* 44.

Nguyen, T. 2000. **"The Social Context of HIV Risk Behaviour by Drug Injectors in Ho Chi Minh City, Vietnam."** *AIDS Care* 12, no. 4: 483–495.

Petraitis, J., B. Flay, T. Miller, E. Torpy, and B. Greiner. 1998. **"Illicit Substance Use Among Adolescents: A Matrix of Prospective Predictors."** *Substance Use and Misuse* 33, no. 13: 2561–2604.

Russell, A. 1992. **"Making America Drug Free: A New Vision of What Works."** *Carnegie Quarterly* 37, no. 3 (summer).

Schapiro, M. 2002. **"Big Tobacco."** *The Nation* (May 6). Available at http://www.thenation.com/doc.mhtml?i=20020506&s= schapiro (accesed January 1, 2004).

Schlosser, E. 1997. **"More Reefer Madness."** *Atlantic Monthly* 279, no. 4 (April): 90–120.

Sweet, R. 1996. **"The War on Drugs is Lost."** *National Review* (February 12): 35–48.

Government Publications and Other Reports

Adelekan, M. 2001. **"Injection Drug Use and Associated Health Consequences in Lagos, Nigeria: Findings from WHO Phase II Injection Drug Use Study."** In *2000 Global Research Network Meeting on HIV Prevention in Drug-Using Populations, Third Annual Meeting Report, July, 2000, Durban, South Africa.* Washington, DC: Department of Health and Human Services

Alcohol and Drug Information Clearinghouse. 2003. **"A Parenting Perspective: Children of Alcoholics."** Available at http://www.prevlink.org/getthefacts/facts/coa.html (accessed January 21, 2004).

American Academy of Child & Adolescent Psychiatry. 1999. **"Children of Alcoholics."** AACAP Facts for Families #17. Available at http://www.aacap.org/publications/factsfam/alcoholc. htm (accessed January 15, 2004).

American Lung Association. **"Multidrug-Resistant Tuberculosis Fact Sheet."** Available at http://www.lungusa.org/diseases /mdrtbfac.html (accessed January 21, 2004)

Ball, A. 2000. **"Epidemiology and Prevention of HIV in Drug-Using Population: Global Perspective."** In *1999 Global Research*

Network Meeting on HIV Prevention in Drug-Using Populations, Second Annual Meeting Report, August 26–28, 1999, Atlanta, Georgia. Bethesda, MD: National Institute on Drug Abuse.

Center for Substance Abuse Prevention (CSAP). 1993. *A Discussion Paper on Preventing Alcohol, Tobacco, and Other Drug Problems.* United States Department of Health and Human Services. Rockville, MD: SAMHSA.

———. 1994. *Prevention Primer: An Encyclopedia of Alcohol, Tobacco, and other Prevention Terms.* United States Department of Health and Human Services. Rockville, MD: SAMHSA.

Centers for Disease Control and Prevention (CDC). 2001. *CDC Fact Book 2000/2001.* Washington, DC: U.S. Public Health Service, Office of the Surgeon General.

———. 2001. **"Women and Smoking: A Report of the Surgeon General."** Washington, DC: U.S. Public Health Service, Office of the Surgeon General.

———. 2002. **"Drug-Associated HIV Transmission in the United States."** Available at http://www.cdc.gov/hiv/pubs/facts/idu.htm (accessed January 15, 2004).

———. 2002. **"World TB Day 2002."** March 24. Available at http://www.cdc.gov/nchstp/tb (accessed January 19, 2004).

Clines, F. 2001. **"Fighting Appalachia's Top Cash Crop, Marijuana."** *New York Times,* February 28, Sec. A, 10.

European Monitoring Centre for Drugs and Drug Addiction. 2000. *Annual Report on the State of the Drug Problem in the European Union.* Lisbon, Portugal: European Monitoring Centre.

Hibell, B., B. Andersson, T. Bjarnason, A. Kokkevi, M. Morgan, and A. Narusk. 1997. *The 1995 Espad Report: Alcohol and Other Drug Use Among Students in 26 European Countries.* Stockholm: Swedish Council for Information on Alcohol and Other Drugs.

Horgan, C. 2001. *Substance Abuse: The Nation's Number One Health Problem.* Princeton, NJ: Robert Wood Johnson Foundation.

Hornik, R. 2002. *Evaluation of the National Youth Anti-Drug Media Campaign: Fifth Semi-Annual Report of Findings, Executive Summary.* Rockville, MD: Westat.

Johnston, L., P. O'Malley, and J. Backman. 1999. **"The Monitoring the Future National Results on Adolescent Drug Use: Overview of Key Findings."** Bethesda, MD: National Institute on Drug Abuse.

Kazancigil, A., and C. Milani. 2002. *Globalisation, Drugs and Criminalisation: Final Research Report on Brazil, China, India and Mexico.* New York: United Nations Office for Drug Control and Crime Prevention.

Lettieri, D., M. Sayers, H. Pearson, eds. 1980. *Theories on Drug Abuse: Selected Contemporary Perspectives.* Rockville, MD: National Institute on Drug Abuse.

MADD—Mothers Against Drunk Driving. **"General Statistics."** Available at http://madd.org/stats/0,1056,1789,00.html (accessed January 15, 2004).

Moulson, G. 2000. **"U.N. Warns of AIDS Complacency, Says Epidemic Explodes in Russia."** *Associated Press,* November 28.

National Highway Traffic Safety Administration (NHTSA) U.S. Department of Transportation. 2001. **"Traffic Safety Facts 2000: Alcohol."** Washington, DC: NHTSA. Available at http://www.nrd.nhtsa.dot.gov/pdf/nrd-30/ncsa/tsf2000/2000alcfacts.pdf (accessed May 1, 2002).

———. 2003. **"DOT Releases Preliminary Estimates of 2002 Highway Fatalities."** News Release April 23, NHTSA 13-03.

National Institute on Drug Abuse (NIDA). 1996. *Epidemiologic Trends in Drug Abuse.* **Vol. 1:** *Highlights and Executive Summary.* Rockville, MD: National Institutes of Health.

———. 1999. *NIDA Notes* 14, no.2.

———. 1999. *Principles of Drug Addiction Treatment: A Research-Based Guide.* Rockville, MD: National Institutes of Health.

———. 2000. *Epidemiologic Trends in Drug Abuse, Vol. 1: Highlights and Executive Summary.* Rockville, MD: National Institutes of Health.

———. 2001. *Epidemiologic Trends in Drug Abuse, Vol. 1: Highlights and Executive Summary.* Rockville, MD: National Institutes of Health.

Nolin, P., C. Kenny. 2002. *"Cannabis: Our Position for a Canadian Public Policy."* Special Committee on Illegal Drugs. Senate of Canada. Available at http://www.ukcia.org/research/CanadianPublicPolicy/default.html (accessed January 21, 2004).

Office of Substance Abuse Prevention (OSAP). 1991. *Prevention Plus III: Assessing Alcohol and Other Drug Prevention Programs at the School and Community Level.* Rockville, MD: ADAMHA.

Pan American Health Organization. 2001. *HIV and AIDS in the Americas: an Epidemic with Many Faces.* Washington, DC: Pan American Health Organization.

Reid, G., and G. Costigan. 2002. *Revisiting "The Hidden Epidemic": A Situation Assessment of Drug Use in Asia in the Context of HIV/AIDS.* Fairfield, Victoria, Australia: The Centre for Harm Reduction/The Burnet Institute.

Sammud, M. 2002. **"Libyan Arab Jamahiriya Report."** Presented at the Twelfth Inter-Country Meeting of National AIDS Programme Managers, Beirut, Lebanon, April 23–26.

Selwyn, P., and S. Batki. 1995. *Treatment for HIV-Infected Alcohol and Other Drug Abusers.* Treatment Improvement Protocol (TIP) Series. Rockville, MD: Substance Abuse and Mental Health Services Administration, U.S. Department of Health and Human Services.

Shepard, E. 2001. *The Economic Costs of DARE.* Syracuse, NY: Institute of Industrial Relations.

Substance Abuse and Mental Health Services Administration (SAMHSA). 1999. *National Household Survey on Drug Abuse Main Findings.* Rockville, MD: United States Department of Health and Human Services.

————. 2001. *Summary of Findings from the 2000 National Household Survey on Drug Abuse.* Rockville, MD: United States Department of Health and Human Services.

————. 2002. *National Household Survey on Drug Abuse.* Rockville, MD: United States Department of Health and Human Services.

————. 2003. *Results from the 2002 National Survey on Drug Use and Health: National Finding,* Rockville, MD: United States Department of Health and Human Services.

Swan, N. 1998. **"Drug Abuse Cost to Society Set at $97.7 Billion, Continuing Steady Increase Since 1975."** NIDA Notes, NIH Publication No. 98-3478.

Switzerland Addiction Research Institute. 2003. **"Tobacco, Alcohol, Drugs Killing 7 Million a Year."** Available at http://www.abc.net.au/science/news/health/HealthRepublish_792982.htm (accessed February 26, 2003).

Touze, G. 2001. **"HIV Prevention in Drug-Using Populations in Latin America."** In *2000 Global Research Network Meeting on HIV Prevention in Drug-Using Populations, Third Annual Meeting Report, July 2000, Durban, South Africa.* Washington, DC: Department of Health and Human Services.

UNAIDS. *Report on the Global HIV/AIDS Epidemic.* Geneva, June 2000.

UNAIDS/WHO. *AIDS Epidemic Update.* Geneva, December 2002.

United Nations. 2001. *Drug Abuse and HIV/AIDS: Lessons Learned.* Case Studies Booklet, Central and Eastern Europe and the Central Asian States. Vienna: United Nations Office on Drugs and Crime.

United Nations General Assembly Political Declaration. 1998. **"Declaration on the Guiding Principles of Drug Demand Reduction."** New York, June 8–10.

United Nations Office for Drug Control and Crime Prevention (ODCCP). 2002. *Global Illicit Drug Trends.* New York: ODCCP Studies on Drugs and Crime.

United States Department of State, Office of International Information Agency. 1992. *Consequences of Illegal Drug Trade: The Negative Economic, Political, and Social Effects of Cocaine in Latin America.* Washington, DC: United States Department of State, Office of International Information Agency.

United States General Accounting Office. 2003. **"Youth Illicit Drug Use Prevention."** Washington, DC: USGAO. Available at http://www.gao.gov/new.items/d03172r.pdf (accessed January 19, 2004).

United States Office of Applied Studies. 2002. *Summary of Findings from the 2000 National Household Survey on Drug Abuse— DHHS Publication No. SMA 01-3549.* Available at http://www.samhsa.gov/oas/NHSDA/2kNHSDA/2kNHSDA.htm (accessed January 19, 2004).

Willard, J., and C. Schoenborn. 1995. **"Relationship Between Cigarette Smoking and Other Unhealthy Behaviors Among Our Nation's Youth: United States, 1992."** In *Advance Data* no. 263. Washington, DC: National Center for Health Statistics, April 24.

World Health Organization (WHO). 2000a. **"Fact Sheet No. 164: Hepatitis C."** Rev. October. Geneva: WHO.

———. 2000b. **"Fact Sheet No. 204: Hepatitis B."** Rev. October. Geneva: WHO.

———. 2001. **"Women and the Tobacco Epidemic—Challenges for the 21st Century."** Geneva: WHO.

———. 2002. **"Hazardous Harmonization in Smoking by European Youth."** Available at http://www.who.dk/document /cma/PB032002e.pdf (accessed January 19, 2004).

World Health Organization, Regional Office for the Eastern

Mediterranean. 2001. *The Work of WHO in the Eastern Mediterranean Region.* Annual Report of the Regional Director (January 1–December 31, 2002), Regional Office for the Eastern Mediterranean, Cairo, Egypt: WHO.

Yoon, Y., H. Yi, B. Grant, F. Stinson, and M. Dufor. 2002. **"Surveillance Report #60: Liver Cirrhosis Mortality in the United States, 1970–99."** Rockville, MD: National Institute on Alcohol Abuse and Alcoholism, Division of Biometry and Epidemiology, December.

Glossary

Abstinence   The conscious choice not to use drugs. The term *abstinence* usually refers to the decision to end the use of a drug as part of the process of recovery from addiction.

Abuse   A term with a range of meanings. In international drug-control conventions, *abuse* refers to any consumption of a controlled substance no matter how infrequent (see also **Drug abuse**).

Adaptive behaviors   Useful behaviors we acquire as we respond to the world around us. Adaptive behaviors help us get the things we want and need for life.

Addiction   A brain disorder characterized by the loss of control of drug-taking behavior, despite adverse health, social, or legal consequences to continued drug use. Addiction tends to be chronic and to be characterized by relapses during recovery.

Addictive drugs   Drugs that change the brain, change behavior, and lead to the loss of control of drug-taking behavior.

Alcohol   The world's most popular drug, legally used in most countries. Alcohol is produced through the fermentation of fruits, vegetables, and grains.

Alcoholics Anonymous   One of the earliest forms of addiction treatment in the United States, AA developed the twelve-step approach to assist recovery from alcohol addiction (alcoholism). Several other anonymous groups have adapted the twelve-step approach to help people recover from addiction to other drugs (for example, Narcotics Anonymous, Cocaine Anonymous, Pot Smokers Anonymous).

Amotivational syndrome   A constellation of effects said to be associated with substance use (especially of cannabis), including apathy, loss of effectiveness, diminished capacity to carry out complex or long-term plans, low tolerance for frustration, impaired concentration, and difficulty following routines.

241

Amphetamines Stimulant drugs whose effects are very similar to cocaine. Often called "speed," this drug is a synthetically produced central nervous system stimulant with cocainelike effects.

Analgesic A substance that reduces pain and may or may not have psychoactive properties.

Antagonist A substance (such as Naloxone) that counteracts the effects of another agent (such as an opiate drug).

Barbiturates Depressant drugs that produce relaxation and sleep. Barbiturates include sleeping pills such as pentobarbital (Nembutal) and secobarbital (Seconal).

Benzodiazepines The so-called minor tranquilizers; depressants that relieve anxiety and produce sleep. Benzodiazepines include tranquilizers such as diazepam (Valium) and alprazolam (Xanax) and sleeping pills such as flurazepam (Dalmane) and triazolam (Halcion).

Binge Uninterrupted consumption of a drug for several hours or days.

Brief intervention A treatment strategy in which structured therapy of a limited number of sessions (usually one to four) of short duration (typically five to thirty minutes) is offered with the aim of assisting an individual to cease or reduce the use of psychoactive substances or to deal with other life issues.

Buprenorphine A long-lasting opiate analgesic that has both opiate agonist and antagonist properties. Buprenorphine shows promise for treating heroin addiction.

Caffeine A mild stimulant, the most widely used drug in the world.

Cannabinoid receptor The receptor in the brain that recognizes THC, the active ingredient in marijuana. Marijuana exerts its psychoactive effects via this receptor.

Cannabis The botanical name for the plant from which marijuana comes.

Cocaine A bitter crystalline drug obtained from the dried leaves of the coca shrub; it is a local anesthetic and a dangerous, illegal stimulant. It is the primary psychoactive ingredient in the coca plant and a behavioral-affecting drug.

Codeine A natural opioid compound that is a relatively weak but still effective opiate analgesic. It has also been used to treat other problems (for instance, to relieve coughing).

Controlled substance A term that refers to a psychoactive substance and its precursors whose availability is forbidden under the international drug-control treaties or limited to medical and pharmaceutical channels.

"Crack" cocaine The chemical cocaine is found in the oil of the coca plant leaf; when processed, cocaine is chemically turned into a water-soluble powder form called cocaine hydrochloride; "crack" cocaine, much like "freebasing" cocaine, is cocaine powder that has been turned back into an oil form of smokable cocaine.

Craving Hunger for drugs. It is caused by drug-induced changes that occur in the brain with the development of addiction and arises from a need of the brain to maintain a state of homeostasis that includes the presence of the drug.

Cutting agents These are various powders that are used to dilute cocaine, heroin, and other drugs used in powder form. Lactose (milk sugar) is an example; another is mannitol.

Demand reduction This approach reflects the policy that reducing the supply and availability of illicit drugs is an essential component of the fight against drug abuse. Efforts to limit the cultivation, production, trafficking, and distribution of drugs are strategies to implement this approach. Supply-reduction projects also seek to broaden regional cooperation between governments in response to cross-border trafficking, strengthen border controls by providing modern equipment, and develop training in "best practice" law enforcement procedures.

Depressants Drugs that relieve anxiety and produce sleep. Depressants include barbiturates, benzodiazepines, and alcohol.

Designer drug An illegally manufactured chemical whose molecular structure is altered slightly from a parent compound to enhance specific effects. Examples include DMT, DMA, DOM, MDA, and MDMA (Ecstasy).

Detoxification The process of removing a drug from the body. This is the initial period addicts must go through to become drug-free. Withdrawal symptoms appear early during this process. Depending on the drug, detoxification lasts for a few days to a week or more.

Diversion Taking legally prescribed medications (such as methadone or tranquilizers) and selling them illegally. The term is also used to mean the provision of an activity or activities that move a person away from drug use.

Drug A term of varied usage. In various UN conventions and in the Declaration of Drug Demand Reduction, it refers to substances subject to international control. In medicine, it refers to any substance with the potential to prevent or cure disease or enhance physical or mental well-being. In pharmacology, the term refers to any chemical agent that alters the biochemical or psychological processes of tissues or organisms. In common usage, the term often refers specifically to psychoactive drugs, and often, even more specifically, to illicit drugs.

Drug abuse   Using illegal drugs; using legal drugs inappropriately. The repeated high-dose self-administration of drugs to produce pleasure, to alleviate stress, or to alter or avoid reality (or all three).

Drug-free treatment   Approaches to helping addicts recover from addiction without the use of medication.

Drug treatment   A combination of detoxification, psychosocial therapy, and, if required, skill acquisition to help people recover from addiction.

Dual diagnosis (comorbidity)   A person diagnosed as having an alcohol- or drug-abuse problem in addition to some other diagnosis, usually psychiatric (for example, mood disorder or schizophrenia).

Ecstasy (MDMA)   A chemically modified amphetamine that has hallucinogenic as well as stimulant properties.

Ephedra   A plant genus comprising some forty distinct species that grow wild in various regions of the world. Ephedra has a long history of medical and ceremonial purposes. The herbs of various species have been used in traditional medicines in China under the name of Ma Huang and also in India to treat symptoms of asthma and respiratory infections. Ephedra contains two principle alkaloids, ephedrine and pseudoephedrine. Both alkaloids are used in medicines worldwide. At the end of 2000, the U.S. Food and Drug Administration (FDA) advised consumers to immediately stop using food supplements containing ephedra. In order to protect consumers, the FDA initiated action to ban the sale of dietary supplements containing ephedrine alkaloids.

Gateway theory   A model of the progression of drug use that has grown out of research with adolescents that has identified a sequential patterns of involvement in various legal and illegal drugs.

GHB   Gamma hydroxybutyrate (GHB) was originally developed as an anesthetic but was withdrawn due to unwanted side effects. At small doses, GHB tends to reduce social inhibitions, similar in action to alcohol, and it is also reported to increase libido.

Hallucinogens   A diverse group of drugs that alter perceptions, thoughts, and feelings. Hallucinogens do not produce hallucinations. These drugs include LSD, mescaline, MDMA (Ecstasy), PCP, and psilocybin (magic mushrooms).

Harm reduction   Harm reduction is a set of practical strategies that reduce negative consequences of drug use, incorporating a range of strategies from safer use to managed use to abstinence. Because harm reduction demands that interventions and policies designed to serve drug users reflect specific individual and community needs, there is no universal definition of or formula for implementing harm reduction.

Hashish   Cannabis preparation more potent than marijuana. It comes from the resinous secretions of the marijuana plant's flowering tops.

Heroin   The potent, widely abused opiate that produces a profound addiction. It consists of two morphine molecules linked together chemically.

Ice   A smokable form of methamphetamine. By smoking the drug, the effect on the body occurs more quickly.

Inhalants   Any drug administered by breathing in its vapors. There are a number of substances that produce strong intoxicating vapors such as paint, paint thinner, modeling glue, gas liquid, correction fluid, markers, and many others. These substances are very dangerous and are often used by young people.

Intoxication   Being under the influence of, and responding to, the acute effects of a psychoactive drug. Intoxication typically includes feelings of pleasure, altered emotional responsiveness, altered perception, and impaired judgment and performance.

Khat   The leaves and buds of an East African plant used to suppress appetite and combat fatigue.

LAAM   A very long-lasting opiate agonist recently approved for the treatment of opiate addiction.

Long-term effects   The effects seen when a drug is used repeatedly over weeks, months, or years. These effects may outlast drug use.

LSD   These letters stand for d-lysergic acid diethylamide. This chemical was synthesized from ergot in 1938 by Albert Hofmann of the Sandoz Laboratories in Switzerland; a powerful hallucinogen whose effective dose is 200 to 400 micrograms, a mere speck in size.

Marijuana   The Cannabis sativa plant that produces a mild euphoric effect. The active ingredient that produces the euphoric effect is delta-9-tetrahydrocannabinol, or THC. Marijuana can be eaten or smoked in cigarette form or pipes. The oily resin of the marijuana plant can be produced into hashish or hashish oil.

Marinol   The trade name of dronabinol, a synthetic version of THC used as medicine.

MDA   One of several hallucinogenic "designer drugs" with psychedelic properties that are manufactured by basement chemists.

MDMA (Ecstasy)   A hallucinogenic "designer drug" with psychedelic and stimulant properties.

Mescaline   A naturally occurring hallucinogenic drug that acts on the serotonin receptor. This is the major hallucinogenic chemical found in the peyote cactus. Mescaline is not found in the mescal cactus from which tequila is acquired. To add to the potential confusion, there is another hallucinogen found in the highly toxic "mescal bean" of the evergreen shrub named *Sophora secundiflora*.

Methadone   A long-lasting synthetic opiate used to treat cancer pain and heroin addiction.

Methamphetamine   A commonly abused, potent stimulant drug that is part of a larger family of amphetamines.

Morphine   A powerful narcotic that comes from the opium plant. Heroin is derived from morphine. It is named after the Greek god Morpheus, the god of dreams.

Motivational interviewing   A counseling and assessment technique that essentially follows a nonconfrontational approach to questioning people about difficult issues like alcohol and other drug use and assisting them to make positive decisions to reduce or stop their drug use altogether.

Naloxone   A short-acting opiate antagonist that binds to opiate receptors and blocks them, preventing opiates from binding to these receptors. Naloxone is used to treat opiate overdoses.

Narcotic drug   A chemical agent than can induce stupor, coma, or insensibility to pain.

Nicotine   The drug in tobacco that is addictive. Nicotine also activates a specific kind of acetylcholine receptor.

Nicotine gum, nicotine patch   Two methods of delivering small amounts of nicotine into the bodies of people who are addicted to nicotine to help them quit smoking cigarettes by preventing nicotine withdrawal.

Opiates   Any of the psychoactive drugs that originate from the opium poppy or that have a chemical structure like the drugs derived from opium. Such drugs include opium, codeine, and morphine (derived from the plant), and hydromorphone (Dilaudid), methadone, and meperidine (Demerol) that were first synthesized by chemists.

Opioids   Any chemical that has opiate-like effects; commonly used to refer to endogenous neurochemicals that activate opiate receptors.

Outpatient treatment   Nonresidential treatment for drug addiction. Patients live at home, often work, and come to a clinic for treatment.

Overdose   The condition that results when too much of a drug is taken, making a person sick or unconscious and sometimes resulting in death.

Oxycodone or OxyContin   An opiate painkiller, it is a semisynthetic opioid derived from the opioid alkaloid thebaine that is similar to codeine, methadone, and morphine in producing opiate-like effects. Oxycodone is a Schedule II drug under the Controlled Substances Act because of its high propensity to cause dependence and abuse.

Paranoid schizophrenia   A severe form of mental illness typically characterized by delusions of persecution and hallucinations. This condition may be induced by binge use of stimulants.

PCP   The full name of this drug is phencyclidine. PCP has an array of effects. Originally developed as an anesthetic, it may act as a hallucinogen, stimulant, or sedative.

Percocet   A narcotic analgesic, it is used to treat moderate to moderately severe pain. It contains two drugs—acetaminophen and oxycodone.

Percodan This is a synthetically produced narcotic that acts like morphine or heroin. It is the brand name of aspirin and oxycodone.

"Persian" heroin   This is heroin in a smokable form. Smoking heroin is often called "chasing the dragon."

Peyote   This is the name of the cacti that contain the hallucinogenic chemical mescaline.

Prevention   Stopping drug use before it starts, intervening to halt the progression of drug use once it has begun, and changing environmental conditions that encourage addictive drug use.

Primary reinforcers   Stimuli, such as food and water, that produce reward directly, with no learning about their significance or other intervening steps required. Most drugs of abuse are primary reinforcers.

Psilocybe   Often referred to as "magic mushrooms," this fungus contains two hallucinogens named psilocybin and psilocin. There are a number of other poisonous and hallucinogenic mushrooms.

Psilocybin   A natural hallucinogenic drug derived from a mushroom. It acts on the serotonin receptor.

Psychedelic drug   Drugs that distort perception, thought, and feeling. This term is typically used to refer to drugs with actions like those of LSD.

Psychoactive drug   A drug that changes the way the brain works.

Psychological dependence   When drugs become so central to a user's life that the user believes he must use them.

Psychosis   Severe mental illnesses characterized by loss of contact with reality. Schizophrenia and severe depression are psychoses.

Psychosocial therapy   Therapy designed to help addicts by using a combination of individual psychotherapy and group (social) therapy approaches to rehabilitate or provide the interpersonal and intrapersonal skills needed to live without drugs.

Rapid assessment A variety of methods for rapid or focused data collection that since the 1980s have grown out of a sense of urgency for social science input in disease-control programs.

Rehabilitate Helping a person recover from drug addiction. Rehabilitation teaches the addict new behaviors to live life without drugs.

Relapse In general, to fall back to a former condition. With substance abuse, it means resuming the use of a drug one has tried to stop using. Relapse is a common occurrence in many chronic disorders that require behavioral adjustments to treat effectively.

Residential treatment Treatment programs that require participants to live in a hostel, home, or hospital unit.

Reward The process that reinforces behavior.

Risk reduction Describes policies or programs that focus on reducing the risk of harm from alcohol or other drug use.

Rock A small amount of crack cocaine in a solid form; freebase cocaine in solid form.

Route of administration The way a drug is put into the body. Eating, drinking, inhaling, injecting, snorting, smoking, and absorbing a drug through mucous membranes all are routes of administration used to consume drugs of abuse.

"Run" A binge of (more or less) uninterrupted consumption of a drug for several hours or days. This pattern of drug use is typically associated with stimulants, but is seen with alcohol as well.

Rush Intense feelings of euphoria a drug produces when it is first consumed. Drug users who inject or smoke drugs describe their rush as being sometimes as intense as, or even more intense than, sexual orgasm.

Seconal A depressant drug of the barbiturate family that induces sleep.

Sedative/Hypnotic Any of a group of central nervous system depressants with the capacity of relieving anxiety and inducing calmness and sleep.

Sinsemilla There are male and female marijuana plants. The flowers of the female marijuana contain the highest concentration of THC. Growers have learned that if the female plants are not allowed to be pollinated, the flowers cluster and excrete greater quantities of resin. Marijuana grown like this is called sinsemilla, which simply means "no seeds."

Skin-popping Injecting a drug under the skin.

Snowballing A method of recruitment of illicit-drug users either for research purposes or for peer-based prevention purposes.

Stimulants A class of drugs that elevates mood, increases feelings of well-being, and increases energy and alertness. These drugs also produce euphoria and are powerfully rewarding. Stimulants include cocaine, methamphetamine, and methylphenidate (Ritalin).

STP This synthetically produced hallucinogen is a variation of mescaline and amphetamines. It is generally less potent than LSD, but it takes longer to break down in the body and therefore lasts much longer, in some instances twenty-four hours to several days.

Supply reduction A broad term used for a range of activities designed to stop the production, manufacture, and distribution of illegal drugs. Production can be curtailed through crop eradication or through large programs of alternative development.

Therapeutic communities Communities that provide long-term residential treatment for drug addiction, offering detoxification, group therapy, and skill acquisition.

Tolerance A physiological change resulting from repeated drug use that requires the user to consume increasing amounts of the drug to get the same effect a smaller dose used to give.

Tranquilizers Depressant drugs that relieve anxiety.

Transdermal absorption Absorption through the skin.

Triggers Formerly neutral stimuli that have attained the ability to elicit drug craving following repeated pairing with drug use; also called cues.

Twelve-step group A mutual-help group organized around the twelve-step program of Alcoholics Anonymous or a close adaptation of that program.

Valium A depressant drug of the benzodiazepine family that relieves anxiety.

Withdrawal Physical symptoms in the body and brain that occur after cessation of drug use in a person who is physically dependent on that drug.

Xanax (aprazalom) A depressant drug of the benzodiazepine family that relieves anxiety.

Appendix

Commonly Abused Drugs: Categories and Street Terms

The following list has been drawn from *Commonly Abused Drugs*, National Institute on Drug Abuse (http://www. drugabuse.gov). A detailed list called "Street Terms: Drugs and the Drug Trade" may be found at the following Web site provided by the White House Office of Drug Control Policy: http://www. whitehousedrugpolicy.gov/streetterms/ByAlpha.asp.

Cannabinoids

Hashish   boom, chronic, gangster, hash, hash oil, hemp

Marijuana   blunt, dope, ganja, herb, joints, Mary Jane, pot, reefer, sinsemilla, weed

Depressants

Barbiturates   *Amytal, Nembutal, Seconal, Phenobarbital;* barbs, reds, red birds, phennies, tooies, yellows, yellow jackets

Benzodiazepines (other than flunitrazepam)   *Ativan, Halcion, Librium, Valium, Xanax;* candy, downers, sleeping pills, tranks

Flunitrazepam *Rohypnol;* forget-me-pill, Mexican Valium, R2, Roche, roofies, roofinol, rope, rophies

GHB *gamma hydroxybutyrate;* G, Georgia home boy, grievous bodily harm, liquid ecstasy

Methaqualone *Quaalude, Sopor, Parest;* ludes, mandrex, quad, quay

Dissociative Anesthetics

Ketamine *Ketalar SV;* cat Valiums, K, Special K, vitamin K

PCP and analogs *phencyclidine;* angel dust, boat, hog, love boat, peace pill

Hallucinogens

LSD *d-lysergic acid diethylamide;* acid, blotter, boomers, cubes, microdot, yellow sunshines

Mescaline buttons, cactus, mesc, peyote

Psilocybin magic mushroom, purple passion

Opioids and Morphine Derivatives

Codeine *Empirin with Codeine, Fiorinal with Codeine, Robitussin A-C, Tylenol with Codeine;* Captain Cody, Cody, doors and fours, loads, pancakes and syrup

Fentanyl *Actiq, Duragesic, Sublimaze;* Apache, China girl, China white, dance fever, friend, goodfella, jackpot, murder, 8, TNT, Tango and Cash

Heroin *diacetylmorphine;* brown sugar, dope, H, horse, junk, skag, skunk, smack, white horse

Morphine *Roxanol, Duramorph;* M, Miss Emma, monkey, white stuff

Opium *laudanum, paregoric;* big O, black stuff, block, gum, hop

Stimulants

Amphetamine *Biphetamine, Dexedrine;* bennies, black beauties, crosses, hearts, LA turnaround, speed, truck drivers, uppers

Cocaine   *Cocaine hydrochloride;* blow, bump, C, candy, Charlie, coke, crack, flake, rock, snow, toot

MDMA (methylenedioxymethamphetamine)   *DOB, DOM, MDA;* Adam, clarity, Ecstasy, Eve, lover's speed, peace, STP, X, XTC

Methamphetamine   *Desoxyn;* chalk, crank, crystal, fire, glass, go, fast, ice, meth, speed

Methylphenidate   *Ritalin;* JIF, MPH, R-ball, Skippy, the smart drug, vitamin R

Nicotine   bidis, chew, cigars, cigarettes, smokeless tobacco, snuff, spit tobacco

Other Compounds

Anabolic steroids   *Anadrol, Oxandrin, Durabolin, Depo-Testosterone, Equipoise;* roids, juice

Inhalants   *Solvents (paint thinners, gasoline, glues), gases (butane, propane, aerosol propellants, nitrous oxide), nitrites (isoamyl, isobutyl, cyclohexyl);* laughing gas, poppers, snappers, whippets

Resources

Friedman, D., and S. Rusche. 1999. *False Messengers: How Addictive Drugs Change the Brain.* Amsterdam: Harwood Academic Publishers. Available at http://www.addictionstudies.org/glossary.html (accessed January 15, 2004).

"Glossary of Drug and Alcohol Terms." 2003. Available at http://www. cocc.edu/lisal/health/drug_terms.htm (accessed January 15, 2004).

United Nations International Drug Control Programme. 2000. *Demand Reduction: A Glossary of Terms.* Vienna, Austria: UNODC.

Index

About the Author

Richard Isralowitz is professor and director of the Regional Alcohol and Drug Abuse Resources (RADAR) Center, Department of Social Work, Ben Gurion University in Israel. Professor Isralowitz received his Ph.D. from the Heller School for Advanced Studies in Social Policy and Management from Brandeis University. He has served as director of social research at the Graduate School of Applied Social Sciences, Case Western Reserve University in Cleveland, Ohio, and director of the Hubert H. Humphrey Institute for Social Research, Ben Gurion University.

Professor Isralowitz has received the Distinguished International Scientist Award from the U.S. National Institute on Drug Abuse for his professional work. Also, he has received recognition for his work on the drug problem as a Fulbright Scholar at the National University of Singapore; the Hallsworth Scholar for Social Policy at the University of Manchester, England; and the International Visiting Scholar at New York University. Among his recent books are *Drug Use, Policy and Management* (2002), and *Drug Problems: Cross Cultural Policy and Program Development* (2002).